PB

£75

The European Commission

CN 337.142
AN 7113

LIBRARY AND LEARNING RESOURCES CENTRE
Northern College, Barnsley. S75 3ET

Please return this book by the last date stamped below.

24/1

Northern C
Librar

NC00593

D1354197

LEGI

ARNSLEY

COLLEGE
CANCELLED
BINGLEBY

The European Commission

Leadership, organisation and culture in the EU administration

Michelle Cini

Manchester University Press

Manchester and New York

distributed exclusively in the USA by St. Martin's Press

Copyright © Michelle Cini 1996

Published by Manchester University Press
Oxford Road, Manchester M13 9NR, UK
and Room 400, 175 Fifth Avenue, New York, NY 10010, USA

Distributed exclusively in the USA
by St. Martin's Press, Inc., 175 Fifth Avenue, New York, NY 10010, USA

British Library Cataloguing-in-Publication Data
A catalogue record for this book is available from the British Library.

Library of Congress Cataloging-in-Publication Data
Cini, Michelle
    The European Commission : leadership, organisation, and culture in the
    EU administration / Michelle Cini.
        p.   cm.
    Includes bibliographical references and index.
    ISBN 0–7190–4148–1.—ISBN 0–7190–4149–X
    1. European Commission.   I. Title
JN33.5.C56   1997
341.24'22—dc20   96–28197
                                                                              CIP

ISBN 0 7190 4148 1 hardback
    0 7190 4149 X paperback

First published in 1996

00 99 98 97 96   10 9 8 7 6 5 4 3 2 1

Typeset in Sabon
by Northern Phototypesetting Co. Ltd, Bolton
Printed in Great Britain
by Bell & Bain Ltd, Glasgow

Contents

List of tables and figures

Tables

Figures

To my parents, Sylvia and Georges Cini

Acknowledgements

Much of the formulation and drafting of this book took place over a period of study leave spent at the Centre de Recherche sur le Politique, l'Administration et le Territoire (CERAT) at the Institut d'Etudes Politiques de Grenoble in France. I would like to thank the director, Guy Saez, for welcoming me so readily to the Centre; the support staff of CERAT for their helpfulness; and Sylvie and Andy Smith (and Charlie) for taking time out to introduce me to Grenoble and its environs, and for providing distraction and support when I was working too hard. Most of all I would like to thank Edith Brenac, for the initial invitation to Grenoble, for her kindness during my visit, and for her reassuring compliments about the standard of my French. Back at home, I would like to thank family, friends and my colleagues in the Politics Department at Bristol University for putting up with months of moaning and groaning as I put the seemingly never-ending 'finishing touches' to the book. I would also like to thank Richard Purslow at MUP for his patience and his helpful suggestions which were much appreciated.

Michelle Cini
January 1996

List of abbreviations

ACP	African Caribbean Pacific countries
Bull-EC	Bulletin of the European Community
CAP	Common Agricultural Policy
CCEE	Countries of Central and Eastern Europe
CFSP	Common Foreign and Security Policy
COR	Committee of the Regions
COREPER	Committee of Permanent Representatives
DG	Directorate-General
EBRD	European Bank for Reconstruction and Development
EC	European Community
ECB	European Central Bank
ECHO	European Community Humanitarian Office
ECSC	European Coal and Steel Community
ECU	European Currency Unit
EEA	European Economic Area; or European Environmental Agency
EEC	European Economic Community
EFTA	European Free Trade Association
EMS	European Monetary System
EMU	Economic and Monetary Union
EP	European Parliament
EPC	European Political Co-operation
ERM	Exchange Rate Mechanism
ESCB	European System of Central Banks
ESPRIT	European Strategic Programme for Research and Development in Information Technology
EU	European Union

EURATOM	European Atomic Energy Community
G7	Group of Seven
G24	Group of Twenty-four
GATT	General Agreement on Tariffs and Trade
IGC	Intergovernmental Conference
IMF	International Monetary Fund
IT	Information Technology
JHA	Justice and Home Affairs
LA	Linguist Grade
LS	Legal Service
MEP	Member of the European Parliament
OECD	Organisation for Economic Co-operation and Development
OEEC	Organisation for European Economic Co-operation
OJ	Official Journal of the European Communities
PASOK	Greek Socialist Party
PHARE	Poland and Hungary: aid for economic Reconstruction
PQs	Parliamentary Questions
R&D	Research and Development
SEA	Single European Act
SEM	Single European Market
SG	Secretariat-General
SME	Small and Medium-sized Enterprise
TACIS	Technical Assistance to the Commonwealth of Independent States
TEU	Treaty on European Union
UK	United Kingdom
UKREP	United Kingdom Permanent Representation
UNICE	Union of Industrial and Employers' Confederations of Europe
US	United States of America
VAT	Value Added Tax

Introduction

In spite of the wealth of books and articles written on European Union (EU) politics, there is relatively little that deals in any detail with the European Commission. One reason for this, though an unjustifiable one, is that as its importance and prominence seemed to decline over the course of the 1970s, researchers found their attention drawn to other institutional arenas and to more specific policy fields. For whatever reason, the Commission as an institution (rather than the discrete policy sectors attached to it) has suffered from severe academic neglect. However, like buses, whilst no studies have come along for ages, three (or more) are now likely to arrive within a short space of time. These are long overdue.[1] There is little enough understanding of the functioning of the EU institutions. And the Commission, more than any other European body, has frequently been subject to ill-informed and outlandish scare-mongering.

Studying the EU through its institutions now seems a rather conventional approach to the dynamics of what might be seen as an emergent European polity. Indeed, while the first fifteen years or so of European integration studies largely dealt with institutional questions, this approach has more recently fallen out of favour. The backlash against what were often seen as descriptive and rather boring historical and structural accounts of the European institutions was part of a wider rejection within social science of the study of organisation.

Rejecting out of hand all studies of European institutions might seem therefore to be an understandable reaction to various academic and governmental trends. It is no excuse, however, for playing down the importance of the European Commission. Of course, this is largely a matter of preaching to the converted, given that we have all witnessed its activism in following through plans to create a Single European Market (SEM), and in its commitment and participation in subsequent political and policy developments at the European level. Even though speculation is rife as to whether the Commission has once again reverted to pre-1985 mode, what has been learnt from the Commission's post-1985 assertiveness is that the institution still has the *potential* to play an important, indeed a crucial and central role in determining the shape and form of the new European polity.

Discussion of the roles played by the Commission, and the objectives it seeks to achieve raises a host of interesting and important questions that challenge popular conceptions of administrative agency. So far commentators have only scraped the surface of many of these issues, and have looked at them only in rather abstract and general ways. Without more empirical evidence and concrete examples of what it is the Commission does and how it organises itself, there is little hope of uncovering what it is about the institution that makes it a novel, dynamic and controversial body. Such an empirical approach does not mean, however, that there is no place in this study for theoretical or conceptual insights. Indeed, theories of integration and, more recently, models of comparative politics, have been used to excellent effect as a way of describing, explaining and even predicting the dynamics of EU politics and the process of European integration. Although some have bemoaned the absence of a successful all-encompassing general macro-level theory that could be used as a conceptual guidebook through the EU maze, most writers on the subject would agree that there is, all the same, much that can be learnt from the theoretical efforts of the past. This book does not associate itself therefore with any one theoretical approach, be it neo-functionalism, intergovernmentalism, federalism or interdependence theory, but prefers to 'pick and mix', to make use of theoretical insights as and when they seem appropriate.

If there is a conceptual bias within this book, it lies in the now fashionable view that it is by taking advantage of comparative politics, public administration and public policy concepts that new insights into the workings of the European institutions can be uncovered. Looking at the Commission as a distinctive and original institution, the book focuses on questions of governance, accountability, legitimacy and bureaucracy: indeed many of the questions political scientists have long been dealing with as part of their domestic politics armoury. Although Anglo-Saxon political studies has over past decades focused much more on behavioural and non-institutional matters, this book (almost by definition it seems) places an institution, the European Commission, centre-stage. Although still considered by many to be an unfashionable and limiting approach, there is room and indeed a need for an institutional focus in political studies. This has been recognised over the last decade or so by numerous authors who have adopted what has been termed a *new institutionalist* or *neo-institutionalist* approach to the study of politics. Much more a set of perspectives than a full-blown theory,[2] this approach is interesting as it seeks to reinsert an institutional dimension into political research. Care must be taken, however, not to make too many assumptions about the importance and centrality of institutions. For that reason alone it is worthwhile considering in a little more detail what it is that the new institutionalists have been trying to do.

The notion that institutions are important is hardly controversial. But whilst in the past there has been a tendency to see institutions merely as arenas within which political activity occurs, or as instruments to be used by individuals and groups, the new institutionalists go beyond this to consider institutions as political actors in their own right. As such, institutions provide social and political order and influence change in politics. In seeking to move away from purely behaviouralist accounts of political life, the new institutionalists at the same time reject the historical and descriptive institutional approaches of the past. In a sense, therefore, they seek the best of both worlds, combining at one and the same time behavioural and institutional perspectives, acknowledging the state's impact on society and the importance of social forces on institutions as a means of offering what they see as a more complete picture of political life.

The emphasis here is important, if only to the extent that our attention can now be drawn to certain features of internal institutional life that have in the past been neglected or, at the very least, underestimated. As such, the formal aspects of the institution are played down, as the focus shifts to such matters as organisational history and memory; leadership: informal structures and decisional processes; the rules of the game, norms and accepted working practices; morale and environment; and the stated and unstated purposive and reflexive goals of the institution. Of course, this is not to argue that formal organisational elements should be ignored, or indeed that this approach effectively *replaces* the former *old* institutionalism. More accurately, the new institutionalists have given the study of institutions a certain *value-added*. This value-added has allowed institutions once again to become a pivotal focus of research – with no apologies!

The new institutionalists are not, however, without their critics. First and foremost, they are criticised for overstating their case, placing too much emphasis on the institutional context. More specifically, the claim is often made that the new institutionalism presumes some sort of direct causal relationship between the institution and policy outcomes. Although the question of the institutional input into policy is certainly one that deserves further attention, simplistic explanations are far from helpful. Such criticism is largely unjustified, however, as it fails to acknowledge the complexity of new institutionalist arguments and the fact that institutions are clearly only one factor in the policy equation. More substantial is the argument that the new institutionalists invite a certain anthropomorphism.[3] In seeing the institution, potentially at least, as a political *actor*, there is a sense in which the new institutionalists might seem to focus on the cohesive rather than on the fragmentary elements of institutional life, and on its autonomy rather than on its dependent characteristics. So what, then, are the advantages in using new institutionalist insights applied to the case of the European Commission – and what are the potential pitfalls of such an approach? The advantages are clear: on one hand the new institutionalism acts as a sort of umbrella under which other theoretical and conceptual models can be applied to our case. Rather than blinkering us against non-compatible theoretical insights, the new institutionalist perspective allows us a certain freedom to learn from past theories whilst acknowledging their limitations. In addition, this approach helps us to delve deeper into the workings of the Commission, to go beyond facile and superficial interpretations of its roles, and to explore the institution from a number of novel dimensions. In short, the new institutionalists provide an avenue for institutional research that allows for the original, non-structural, ideational and informal characteristics of the Commission to be stressed. The Commission, therefore, is considered not just as a set of structures or as an organisation in the functional and instrumental sense, but as a dynamic, living, changing set of 'arenas for contending social forces, ... collections of standard operating procedures and structures that define and defend values, norms, interests, identities and beliefs'.[4]

But in spite of having painted this somewhat rosy picture, it is acknowledged that there are problems in applying a new institutionalist approach to the Commission alone. New institutionalist insights and frameworks are at their most useful when they explore the interaction between various institutions and actors on a more macro-level. Such insights have been used in the case of European merger control, for example, to explore how institutional characteristics define decisional processes. They have also helped to explain the dynamism of particular policy sectors or issues, such as fraud or the environment.[5] Applying the new institutional framework solely to the Commission, and without any specific policy focus, is bound to give a somewhat distorted view of the policy process at the European level. It may serve us better therefore to be less ambitious and to content ourselves with using elements of the approach as a window through which to understand better the Commission. The bulk of the book therefore concentrates on doing just that, seeking to answer questions about the internal functioning and effectiveness of the institution and its relationship with its external environment. We must therefore accept that this book seeks only to provide one paragraph in a chapter on EU politics.

Informed by new institutionalist thinking and by work on organisational theory,[6] the following framework seeks to structure much of the content of the chapters below. Three internal aspects of institutional life provide headings under which the Commission is examined.[7] The first element is that of *leadership*. Here the changing involvement and behaviour of individual actors and groups within the Commission are assessed in order to determine the extent to which leaders are able to contribute to and mould meaning within the institution. Individuals, and not just those in leadership positions, do not only act collectively within an institutional context. Personality, personal motivation and interests are also important. Naturally, leaders have more potential for making use of their own visions and projects than officials. Indeed, they are often appointed for that very purpose. But this does not mean that officials are irrelevant here. This is especially the case where a certain amount of administrative discretion is permitted.

The second perspective relates to the *socio-structural* aspects of the institution. Here we are concerned with the structures within and the organisation of the institution and the manner in which these alter over time. This includes not just formal organisational features, but also such elements as the power structure within the institution; informal channels of communication; questions of recruitment and promotion; and the working practices that affect the day-to-day lives of officials. In other words, the socio-structural elements are those aspects of institutional life that involve both formal and informal structures and processes, the concrete and the more ephemeral realities of recruitment, socialisation, communication and decision.

The third and final element deals with the cultural concerns. Administrative culture is far from an easy concept to define or, for that matter, to research. Within an institutional context the notion of culture is taken to mean *that which gives meaning to human actions*. As such, culture is defined not in terms of what it is, but in terms of what it does. It is administrative culture that provides *shared* interpretations of the world, that shapes the way in which officials communicate with one another and how they perform the tasks entrusted to them. It is clear that under the heading of administrative culture we might see a wide variety of aspects of institutional life and that this may provide fodder for critics of the concept. But if we are looking for something of a checklist, it may be helpful to note that

> the *cultural* system ... embodies the organisation's expressive and affective dimensions in a system of shared and meaningful symbols manifested in myths, ideology and values and in multiple cultural arte-facts (rites, rituals and customs; metaphors, glossaries, acronyms, lexicon and slogans; sagas, stories, legends and organisational lore; logos, design, architecture). This cultural system is shaped by ambient society, the history of the organisation and the particular contingency factors impinging upon it; it changes and evolves under the influence of contemporary dominant actors and the dynamic interplay between cultural and structural elements.[8]

More specifically, the cultural system of an institution comprises three central components: *myth*, which provides 'tenacious and affective links between a valued, often glorified past and contemporary reality, bestowing legitimacy and normalcy upon present actions and modes of organisation'; *ideology*, which is a 'unified and symbolic system of beliefs which provide encompassing, compelling, often mythical, explanations of social reality'; and *values*, which are the constitutive parts, as well as the tangible expressions of an ideology.[9]

These three internal elements provide a focus for discussion within the chapters below, although it is clear that the weight given to leadership/individual, socio-structural or cultural insights will be dependent upon the particular aspect of the institution under scrutiny. The framework requires some further fine-tuning, however. First, we need to give consideration to the relationship between the internal features of the Commission and its external environment. Clearly, external factors beyond the institution's control affect the choice of leaders and structures, and influence the cultural and symbolic character of the Commission. It is important, however, to take into account not only the impact of exogenous factors, but also the way in which the Commission itself is able to mould and re-form its own environment. Clearly, individual actors, organisational and cultural factors are also able to impinge upon institutions and actors outside the bounds of the Commission itself.

It is also important to remind ourselves that the Commission involves a living, changing, dynamic set of relationships. An emphasis on change will therefore be drawn out in the chapters that follow. Leaders and individuals, structures and the symbolic dimension of the institution cannot be treated as constants that explain how the institution *is*. Leaders and officials come and go, structures are reformed or sidelined and cultures redefined or consciously moulded. Likewise, the dynamism of external environmental factors must also play a part in altering the context within which the Commission acts and reacts. For without taking into account the importance of *change*, we could learn little of value about the institution.

Finally, it will become clear throughout the course of the book that the perspectives highlighted above do not exist isolated from one another. Recognition of the complex relationships between individuals, structures, cultures and environment is crucial if our objective is to gain a better understanding of the European Commission and to make some judgement as to the effectiveness of that institution. Indeed, it should come as no surprise that the empirical examples often fail to fit neatly into the boxes created above. There is a fair amount of overlap and not a few grey areas to cope with. However, this should not deter us from making use of the framework if only as a heuristic device. The framework is present throughout the book, not as a constraint, but as an aid to explaining and accounting for the empirical evidence.

Finally, a word about the nature of the institution itself. There is a danger in dealing with something that we identify as *the Commission*, that assumptions are made as to the boundaries between those elements inside the institution and those outside or excluded from it. Although this is perhaps in the nature of a study of this sort, it should be made clear at this point that this in no way precludes the existence of networks and channels of communication that cut across and through the often chimeric Chinese walls of the institution. Where the institution begins and ends is not always as clear as we might imagine at first sight. And, to some extent at least, it is by writing a book of this sort that the Commission (in our own minds) is in fact created. Such musings do not necessarily act as an intellectual or methodological barrier to our efforts to understand more about the European Commission. But we should nevertheless be aware of the fact that in creating frameworks to explain reality, we are creating order where (possibly) none exists. We should not perhaps be too critical of this approach, however, given that institutions themselves are attempts to order and simplify the complexities of political life.[10]

The chapters that follow are divided into three main parts, each of which serves to explore further the relationship between institutional dynamics, policy leadership and European integration. The first part serves various functions. It provides a contextual underpinning to the later chapters on organisation; it introduces the Commission as a dynamic, evolving institution; and seeks to explain both how it has affected its external environment, and how that environment has itself impacted upon the Commission. Part one is divided into three chapters, the first of which asks the question: what is it that the Commission does? The second chapter goes on to explore the evolution of the Commission over the period 1958 to 1984, whilst the third focuses, more specifically, on the Delors Commissions of 1985–88, 1989–92 and 1993–94.

The second part of the book turns its attention to what might be called the *organisational* aspects of the Commission's work. Perhaps a more accurate label would refer to its *internal dynamics*. Here the intention is to explore not just formal structures and procedures, although these are indeed important. It is also the aim here to make full use of the new institutionalists' conceptual armoury, so that such elements as norms, working practices, belief systems and ideology are considered. Part two is divided into three chapters: the first dealing broadly with organisational structures; the second with decisional processes; with the third focusing attention on leadership, structural and procedural issues that coloured Delors's internal management of the Commission.

The third and final part of the book draws broad conclusions whilst, at the same time, adding new insights on questions of institutional reform and more recent developments within the Commission. Although it is too early at the time of writing for any conclusive assessment of the Santer presidency, it may still be possible to point to some interim markers on the style and substance of the post-Delors Commission. This is dealt with in the first chapter, while the second draws together some of the key strands and themes within the book, using the framework outlined above to seek to establish broader conclusions about the internal dynamics of the Commission: the role of leaders within it, its organisational and structural characteristics, the importance of symbolism in this context and the impact of all these aspects of institutional life on the Commission's external environment.

Notes

1   See Edwards and Spence (1994); and Ross (1995).

2   Peterson (1995).

3   Anthropomorphism endows non-human entities with human characteristics.

4   March and Olsen (1989, p. 17).

5   See Bulmer (1994); Menindrou (1994); and Lenchow (1995).

6   Organisation theory is a branch of industrial sociology which tends to focus on explanations of organisational structure, process and performance, whilst at the same time prescibing ways in which organisations may be altered so as to improve them.

7   I am indebted to the staff of CERAT, IEP de Grenoble, for their comments on this framework during a departmental seminar presentation on this subject.

8   Allaire and Firsirotu (1984, p. 213).

9 *Ibid.* (pp. 213–14).
10 March and Olsen (1989, p. 16).

I

The functions and history of the Commission

1

'What does the Commission *do*?'

There is a great deal of confusion about what the European Commission actually does. Ignorance about the institution clearly extends far beyond the misrepresentations of the tabloid press. Generalisations about the European Commission abound as commentators search for simple analogies with more familiar bodies. The confusion begins, however, in the Treaty of Rome itself. This is not surprising given that institutional questions were given perhaps the lowest of priorities during the negotiations setting up the European Economic Community (EEC) in the late 1950s. As such, in Article 155, the Treaty states only that:

> In order to ensure the proper functioning and development of the common market, the Commission shall ...
> – ensure that the provisions of this Treaty and the measures taken by the institutions pursuant thereto are applied;
> – formulate recommendations or deliver opinions on matters dealt with in this Treaty, if it expressly so provides or if the Commission considers it necessary;
> – have its own power of decision and participate in the shaping of measures taken by the Council and the European Parliament in the manner provided for in this Treaty;
> – exercise the powers conferred on it by the Council for the implementation of the rules laid down by the latter.[1]

Neither the Single European Act (SEA) nor the Treaty on European Union (TEU) make any alteration to this broad framework.[2] There was, as such (and still is), little in the treaties to suggest the precise role that the Commission might play within the European integration and policy process, although they certainly did suggest that the

Commission was to be something more than just a European civil service. To a certain extent, the fortunes of the Commission have mirrored broader institutional and political developments at the European level. It could quite easily be argued therefore that the Commission has tended to be a rather reactive body. But in spite of the crystal-clear fact that external events and circumstances are bound to have an impact upon the institution, this would still be a gross simplification. What the Treaty did give the Commission, whether intentionally or by default, was a certain flexibility, or even a malleability, a capacity to adapt to a variety of external conditions. These may have proved at times to be double-edged swords, but they have meant that the Commission, chameleon-like, has been able to survive the proactive first decade of the EEC, the more cautious and reserved post-1966 era, and more recently, the super-activism of the Delors years. However, it has also meant that reform of the institution has never really been a high priority, even though there seems to be a general consensus that the Commission is much in need of it. Change, where it has occurred, has tended to come about as a result of a process of incremental muddling through.

It is perhaps surprising, then, that there should be a fair amount of consensus on the various functions that the Commission performs. Differences of opinion, where they do occur, tend to focus on the relative importance of some tasks over others. Whilst a number of commentators have divided the functions of the Commission into four discrete areas, others have sought to highlight six or more elements of its work. These can often be reduced to the following: the Commission as *initiator* and proposer of legislation (and more generally of policy); the Commission as executor or *administrator*, carrying out the wishes or the mandate of the Council and the Parliament; the Commission as *guardian of the legal framework*, ensuring laws are implemented and enforced; the Commission as the *external representative* of the member states and negotiator on their behalf; the Commission as *mediator* between member states, the European institutions and other sectional interests; and the Commission as the *conscience* and voice of the Union as a whole.

There exists a number of variations upon this theme, and there is no one definitive way of breaking up or pigeon-holing the Commission functions. A noteworthy, though a rather traditional, approach has involved the breakdown of Commission tasks into their political and bureaucratic elements. On the political front, the policy initiation role is lumped together with the Commission's more normative functions, which involve the *filling in* of Community policies; on the bureaucratic front, by contrast, the Commission's administrative and mediative roles are highlighted.[3] This distinction raised interesting questions as to whether (or not) the Commission could be defined in any meaningful sense as a bureaucracy.[4]

We should not be surprised to find that conceptual distinctions often disguise themselves as functional differences in studies of this sort, and we may need to ask ourselves about the agenda being pursued in adhering to one or other form of categorisation. In any case, it should always be borne in mind that to overemphasise the differences between the Commission's functions at the expense of the overlaps that exist is to take these distinctions far too seriously. They are there to help us, and not to constrain our understanding of the institution.

In the past, the so-called politics/administration dichotomy was often used as a framework for analysing institutional contexts.[5] However, the question of the interplay between politics and administration is now well worn, and the distinction remains useful only as a heuristic device. In the past, this debate was rehearsed along the lines of a number of scenarios envisaging the future development of the EU. In short, it centred on whether the Commission could be considered in any sense a future European government, or whether it could amount to little more than a glorified European civil service, not unlike the relatively powerless secretariats of other international organisations.[6] Inevitably, the normative context of such distinctions was omnipresent in these discussions. The question remains, however, an interesting, though overly simplified one as it touches on all the raw theoretical nerves that have coloured the intergovernmentalist versus integrationist debate.[7] One might justifiably argue nevertheless that the question itself may well be somewhat out of date now. Certainly, there are new questions to ask, and new perspectives to take.

A *European* institution?

It is perhaps unusual to begin by considering the Commission as the representative of some sort of European or European Union interest. More often than not, this role, often labelled that of 'conscience of the Community', appears way down the list of what the Commission does. This is largely due to the fact that in performing this role, the Commission is not endowed with any formal powers. Nevertheless, it is clear that to question the importance of the Commission's Europeanism provides an excellent starting-point, as most of what the Commission does either flows from this function, or at the very least is shaped by it.

In the early years of the Community it was believed that the Commission was to be an institution that would eschew sectional interests, rising above the divisive day-to-day political wrangling that dominated national political agendas.[8] This aspiration was overly optimistic and perhaps even naive given the manner in which the Community system was to evolve. This is clear with the benefit of hindsight. Drawn largely from functionalist writings that saw the Community developing along the lines of a non-political technocratic and functional set of structures, the notion of *general* interest came to suggest an objectivity and rationality which would counter the partisanship of the member state governments.

The difficulty lies, then, in trying to understand how this perception of the Commission fits with the avowed European character of the institution; how the general interest represented by the Commission came to be equated with a common or, indeed, a specific and distinctive *European* interest. The apparent contradictions here are highlighted in the labelling of the Commission as a 'protagonist',[9] though it is often unclear what exactly the Commission is a protagonist for or of. Part of the problem lies in the fact that this particular function of the Commission is largely self-proclaimed:[10] that is, that it is not spelt out in any treaty. Does representation of the European interest imply a bias in favour of further European integration, for example? And if so what kind of integration? These sorts of questions remain unanswered, even though the Commission's role may well be one of informing the world about possible European futures.

It is clear that the role of 'conscience of the Community' invites a host of different interpretations and definitions. Four distinct strands can be identified which together help explain the interests of the institution. First of all, the Commission may be viewed as a multinational organisation which does not seek to represent any one particular governmental position within the Union. As such, it finds itself in an excellent position to present to member state actors an *overview* of the EU-wide situation and to adopt an EU-wide perspective on policy issues. Translated into the currency of EU negotiation and decision-making, this overview becomes an *interest* in its own right. In fact, the Commission is often talked of as though it were a sixteenth member state. Even so, it is simplistic in the extreme to accept this at face value. The European interest, as defined by the Commission, is the product of a much more complicated process of bargaining at the European level, and indeed within the confines of the Commission services. Behind the slogan of conscience of the Community, then, lies a larger story about the Commission and its internal dynamics.

Secondly, it is possible to identify a more specific interest: that of the promotion of European integration in the most general of senses. This is an inherently teleological role, and is one of the foundations upon which all other Commission functions rest. It is in essence vague and undefined, attaching itself largely to a process of incremental change, with no necessary commitment to any end result. The federalist rhetoric of the early years of the Community is not much in evidence in the Commission nowadays, but this does not preclude the existence of a more diffuse pro-European ethos. Thirdly, interests revolve around specific policy or sectoral distinctions that are dealt with by the Commission. These fragment, potentially at least, the notion of a European or a general interest, with policy functions determining functional allegiances. Here, the Commission services may well see their interests lying with the policy networks to which they belong, or the policy objectives they promote. As such, these contradict the notion that Commission-wide interests necessarily predominate within the institution. Finally, it is also possible to discern a distinctive internal *Commission* interest, a reflexive interest that relates much more to the self-preservation and even the expansion of the Commission than to the collective interest of the EU member states or a distinctive pro-European line. This, too, may be fragmented to the extent that even within the Commission, institutional interests rest with individual administrative units rather than with the Commission as a whole.

Clearly there is no either/or choice to be made when it comes to examining interests. It may well be that all four distinctions made here tell us something about what motivates the Commission. What is interesting for our purposes, however, is that through exploring interests in this way, it is possible to direct our attention to some of the most important Commission roles: those of think-tank and policy formulator; manager, administrator and executive; legal watchdog; and consensus-builder. As will become apparent, an understanding of the Commission as the representative of the European or the common interest, of a sectoral or of its own self-interest cannot be divorced from a more specific understanding of what the Commission staff actually do in their daily work. Indeed, it would be fair to say that the Commission's 'conscience' is what pervades all of the roles it assumes and the functions it performs.

Think-tank and policy formulator

A debate at the heart of many theories of integration and international co-operation has been the relationship and interaction between economic and political integration, and whether such a distinction is indeed tenable. Whereas pluralists and functionalists made a strong case for *politics* to be considered as a distinct sphere of government, usually involving diplomatic, security and defence aspects, neo-functionalist writers saw politics as part and parcel of all government policies and economic sectors.[11] Politics, from this perspective, had more to do with the allocation of values and social goods within a society, than with any discrete set of policy domains. How we define politics is important if we seek to explore and understand institutional life within the Commission. Simply to call the Commission *political*, without a clear idea of what is meant by this, is pointless. Just as neo-functionalists saw the political in all policies, this chapter suggests that the political comes in many shapes and forms, and is a feature of all Commission functions in one way or another.

However unintentionally, when evidence is sought on the political characteristics of the Commission, it is first and foremost the function of policy initiation or policy formulation that is highlighted. This might imply that the Commission is a crucial 'catalyst in the policy making process',[12] or in broader terms, that the institution has 'a sort of overall responsibility ... for the future development and completion of the Community'.[13] There does seem to be some agreement that the Commission possesses, at least potentially, the ability to act as the driving force of European integration. This identifies not simply the Commission's right to draft legislation, but more generally its obligation to *lead* the Community through the development of grand projects and programmes of action, by means of a strategic goal-setting capacity. This, it is assumed, is used together with its skills in mediation, to push forward the process of European integration and to enhance and develop further the policy role of the EU.

Certain questions are begged here: in particular, is it clear that this is indeed what the Commission is doing? To begin with, it may not be able or may not wish to set the agenda in this way. From the late 1960s on, the Commission was lambasted for demonstrating a distinct lack of leadership. Since then, other institutional actors, the European Council (of heads of government), the Council Presidency, and more recently the European Parliament (EP) have stepped in where the Commission seemed unable to act. Secondly, even if it is possible for the Commission to identify with such a long-term objective as the promotion of European integration, it is far from being a unified body with a single set of aims. End goals are often blurred and vague and are more often than not tied to specific policy sectors or institutional fiefdoms. There is a clear paradox between a Commission obliged to develop strategic and policy objectives, but whose ultimate *raison d'être* remains undefined. Not surprisingly, such strategic developments are often left to visionary leaders to operationalise, and, within the Commission, most usually to the President, or to one or more determined commissioners.

There is no doubt that if there is to be a visionary leadership role for the Commission, it is likely to be tied closely to its role as European conscience – whatever we take that to mean. But there are dangers inherent in this function. The Commission has, in the past, been accused of producing grand statements and making strategic gestures, without having the wherewithal to put plans into practice. Commissioners have at their disposal the capacity to issue recommendations, opinions, reports and programmes as part of their initiation responsibilities. But for the most part they are reliant on the member states for the provision of resources. A clear example of this is found in the Werner Plan of 1970 which foresaw economic and monetary union by 1980. Although, in general, establishing timetables for action may be a useful way of motivating elites and focusing minds within the Community (as it was with the 1992 deadline), the failure to achieve objectives within set time limits, as (potentially) in the case of Economic and Monetary Union (EMU) this time around, can tarnish the image of the Commission and of the Union as a whole. As such, when Commission programmes dissolve into rhetoric, the Commission can only be discredited.[14] The leadership role played by the Commission is one dependent upon favourable external conditions. The success or failure of the goals that are set is often out of its control.

While the political leadership role of the Commission may well be labelled its right of *initiative*, its right of *initiation* is a much more specific function. Indeed this may well be the most important formal power that the Commission possesses.[15] Without a proposal from the Commission no European legislative act can be issued. Although the Commission is often accused of inventing outlandish ideas for legislation, it is certainly constrained in what it can do by the Council and by the EP. Indeed, it would be self-defeating for the Commission to propose legislation which it knew could find no support in one or other of the legislating institutions.

It is however the Commission alone that has the right to draft the proposals that form the basis of discussion, consultation and subsequent European legislation. This does not mean that the Commission operates in some sort of institutional or policy vacuum. Under the Maastricht Treaty, the EP also has the right to initiate, although what this means in practice is that, like the European Council, it can request that the Commission drafts proposals on its behalf. The Commission, according to the new treaty, is obliged to respond. As such, it is still up to the Commission to flesh out general ideas and principles and to make choices about different policy approaches. These practical initiatives 'are key factors in providing the dynamic of the Community and serve as milestones in its development'.[16] The policy stances adopted by the Commission do not emerge out of thin air, however, but are the product of a complex and detailed process of information retrieval and consultation. Under the 1966 Luxembourg Compromise, the Commission has an obligation to consult the member states as well as other interests before proposals are issued, and although there is no assumption that this agreement carries legal or political weight any longer, it is clearly in the Commission's own interest to continue to follow it in spirit.

As already mentioned, Article 155 of the Rome Treaty provides the legal base for this initiation role. It bids the Commission 'have its own power of decision and participate in the shaping of measures taken by the Council and by the European Parliament in the manner provided for in this Treaty'. The initiation of policy is not simply a right, but also a duty. As such, the Commission has a clear legal responsibility to translate into implementable policy the principles set out within the Treaties, advanced by the European Council and now, by the EP. In fact, the Commission has fulfilled this responsibility with gusto, producing in the past around 700 to 800 individual pieces of draft legislation each year. Although quantity is no evidence of effectiveness, the Commission has been rather successful in translating non-specific policy ideas into concrete legislative proposals.

There has been a clear commitment in recent years to reduce the number of proposals issued, however. This is in part evidence of the subsidiarity principle at work, but it also relates more generally to fears of overload or *lourdeur* due to an ever-growing workload. The shift in emphasis from activism to consolidation has been gradual and has not exactly followed a linear path. The turning-point was not the Luxembourg Compromise, but the realisation by Commission staff themselves that neither public opinion nor governments would support increasing the competences of the Commission, when this was perceived as a process of centralisation. There is a certain irony in this shift away from the initiative function, however, to the extent that 'The Commission is quite simply better at proposing than managing'.[17]

In Western liberal-democracies, initiation or policy formulation tends to lie with government. It is an activity that is not the prerogative of any civil service, though of course the input from administrators and bureaucrats may well be explicit as well as implicit. Particularly in the early years of the Community, the notion that the Commission would eventually evolve into a European government was not unthinkable.[18] This is not to say that the Commission has ever come close to living up to such a grand label, however. It is certainly lacking in functions that would normally be part and parcel of a national government. It does not, for example, have a leading role in foreign affairs or defence; and neither does it have the right to use force legitimately, either internally or externally. Perhaps as importantly, the Commission cannot approve legislation to raise revenue if it sees fit; neither does it have a majority in the EP to support it, nor a prime minister, cabinet or ministers, for that matter.[19] Members of the Commission could perhaps be deemed to be European politicians, but there are limits to parallels that can be drawn between them and their national counterparts.

Manager and administrator

Although a great deal of emphasis is placed on the Commission's policy initiation role, this can be misleading as it seems to suggest that most of the Commission's time is spent drafting legislation.[20] It ignores the fact that a great deal of energy goes into what are often rather routine administrative and management tasks. In many senses, the Commission really does play the role of a conventional civil service, and this raises questions about whether there is in fact an identifiable European public service.[21] It is in areas where the Commission is responsible for the *execution* of policy that parallels with national administrations are most pertinent. Whilst policy initiation or formulation is considered essentially to be a political activity, policy execution is generally viewed as a function undertaken by bureaucrats and administrators.

Broadly speaking, the Commission is responsible for 'laying down ground rules, carrying out investigations and giving rulings on significant matters':[22] indeed, all areas of the Commission's work that involve turning treaty commitments and secondary legislation (either of the Council or of the Commission itself) into workable policy or programmes of action. As a result, most of the Commission's administrative work is really concerned with ensuring the smooth running of policies that have already been agreed in the Council. As such, its role involves planning and programming only within those guidelines and frameworks established by member state representatives. In practice this means that where the Council agrees the general rule, the Commission is given the task of filling in the detail.

However, the Commission is not itself responsible for the implementation of legislation in any street-level sense. This task is generally delegated to national or subnational government departments and agencies. As such, Commission officials are often far removed from the application of legislation. In this sense, the Commission lies between a rock and a hard place. It does not have the right to legislate: but neither does it have responsibility for practical implementation. In fact, the Commission plays an intermediary role between these two stages in the policy process, though it is nevertheless involved in or associated with all stages in that process. The specific tasks the Commission is expected to perform in this regard are generally well defined, even though over recent years there has been a general encroachment by national governments on the Commission's field of executive activity.

On the one hand, the Commission has become increasingly irritated by the Council's approach to executive decision-making. More and more, Council bodies have sought to involve themselves in what the Commission considers to be its own field of responsibility. This has largely been achieved through the extension of the Council's multi-layered network of committees which exist largely to keep a check on the Commission.[23] On the other hand, the wholehearted adoption of the principle of subsidiarity by the Commission has meant that any liklihood of more involvement in national and subnational implementation has diminished even further. Indeed, the contrary is more likely, with national governments keen to make sure that the Commission allows them as much flexibility as is possible in applying European rules. This may even be written into individual legislative acts as an obligation. Given the fact that the Commission is being squeezed in this way, it is perhaps surprising to discover that its administrative load has continued to increase in recent years, though this has more to do with the cumulative growth of the body of European law and policy, as well as with constraints placed upon Commission resources by the Council.

It is only in extreme cases, such as under the rules on competition policy, that a delegated legislative role may be part and parcel of this function. Competition policy is somewhat different from other policy areas in that implementation rests with a directorate-general (DG IV) of the Commission and not with the member states. Although the quasi-legislative role performed by the Commission in this respect is *de jure* an executive task, the issuing of individual decisions that are legally enforceable implies that in this policy field the Commission has a measure of discretion which is effectively unique. However, there are other occasions when Commission directives and decisions are issued under procedures that have led to the Commission being labelled a quasi-legislator. The most important example is perhaps the Commission's management of agricultural markets, where a plethora of decisions on agricultural prices are taken practically on a daily basis.[24]

Not surprisingly, this quasi-legislative function of the Commission tends to apply to the management of policy areas that were developed in the early years of the EC's existence. By definition, these are the policy areas that are most centralised – the so-called common policies. On the whole, the law that is issued by the Commission tends to be law that implements broader policy objectives initially agreed by the member states, even though that original agreement could well have been made as far back as the 1950s or 1960s. The distinction between administrative and policy law is one familiar in domestic political circles. And as at national level, the blurring of this distinction has meant that the Commission has on many occasions been accused of acting illegitimately as a sort of legislator, even though this is not permitted by the treaties.

One of the Commission's most important tasks involves the drawing up and administration of the Community's annual budget. Here, the Council and Parliament are the legislating authorities, with the Commission performing a lesser, though crucial, managerial function. The Commission draws up the budget as a proposal to be put to the other EU institutions, and is subsequently involved in all stages of the budgetary process right through from the collection of revenue to the processing of funding applications. Budget matters take up a great deal of Commission time, and the process is literally never-ending: once one year's budget is agreed upon, work begins on the following year's.

At the end of the process, moneys from the EU coffers are distributed to the various funds and budget lines. Although the amount of money available and the broad focus of the funds is restricted by the Council and Parliament, the Commission does have a certain leeway in deciding the application criteria to be used. This gives them at least some flexibility. Likewise, the Commission also has some freedom of manoeuvre in deciding the criteria for other sources of funding available, under the programme approach used in environmental, science, technology and research areas of EC policy. Once again, however, the broad objectives to be attained have been set out beforehand by the Council. This programme approach often stretches well beyond the EU member states themselves. In the case of the PHARE (Poland and Hungary: aid for economic Reconstruction) programme which channels aid and technical assistance from the G24 (Group of Twenty-four) countries, for example, the Commission appears at first sight to be acting as little more than a secretariat. But given the Commission's role in developing criteria for the distribution of these funds, the effect it can have on the policy on the ground and the discretionary scope of officials involved, can be considerable. Administrative discretion is not peculiar to the Commission, of course. But it does underline the fact that we should not be too hasty in assuming that an administrative role implies a non-political role. Even though margins for manoeuvre might be slim, and getting slimmer, Commission officials are still able to wield a fair amount of influence over the content of the policies they administer. This is in spite of constraints placed upon them, not only by the national ministers in the Council, but also, increasingly, by the EP.

This is certainly the case when we consider the external representative role performed by the Commission. Often considered a distinctive function in its own right, the Commission's responsibilities internationally remain, to a large extent, managerial. This is in spite of the fact that here the Commission can act as negotiator on behalf of the member state governments, when deals are to be struck on matters of international trade. Ultimately, however, the flexibility or discretion of Commission actors is constrained by the mandate offered them by the Council. Indeed, one might even go as far as to argue that, in performing this function, the Commission acts much more as a conventional international secretariat than it does in other tasks it undertakes. There is no doubt, nevertheless, that the projection of an external EU image beyond the European continent is an extremely important job for the Commission.[25]

Defender of the legal order

As the conscience of the EU, the Commission is responsible for defending the European legal order, that is, ensuring that member states and in some cases, companies and individuals, comply with the European rule of law. Indeed, the distinction between the Commission's role as *active* conscience of the Community, telling the world of the merits of European integration, and its role as *passive* conscience, ensuring the implementation of European law, is a helpful one here.[26] This latter function, which often sees the Commission labelled the *watchdog* of the Union or the 'guardian of the treaties', comprises a set of supervisory and enforcement functions which highlight the ambivalence of the Commission's position within the European system of governance.

Non-implementation or incorrect implementation is a serious problem for the Commission as it seeks to fulfil its *watchdog* function. Member states may be prepared to sign up to European legislation, but legislative obligations frequently remain unfulfilled. There are a multitude of reasons why this is so. It may be that member state governments or the agencies responsible for implementation do not have the political clout or the administrative structures in place to ensure that the laws are applied on the ground; there may even be cultural or linguistic misunderstandings about the nature of the laws that have been agreed. Even so, it is not unheard of for member states to fail to implement legislation intentionally – either to gain a competitive edge over other member states, or to appease a nationally-based sectional interest. The first problem for the Commission, therefore, is to *detect* this implementation deficit – a supervisory function; the second is to resolve it, which essentially involves enforcement mechanisms.

Detection should not be taken for granted. The Commission is not a large organisation, in spite of rumours to the contrary, and it is more often than not dependent on outsiders for information on breaches of the law. There are several ways in which an illegality of this sort can come to the attention of Commission officials. Law-abiding governments may be eager to make sure that they are not the only ones implementing legislation, especially where there are substantial costs involved that may affect the competitive standing of their country. In such cases, they may be inclined to report on governments that have not been so conscientious. However, when they themselves are accused, they may not be so eager to submit to investigation and accept the Commission's supervisory authority. Likewise, interest groups and other non-governmental organisations (or indeed individuals) may report breaches to the Commission. In Britain, for example, environmental interests have been quick to report the non-implementation of European environmental law.

In some cases, regulations and directives have a process of self-notification written into them. The Commission may become aware of non- or incorrect implementation through this route. If the notification procedure is not complied with, a potential substantive breach of the rules is compounded by a lesser procedural breach. Ultimately, the Commission does its best to keep a check on what is happening at the implementation stage, although it is impossible to

keep track of all laws in all member states. The task at hand, therefore, may amount to little more than keeping a watchful eye on the
financial and trade press. Commission officials are as reliant on the
investigative capabilities of journalists as they are on interest groups
when they seek to uncover ineffective implementation.

It is only really in the competition policy field that the Commission's powers of investigation are really to be taken seriously. Here,
Commission officials, with the assistance of national cartel officers
are able to raid the offices of companies they suspect of breaching
European competition law.[27] Not surprisingly, demands for these
sorts of powers to be extended into other policy areas have so far
been resisted. In the case of anti-fraud action, an issue that has been
much in the headlines in recent years, the Commission is solely
dependent on national governments for the investigation of the
illicit use of European funds or any other potentially fraudulent
activities involving the EC budget.

Regardless of their powers of investigation, discovering that a
breach has occurred is only half the story. The enforcement of EC
law is also problematic for the Commission, as although it is obliged
to perform this task by the treaties, it possesses very few mechanisms through which it can force those in breach of the rules to
comply. If the legal watchdog role of the Commission is a substitute
for an effective EU-wide implementation framework, it is a rather
inadequate one. Solutions to this problem are not difficult to envisage, but it is unlikely that the political will exists to make substantial changes to enforcement mechanisms. So even though 'national
governments will probably have to be ready to allow the Commission greater powers of enforcement if rigorous standards are to be
secured throughout the Community',[28] it is doubtful, with the adoption of the subsidiarity principle, that the member states will be prepared to accept what they would most likely see as a centralising
move.

The Commission is therefore in an extremely vulnerable position
when it comes to playing out its role as guardian of the treaties. It is
reliant upon the goodwill of the member states, even if its position
is strengthened somewhat by the support of the European Court.
This weakness does not reflect any lack of commitment on the part
of the Commission. What it does reflect is the resource strain the
Commission is under in terms of time, money and staff. As the legislative load the Commission must bear has expanded, demands

placed on its officials have multiplied. It is not surprising that the
Commission itself has been in the forefront of calls for a reduction
in the quantity of legislation issued.

Political considerations are also crucial. The Commission is well
aware of the criticisms it faces when it tries to fulfil its supervisory
obligations. In particular, accusations of non-accountable elitism
and technocratic decision-making often hit raw Commission
nerves. In order to challenge these accusations the Commission has
had to become an astute political actor, even though this may imply
a certain ambivalence when contrasting the institution's legal as
against its political position. Ironically what this tends to mean in
practice is a playing down of its overtly political role, adopting a less
aggressive and less confrontational style when pursuing breaches of
the rules. There are numerous examples of the Commission backing
down when faced with recalcitrant member states. However, caution itself must be used with caution, as it is likely to backfire if
taken to extremes. A playing down of the Commission's *watchdog*
role could very easily lead to the undermining of the entire European rule of law. The Commission has a careful balancing act to perform.

Consensus-building

The construction of consensus within the EU is perhaps the most
underrated function performed by the Commission. Yet, those who
take a more intergovernmentalist line on European integration are
more likely to consider this to be the most important function of the
Commission. It is clear that, given a decision-making process that
continues to place national governments centre-stage, the Commission's 'European' function is largely defined by its relation with the
member states. It is in this sense that the Commission is labelled an
honest broker within a process largely concerned with intergovernmental negotiation.

It would be incorrect, however, to see the Commission's consensus-building function solely in this light. Consensus-building around
specific policy issues, but also around the wider question of European integration, is something that also concerns subnational
actors, transnational actors and non-governmental organisations.
Although the Commission must be careful not to tread on national
governmental toes, there is still much it can do to facilitate Europe-

wide agreement. In terms of interest group activity, for example, this is well developed, while on the question of trade union-management relations, there has been much less success.

Likewise, the growing importance of the EP must not be neglected. This is exemplified most clearly in the role that the Commission performs within the co-decision procedure introduced in the Maastricht Treaty. Here, at the final stage in the process of decision-making, when agreement has still not been reached, the Council and Parliament meet in a conciliation committee to attempt to come to a mutually satisfactory agreement. The Commission's role may well be minimal, but it does have a legal obligation to help facilitate agreement between the two legislative bodies. As such, it finds itself clearly in the role of inter-institutional go-between.

Nevertheless, the consensus-building activities of the Commission often tend to focus on governmental actors. Here, promotional, political input is downplayed in favour of a perspective that sees the Commission much more as an international secretariat than as a policy actor in its own right. But to claim that this implies a non-political role for the Commission is way off the mark. In working to explore the common ground between the member states and other interests, the Commission does not content itself with seeking to 'split the difference' between parties; and neither is the game seen as zero-sum. The Commission clearly aims to reach beyond basic lowest common denominator solutions, in order to upgrade the common interest and raise the stakes at the European level.

Not surprisingly, the Commission has an interest in performing this function well. On a policy or decisional level, what is at stake is a proposal which has been initiated and drafted by Commission staff. As such, the officials involved have a vested interest in seeing their hard work translated into concrete legislation. However, a fine balance must be sought. The need to arrive at a political bargain, a compromise, may in the last resort make the legislation itself more inflexible and difficult to implement, thus making life harder for the Commission when it comes to policy execution. These are the things that the Commission must take into consideration at the policy formulation stage, by presenting proposals that are technically feasible, yet politically well informed. It is in achieving this balance between the technical and the political that the Commission gains the upper hand. It can present itself as having a monopoly of knowledge on a given subject, having undergone a rigorous process of consultation at European, national and subnational levels, and having dealt extensively with relevant interest groups. However, at the same time, the political elements within proposals are played down. Where the ideological content is explicit, member states are going to find it all the easier to muster opposition. The image of an apolitical, technocratic Commission may be illusory, but it remains an illusion that it is often in the Commission's best interest to perpetuate.

In terms of grander policy objectives, including those initiated by the European Council, the Commission is likely to see its role as one of facilitating not only European integration *per se*, but also the resolution of European problems and amicable relations between states and non-state actors in the region. As such, the Commission's role here goes beyond merely smoothing the path of regulations and directives. It refers much more to the overview functions already mentioned, that is, the capacity of the Commission to act simultaneously as think tank, research unit *and* consensus-builder. It is indeed a difficult and rather contrived task to separate out neatly all of these Commission functions.

The Commission has many strategies and tactics at its disposal for building a consensus which, as stated, goes beyond striving for lowest common denominators. One familiar tactic it has used involves grouping policies and issues together so as to push a set of proposals through the Council. In this way the Commission seeks to convince all member states that there is something in the package for them. Such a strategy can be helpful even if it is only really important at the margins of policymaking.[29] The Commission constructs package deals to placate aggrieved states or to give the illusion of a *fair deal*. When it comes to more controversial political issues, however, package deals are not always possible. This has been clear ever since the infamous failure of the 1965 package, which linked the funding of the Common Agricultural Policy (CAP), the creation of an independent Community budget, and the extention of powers for the EP.[30] Given De Gaulle's overriding reluctance to see majority voting introduced in the Council of Ministers, it soon became clear that these matters were too controversial to be tied together. The crisis that ensued, prompted by the French withdrawal from the Council (the so-called *empty chair* policy) subsequently made the Commission wary of becoming too dependent on these types of arrangement.

There may of course be a more malevolent and manipulative interpretation of the Commission's package dealing approach. It has, for example, been suggested that the Commission seeks to push forward the frontiers of integration by 'the deliberate engineering of regular crises'.[31] This is interesting, as it suggests that the Commission intentionally constructs threats to the broader structures of European integration in order to argue that the only way to consolidate what has been achieved so far is to reach a *new* consensus over integration.

However, a rather different approach that is still frequently used by the Commission is that of postponing the adoption of decisions to a future date when circumstances are likely to be more favourable. Consensus-building, where there is no immediate hope of a consensus, is time-wasting. The Commission must be astute enough to realise when and where there is no prospect of an agreement. Instead of focusing on the final substantive outcome, therefore, the Commission, in the meantime, concerns itself with the more technical business of setting deadlines and putting procedures into effect, with the ultimate objective pushed temporarily out of view. Here once again the Commission puts on its technocratic cloak and presents political proposals as matters for simple bureaucratic solutions. Ideological or national opposition to elements in the policy are dismissed as irrelevant to the technical business at hand, or, at the very least, are considered as something apart from the *political* controversy. Once the procedural machinery is in place and the policy already has some sort of institutional foundation it is hoped that it will be much easier to overcome resistance. Likewise, circumstances may alter, and consensus may be more easily achieved at a later date – by which time swift action can be taken.

We see therefore that what is labelled here as the *consensus-building* role of the Commission is a term used rather loosely. What is really being discussed is the way in which the Commission can facilitate political solutions within a multinational inter-institutional political arena. But it goes beyond this, if we consider the Commission's role as one of promoting agreement on broader issues across European society at large. The extent to which the Commission can do this really depends on how it is able to make use of both its institutional skills at consensus-building, and its agenda-setting capacity. Increasingly we come to recognise that it is not really possible to make clearcut distinctions between the different functions the

Commission performs. As such, the image of the Commission as 'honest broker' can be much overplayed.

Conclusions: defining the Commission

If the intention of this chapter was to answer the question 'what is it that the European Commission does?', some headway has been made in furnishing a preliminary response. It is, as such, possible to draw some conclusions as to how one might define the Commission as an institution. Several perspectives deserve our attention here.

It is clear that what the Commission does seems initially to be determined or at least constrained by the legal framework, that is, by the Treaty of Rome and its subsequent revisions. This framework may not be spelt out in much detail, but it nevertheless provides the perimeters within which the Commission's work is done. It is clear, though, that a constitutional definition of the Commission's role is often neglected. Indeed, whilst a great deal of fuss has been made about the Commission's administrative and political functions, there has been less emphasis on its legal character (by political scientists, in any case). This refers not only to the fact that the Commission is subject to certain legal obligations and responsibilities, but also that it functions as a quasi-judicial body in several policy domains. Indeed, the Commission is as much a legal animal as it is a political one.

Falling between attempts to uncover a legal and a political definition, it is also possible to consider the Commission as a regulatory body. This amounts to much more than simply a restatement of the managerial and administrative functions identified above. The regulatory strand pervades the ethos of the institution, focusing attention on the quasi-legislative, quasi-judicial as well as the executive components within the Commission's competences and, in so doing, seeks to define the institution as a 'quasi-agency'.

After mention of constitutional, judicial and regulatory definitions, it may well sound rather conventional to rehearse the view that the Commission is after all a 'political animal'. But this focus is important if we are interested in assessing whether the Commission may be considered an actor in its own right. It is all too easy to label the Commission 'political' without any consideration of what that label really means. One perspective may well focus on the quasi-governmental nature of the institution's work. We have clearly already identified the similarities and the differences between the roles played by national governments and those performed by the Commission. But this does not prevent us defining the Commission in these terms.

Are we any closer, then, to understanding what it is that the Commission does? One difficulty found in addressing these grand questions, exploring the big picture as it were, is that any focus on 'functions' or on 'roles' will tend to turn attention away from the internal characteristics of the institution towards Commission interaction with institutions or individuals beyond its boundaries. A new perspective, albeit one that complements the approach taken above may well be called for: one that focuses attention on the 'interests' of the Commission, rather than upon its functions. Here, we might see a distinction between reflexive or inward-looking priorities, and those more closely related to the attainment of specific policy objectives or to the role of the Commission in the European integration process.[32]

Clearly, unanswered questions remain. So far, there has been little emphasis on organisational, structural or procedural matters, for example. Likewise, no consideration has been given to questions of effectiveness and accountability. Moreover, the themes of 'change' and 'dynamism' in the context of the institution have not been addressed. There are indeed many definitions that remain to be uncovered and many stories yet untold about the European Commission.

Notes

1   *Treaties Establishing the European Communities as Amended by Subsequent Treaties*, HMSO, London, September 1988; *Treaty on European Union*, Office of Official Publications, Luxembourg, 1993.

2   There are other treaty provisions that refer to the Commission, but these focus on organisational and inter-institutional matters. See Articles 156–159.

3   See Coombes (1970).

4   *Ibid.* (p. 235).

5   See, for example, Campbell and Peters (1988).

6   Neunreither (1972).

7   The study of European integration has been shaped theoretically by a debate between integrationists (often neo-functionalists) who have emphasised the importance of the central European institutions in the inte-

gration process, and the intergovernmentalists (neo-realists), who focus their attention much more on the continuing dominance of the member states.

8 Nugent (1991, p. 97).

9 Both Coombes (1970) and Henig (1980) talk about the Commission as a 'protagonist'. In the case of Coombes, he argues that the Commission must be 'partisan and protagonistic' (1970, p. 78), while Henig labels the Commission as the 'protagonist of the common interest' (1980).

10 Henig (1980, p. 59) makes this point.

11 For an overview of various older theories of European integration, see Pentland (1973). Fo a newer overview, see Hix (1994).

12 Henig (1980, p. 51).

13 Neunreither (1972, p. 235).

14 Ludlow (1991, p. 97).

15 Coombes (1970, p. 79).

16 *Ibid.* (p. 235).

17 Ludlow (1991, p. 97).

18 Coombes (1970, p. 84) stated that 'some of the formal powers bestowed upon the commission imply a role similar to that of the typical executive branch of government'. On the other hand, he also stated that 'whatever the behaviour of individual Commissioners, they are performing the function of bureaucrats in relation to the political system of the Community. Their autonomy is strictly delegated and derived. Their purpose is the implementation of a consensus reached by the member governments acting together under the mediative agency of the Commission' (Coombes, 1970, p. 274).

19 Nugent (1991, p. 73).

20 Michelmann (1978a).

21 This notion of a European public service would cover not only the officials of the Commission, but those working within other European institutions too.

22 Nugent (1991, p. 77).

23 Chapter six gives an overview of the committee system within the Commission.

24 Henig (1980, p. 55) noted that over 4,500 agricultural instruments were issued by the Commission in 1980.

25 For further information on the external role of the Commission see Nutall (1992), Nutall (1994) and Smith (1994) for example.

26 Coombes (1970, p. 82).

27 Breaches would usually involve the existence of some sort of cartel or restrictive practice, such as price fixing or market-sharing.

28 Franklin (1990, p. 99).

29 Moravscik (1993).

30 See chapter two.
31 Coombes (1970, p. 286).
32 This question is revived in the concluding chapter of this book.

2

Presidents and policies: a short history of the Commission, 1958–1984

What was, in effect, the first European Commission was set up in 1952 with the creation of the European Coal and Steel Community (ECSC). Although it was not called a commission as such[1] – it was in fact given the grander title of *High Authority* – it was similar in many respects to the equivalent institution set up to administer the EEC after 1958. However, the blatantly supranational elements found in the High Authority were largely excluded from the EEC Commission's make-up. Essentially the executive organ of the ECSC, the High Authority was also in some instances responsible for legislation. This element was absent from the later EEC (and the EURATOM (European Atomic Energy Community)) Commissions. In the EEC, there was more of an attempt to separate legislative and executive functions. And as such, the Council of Ministers was given a much greater role to play.[2]

Structural and procedural factors clearly provide the context within which Commission business is undertaken; indeed, they more often shape the choice and even the form of that business. Exogenous environmental considerations must also be borne in mind, however. Whilst taking into account the impact of structural and external contexts, this chapter focuses its attention more specifically on leadership and personality. As such, it raises questions that relate to the importance of leadership in determining both the speed and quality of the European integration process, and the role of the Commission within it. Commission presidents are undoubtedly important. But they are often important for different reasons; for the very different roles which they choose (or are forced) to play. Above all, Commission presidents are important as they symbolise or personify the institution as a whole. There is no doubt that an effective leadership role performed administratively has tended to go hand-in-hand with an effective leadership role for the Commission externally. It is this assumption that provides an underlying rationale when considering the individual performances of presidents from Walter Hallstein to Gaston Thorn (Figure 1)

Walter Hallstein	1958–67	German
Jean Rey	1967–70	Belgian
Franco Maria Malfatti	1970–72	Italian
Sicco Mansholt	1973–73	Dutch
François-Xavier Ortoli	1973–77	French
Roy Jenkins	1977–81	British
Gaston Thorn	1981–85	Luxembourger
Jacques Delors	1985–95	French
Jacques Santer	1995–	Luxembourger

Figure 1   Presidents of the European Commission

From the setting up of the High Authority, to the arrival of Jacques Delors as President of the Commission in 1985, much changed within the European Community. The Commission, created without any real blueprint, became a force to be reckoned with over this period. Even when criticised as weak and ineffectual, the institution continued to affect the political, economic and legal environments of all the member states. As such, the history of the European Commission, of its fluctuating fortunes and its evolving policies, is one in which individual personalities play an important part.

Hallstein and the administration of the new Commission

The first decade of the Commission's existence was shaped largely by the first Commission president, Walter Hallstein.[3] Indeed, Hallstein left such a lasting imprint on the institution that many have recently compared his influence on the Commission with that of Jacques Delors. Until the Delors Commissions of 1985–94, it was almost an accepted wisdom that no one individual had been able to equal the activism and dynamism of the first ten years. Hallstein came to personify, over this period, not only the Commission, but also the process of European integration more broadly defined. The flexibility of the framework provided within the Rome Treaty meant that the potential for the Commission to play such a role already existed. But it would only be with encouragement from Hallstein that this potential would be fulfilled.

Hallstein was a high-profile candidate for the post of Commission President. His involvement in West Germany's European policy after the end of the Second World War had given him a good grounding in European affairs generally. It was indeed his involvement in the drafting of the Treaty of Rome which had led Jean Monnet[4] to push for his appointment in the first place. There was little controversy over his nomination to the post, though the appointment process did get tied up with certain organisational issues, in particular with the question of where the European institutions would be located.[5] Thankfully, these matters were not an insuperable barrier to Hallstein's appointment. And with the French government making no opposition to the nomination of a German, there was little to stop Hallstein getting down to work. French acquiescence is perhaps not surprising, given that Hallstein was considered more as a European candidate than as a German one. This was an important point to consider given that the Commission was supposed to represent something *above* the national interest alone.

Walter Hallstein, a fifty-six year old professor, who alongside a prestigious career in post-war German politics had held academic posts in international law and economics at the Universities of Berlin, Rostock, Frankfurt and Georgetown, seemed admirably suited to his new position. His appointment greatly pleased the German government who considered acceptance by the five other member states as a 'trophy of national rehabilitation'.[6] Hallstein, himself, was a fervent Europeanist and, in economic terms, a liberal. He had a clear vision of what his task as Commission president would involve. So although the first stages of the integration process concerned the creation of trade and economic agreements, he recognised from the start the ultimate political objectives that were inherent in this process. In a speech made at the end of 1958, he stated, for example, that: 'The unification of the economies is a political act leading to a political union'.[7] Throughout his presidency he was an outspoken advocate of Commission activism, and in particular, of the Commission's right to speak freely and independently. So as to emphasise this, he affirmed, in a much quoted statement, that in the Commission 'We are not in business, we are in politics'.[8]

1958 was largely a settling in period for the new Commission. The priorities were largely organisational, for little could be achieved without Commission staff, structures and procedures in place. In this task, Hallstein benefited from a visionary Secretary-General, Emile Noël,[9] and a strong team of eight commissioners. All eight had been nominated in Paris on the 6 and 7 January 1958, by representatives of the Six, and 'by common accord', and had held their first meeting at Val Duchesse, a chateau outside Brussels a week later. This was where they took their oath of allegiance to the Community, foreswearing any direct representation of national interests.

There were some well-known faces amongst the Hallstein team. Particularly notable were Sicco Mansholt who had previously been the Dutch agriculture minister, Jean Rey who had just resigned as Belgian economics minister, and Robert Marjolin, the French former Secretary-General of the Organisation for European Economic Co-operation (OEEC). Indeed, of the nine commissioners (including Hallstein), five had previously been senior government ministers.[10] This reflected the way in which national governments perceived the role of the Commission. By appointing high-profile political figures, they seemed to suggest a high-profile political role for the institution. However, it is also certain that governments hoped to ensure that their national interest would be well represented by appointing individuals who had, in their previous existences, been deeply immersed in domestic politics.

The setting up of Commission departments and the recruitment of staff needed to be accomplished as quickly as possible, so that policy-making could get under way. The first departments (or directorates-general (DGs)) were set up over the course of 1959. And indeed, by the end of February of that year more than one thousand officials had already been recruited. Although a personnel statute was in the process of being drafted, it would, however, take another three years for the Statute of Service to come into effect. Even so, it is possible to say that by the middle of 1960 the basic organisational machinery of the Commission was in place.

Officials were recruited in a rather informal fashion at this stage, with some countries supplying lists of candidates from their own national administrations, whilst others allowed for personal appli-

cations. The absence of a general entrance examination, which did
not appear until 1962, meant that the quality of Commission staff
varied enormously in the early years. While the French goverment
encouraged the ablest of its staff to join the Commission, thereby
increasing French influence, other member states were unable to
persuade their top grade officials to leave national office for Brussels. Given the fact that salaries were fairly high this might appear
surprising. But it is important to remember that at this stage there
was a great deal of uncertainty about the future of the EEC. Many
officials simply did not see the advantages of risking a secure and
often prestigious post at home for an insecure, unproved and possibly temporary post in the Commission. The implications were
interesting, in that those who did choose to move to Brussels dis-
played certain characteristics that would give the Commission the
beginnings of an administrative culture all its own. On one hand,
those prepared to leave home were often fairly young and without
constraining family ties; they tended to be enthusiastic about their
new career and more adventurous in exploring new career possibilities. In addition, they tended not to take up their posts in order to
represent or serve any national objective. One might go as far as to
say that their mentality was largely a European one.[11]

Staff numbers rose gradually, very much in line with the extension
of Commission duties. Whereas in February 1959 there were 1,108
staff, by the middle of 1961 the total staff complement was 1,848,
and by the end of 1963 it had surpassed 2,000. There was some concern, however, that the Commission could quite easily become overloaded with officials. As such, a decision was taken to keep staff
numbers as low as possible. It was decided at an early stage to balance the Commission staff roughly along national lines and, accord-
ingly, the French, Germans, Italians and Benelux were each given a
25 per cent share of Commission posts.[12] This was to ensure that no
member state would feel that the Commission was an alien or foreign body, but that each would see in it a mirror of its own administration. Even so, there were still considerable problems filling posts.

In spite of certain administrative problems, by the end of 1961
the first phase of organisational construction had been completed.
Although some of the duties that the Commission would perform
had been listed in the Treaty, it was for the Commission itself to
decide upon its own working procedures. The ECSC High Authority was used to provide a rough model for decision-making within

the Commission. Here, a middle route between a strictly collegial style of decision-taking and a more individualistic approach was sought. This involved the setting up of groupings of three commissioners to oversee broad areas of policy. Other elements of Commission decision-making were developed gradually over the course of the first few years. But there is no doubt that the experience of the High Authority of the ECSC was invaluable, and many of the procedures and structures replicated the earlier model.[13]

But even though administrative and organisational questions dominated the first few years of the Community's existence, this did not mean that policy matters were placed on hold. Indeed, it may even be misleading to put too much stress on organisation at this stage. The Commission did not really exist as an institutional entity in the sense that it does today. If, even now, we still call the Commission an *immature* institution, the Hallstein Commission was at this stage little more than *embryonic*. It is clear that:

> The Commission, over the period 1958–62, was more concerned with promoting the Community concept than with seeking an unambiguous institutional identity for itself. Certainly, it did assert the political nature of its own role and it did try to increase its powers, but it did so within the basic institutional framework laid down by the treaty and failed to propose measures designed to change the institutional system to its own advantage.[14]

Even with Hallstein playing a dominant leadership role, the Commission at this early stage in its evolution can be seen in little more than instrumental terms. It was being formed to perform a task and to embody a specific organisational purpose. One may justifiably question therefore whether we can even call the Commission an institution in any meaningful sense at this stage in its development.[15]

Policies and projects

One might argue that it was a mark of the Commission's organisational success that even at this point, it was having to face accusations that it was too 'centralised'.[16] Alongside the inward-looking administrative achievements involved in the creation of a new multinational institution, the newly established EEC Commission had begun to unravel the Treaty of Rome so as to turn some of its general principles and objectives into concrete legislative proposals.

Initially, this involved the preparation of basic studies and the colla-
tion of information on the general economic situation within the
Community. The Commission's primary policy concern over its first
decade was the removal of quotas and tariffs that acted as barriers
to trade between the member states. Most of 1958 had been spent
making preparations for this task, so that the first results were visible as early as 1959. By 1962, after successes in cutting internal tariffs and quotas, the Commission had already shifted its attention to
the creation of a customs union, which would entail the agreement
of a common external tariff on industrial goods entering the EEC
from non-member states.[17] In line with Treaty requirements this was
due to come about by 1 January 1970.[18]

Given the deregulatory bent of integration thus far, it appeared to
the member states that the Commission was committing itself to a
liberal economic policy approach. In this sense it seemed it was
adhering to the spirit of the Treaty. However, there would soon be
claims that the institution was already overstepping the mark in the
strategies it was pursuing. As in the later case of the 1992 single
market project, the removal of tariffs and quotas was not considered
an end in itself, but rather, as Hallstein made clear on many occasions, a first step in a more ambitious project. It should not be surprising therefore that longer-term policy projects were also on the
agenda as early as 1960, with the foundations for common policies
– regional, competition, social and agricultural – already being laid.
The first proposal on agricultural policy was issued in June 1960
and the detailing of a Community policy towards restrictive practices (competition policy) was also an early priority. By 1962, the
increased workload that came about as a result of developments
under these two policy headings alone meant that the Commission
was already facing severe staff shortages. In a supplementary budget
for 1962, they were given an additional 223 posts. They had originally asked for 317.

Action in other policy areas was less successful, if one judges success in terms of policy creation and legislative output. Although
transport policy was clearly a priority within the Treaty, few concrete steps were taken to put plans into practice, even though in a
rather upbeat manner the Commission continued to claim throughout that progress of a sort was being made. Plans to develop a
common energy policy also amounted to very little.[19] In spite of
these failings, the Commission did not escape criticism for launch-

ing itself so early into the drafting of policy proposals. Already attacks focused on the boundaries of Commission competence and the limits to its powers. For example, *The Economist* wrote that:

> Some critics felt that the Commission is something of a Johnny-Head-in-Air. Important details sometimes get lower priority than speeches. Instead of getting proposals ready on time to carry out the road transport arrangements in the treaty, the Commission has been proposing a policy for air transport – which is not in the Treaty at all. There is a certain Carolingian atmosphere abroad in the fine steel and glass building in the avenue de la Joyeuse Entree; political dreams cohabit with a somewhat feudal administrative confusion.[20]

This emphasis on strategic goal-setting, the construction of ambitious new policies and the visionary manner in which many officials and leaders within the Commission came to see their tasks, marked the early years of the Commission's life. Here was a once-in-a-lifetime opportunity to start from scratch, to create policies afresh rather than relying on incremental change. It is clear that many in the Commission relished this opportunity, one made easier as a result of a political and economic climate conducive to change. Administrative difficulties were just part of a learning experience through which the new institution had to pass, before maturing and consolidating its position *vis-à-vis* other institutions and political actors. The minutiae of policy content would become more important once the strategic decisions were taken. Yet, visions depend on visionaries and the engagement of individuals working within the institution. Individuals come and go, whilst institutions retain a certain permanence. The creation of permanent social structures within the Commission would take longer to achieve. But even here, first steps had already been made.

1963: the first challenge

1963 was marked by the first real political crisis faced by the European Commission. The issue that brought it about was the potential enlargement of the EEC to encompass several of the EFTA (European Free Trade Association) states, including Britain.[21] Discussions with prospective member states had in fact begun in 1961 with the Commission taking a key role as EEC negotiator – very much against French wishes. When the French President, General de

Gaulle, announced the suspension of negotiations at a press conference in January 1963, the Commission was left powerless to salvage anything of what had been difficult but potentially fruitful discussions. There had already been concern voiced by Hallstein earlier in the year about the Franco-German Friendship Treaty which had been signed in April, with Hallstein arguing that it was in fact incompatible with Community obligations. However, the Commission's 'regrets' over the manner in which the accession negotiations were broken off were tempered by Hallstein's desire to retain a sense of unity amongst the Six and to focus attention on progress towards economic union. He did not want the question of enlargement to split the EEC. Nevertheless, there was at the time some disagreement within the Commission over De Gaulle's behaviour, with Sicco Mansholt, the Dutch agriculture commissioner, publicly stating that De Gaulle's action had harmed the Community. At the same time, Hallstein, who had not in any case been particularly keen on the idea of British membership, tried to paper over the Community and the Commission cracks. Within a short time it certainly seemed as though the rift had been healed. Indeed, there was even a certain pride within the Commission that they had survived their first Community crisis, to the extent that it was felt that 'if the Community held together during the January crisis, the reason is ... that it is the expression of a new constitutional order'.[22]

The period after the 1963 crisis was marked by a renewed activism, with the Commission launching proposals in transport policy, turnover taxation and free movement of workers. Work continued in the areas of vocational training, the European Social Fund, monetary policy and external relations (notably with former colonies), with attention also turned to the Commission's high-profile role in the Kennedy Round of the GATT (General Agreement on Tariffs and Trade) negotiations, newly opened in May 1964. In spite of Commission successes in managing European trade within this forum, there were, however, only a few limited successes when it came to attempts to develop a common commercial policy.

But the most controversial and yet noteworthy development during this period involved the setting up of the CAP. For the Commission, the workload was immense from the very start. Already by 1965, the agriculture directorate employed a disproportionate 350 officials. And the policy was controversial in that it endowed Commission staff with a certain amount of administrative discretion, albeit delegated from the Council of Ministers. The period after 1963 also marked the beginning of the second stage of the economic integration process. The Commission's Action Programme planned to implement further treaty provisions, whilst at the same time it sought to speed up the introduction of the customs union. The Action Programme had already brought forward the date of completion of the customs union to 1 January 1967 so that it would coincide with the imposition of a single cereals price. As such, progress was to be made simultaneously both on industrial and agricultural fronts. The plan was to free trade in both markets before turning attention to other aspects of economic union. Work on common policy matters also continued, however. The Commission's role seemed to change subtly at this time, with emphasis increasingly placed on resolving what was at the time considered to be a rather difficult economic situation. Economic policies pursued at national level were starting to diverge as conditions began to vary throughout Western Europe. So while Germany continued its balanced growth, France, Italy and the Netherlands were all subject to inflationary pressures. The Commission increasingly came to see its primary role as minimising economic divergence within the Community. What this amounted to in practice was, however, the thankless task of proposing common solutions to differing problems, an approach that found a concrete expression in the medium-term economic policy drawn up to cover the years 1966 to 1970. The medium-term policy programme, which was also to include a social dimension, was essentially an exercise in dirigisme, very much along the lines of French indicative planning. As such, it seemed to mark a move away from the liberal economic approach apparently implicit in the Rome Treaty, towards a more positive statist form of European integration.

The deregulatory and the regulatory, the negative and the positive approaches went hand-in-hand, however. The plan for speeding up the customs union for industrial products had been proposed to the Council in the form of *Initiative 64*, which was essentially a plan for a single European market 'in which goods, services, capital and persons can move across frontiers without let or hindrance of any kind'.[23] This project coincided with efforts by commissioner Marjolin, to persuade the member states to pursue a deflationary economic policy as a means of limiting the impact of recessionary pressures. Although this was very much in line with German economic thinking, the Germans were paradoxically unhappy that *Initiative 64* implied the acceleration of the completion of the customs union. Their concern was largely based on a fear that the speeding up of the internal reduction in tariffs and quotas would mean a growing protectionism towards the outside world. Hallstein, however, gave this fear short-shrift arguing that 'the sooner we (the Six) have achieved the full consolidation of our unity, the sooner we are recognised as a single economic entity, the sooner it will be possible for us to exert the full influence of our trade policy, and to use our economic strength to help others'.[24] *Initiative 64* was eventually agreed in May 1965, although the Council of Ministers extended the timetable so that the customs union would not come into force until 1 July 1968, which is in fact what happened.

Nowhere is the initial Community bargain struck between France and Germany more evident than in the middle years of the 1960s. Here, economic developments, notably the creation of the customs union and the agreement on competition policy matters,[25] were paralleled by the setting up of a common policy in agriculture. But the bargain underpinning the creation of the Community was already showing strains, and it would be the Commission that would have to face the consequences. Gaullist reluctance to entertain the supranationalistic ambitions of some member state governments meant that these underlying tensions could quite easily be brought to the fore. The events of early 1963 had in fact provided just a taster for what was to come a few years later.

The 1965 crisis

By 1964 there was already a fair amount of speculation about the introduction, two years hence, of a system of majority voting in the Council of Ministers. How the EEC was to be financed also had to be resolved before the 1966 deadline. This was necessary so as to allow for the setting up of the CAP, with the Commission hopeful that agricultural levies and customs duties might be treated as independent sources of Community revenue once common external customs tariffs were in place. Given the potential size of any EEC budget, the question of parliamentary scrutiny over European-level expenditures was also raised, even though the EP was not at this time directly elected.[26] As such, proposals for extending the functions performed by the Parliament began to be discussed seriously.

The Commission, not surprisingly, was keen to see the role of the EP extended in parallel with an agreement on budgetary matters.

To ensure that member state governments would not block one or other of these interrelated proposals, the Commission put together a package, which included the completion of the CAP; increased budgetary autonomy for the Community; and a greater scrutiny role for the Parliament. The first sign that there were likely to be difficulties with this arose in the Council in June of 1965, with the French President unwilling to accept the package as it then stood. Although De Gaulle was keen to see the CAP established as quickly as possible, this objective was certainly not to be achieved at any cost. With the benefit of hindsight it is clear that Hallstein misjudged the situation. The Commission's package-dealing strategy, previously so successful, had been pushed too far in this instance. The attempt to use French support for a European-level agricultural policy as a means of strengthening the Community's institutional framework and its autonomy had not paid off.

The events that followed, and, especially, the 'empty chair' policy subsequently pursued, were clearly provoked by substantive issues, not least the extent and type of integration that the EC was to adopt. But the crisis itself was, first and foremost, a showdown between the Commission and the French Presidency – or rather, between Hallstein and De Gaulle.[27] The French President was increasingly irritated by the leadership role adopted by Hallstein as the 1960s progressed. Indeed, Hallstein had even gone so far as to claim that as president of the Commission he could be considered as a sort of European prime minister.[28]

Although on the surface, the commissioners seemed united in their support of the 1965 package, there was behind-the-scenes criticism of Hallstein's judgement in this matter. One of the Commission vice-presidents, Robert Marjolin, was at the time arguing in private that Hallstein had gone too far.[29] And even when the talks broke down, Hallstein still claimed that an agreement could be reached. One week later the French withdrew their representatives from the Council of Ministers. The boycotting of Council meetings did not prevent the Commission continuing much of its work as usual. At the same time, however, Commission staff were striving to resolve the crisis by watering down the original package of proposals. As a result of this work, the first revised set of proposals was presented in a memorandum to the Council on 22 July 1965.

Although this served as the basis for later discussion it was not enough in itself to ensure the acquiescence of the French President.

French opposition to the package rested on two criticisms of the way in which the EC seemed to be developing. Their first complaint concerned the planned introduction of the majority vote in the Council at the start of 1966. The French position was clear. They wanted to exclude the possibility of majority positions carrying weight in the Council.[30] Without the introduction of majority voting, the French would retain their veto over EC legislation, and would thereby be able to vote down any increase in the powers of the EP, or any introduction of independent financing for the Community.

The second French criticism was directed at the Community's central institutions, and in particular, at the European Commission. Power-hungry, unaccountable and alien, an institution which sought to extend its influence by overstepping its constitutional functions, the Commission symbolised for De Gaulle the threat posed to France from the supranational integration process.[31] This was spelt out clearly by De Gaulle in the press conference he held in the September. Here he claimed that the signatories of the Treaty of Rome had taken advantage of the weakness of France at the end of the Fourth Republic (before De Gaulle had come to power), and accused the Commission, 'this embryonic technocracy, for the most part foreign' of the worst of all sins, of introducing majority voting as a means of enhancing its *own* power.

Throughout the crisis, Hallstein's first priority had to be to ensure the survival of the integration process in whatever form possible. There had been no doubt that the Community had been threatened by the events of 1965. There could clearly be no Community without French participation. Whatever the cost, a compromise had to be agreed. When it was eventually agreed to hold meetings to try to resolve the crisis, in Luxembourg in January 1966, the French government presented a list of ten demands, the so-called decalogue. This dealt specifically with the relationship betwen the Commission and the member states. And in the agreement that was reached at the end of this negotiating process, the so-called Luxembourg Compromise, limits were placed on the Commission's autonomy. It was agreed that the Commission should consult national governments through the Permanent Representatives before initiating any new proposals; that the Commission should not make proposals public until the texts had been delivered to the member governments, thus placing a tighter national control over information. Closer co-operation between the two institutions was to be encouraged, particularly in terms of information policy; and restrictions were to be placed on the Commission's relationship with missions from non-member states and international organisations. Budgets were to be decided jointly by the Council and the Commission, and, on the issue of majority voting, the veto in the Council was effectively to be retained by any member state prepared to claim that vital national interests were at stake. At the time, this was considered a major defeat for the Commission. It seemed clear that:

> in the trial of strength the Commission had been chastened and the whole Community spirit had been diluted. The hope behind the Treaty of Rome, that the supranational body would gradually accumulate more power and that the economic 'meshing' of the member countries would draw close together, had been dashed. The Commission had tried to force the pace too quickly. De Gaulle, for the time being, had won.[32]

Even so, this may, in retrospect at least, overstate the change in approach and emphasis that was to take place subsequently within the Commission. Contrary to popular belief, there was no overnight conversion in the functions performed by the Commission. The process of adaptation to the new realities of EC life, and the increasing dependence of the Commission on the goodwill of the member states was a much more gradual evolution. Nevertheless, if we are searching for landmarks in the evolution of the Commission's role within the evolution of the EC, it is clear that 1966 still marks the beginning of a new era for the institution.

Hallstein was placed in a difficult position after the Luxembourg Compromise. With the leadership role of the Commission ostensibly weakened, though formally unaltered, the President's situation changed substantially. De Gaulle held Hallstein personally responsible for the 1965 crisis, placing the Commission President in what soon became an untenable position. Indeed, at the tenth anniversary celebrations of the Treaty of Rome the following year, Hallstein was 'kept in the background: De Gaulle refused even to shake his hand'.[33]

While the 1965 crisis made headline news, a major, yet less high-profile, institutional change was taking place amongst the three

Communities. Discussions over the possible merger of the three Communities[34] and their three sets of institutions had been on the European agenda since the late 1950s when a proposal along these lines had been put forward by the Belgian Foreign Minister, Pierre Wigny. Reports were published and opinions sought over the next few years, but member states differed on how this reform should take place. As a result, it was not until 1963 that an agreement, in principle, was reached in the Council. This was to institute a first step which would involve merging the executives, that is, the High Authority of the ECSC and the two commissions (EEC and EURATOM), followed by a later amalgamation of the three Communities. There were a few problems to be resolved before this could happen. The main sources of disagreement concerned the siting of the unified European Commission and the number of commissioners it should have. With agreement on Brussels as the location and fourteen (in an interim period) as the number of commissioners,[35] a treaty establishing a single Council and Commission was eventually signed on 8 April 1965. The merger itself did not take place, however, until 1967 after the so-caller Merger Treaty had been ratified by all six member states.[36]

A new institutional phase began with the merger, one which would parallel political changes that were taking place at the same time. It should come as no surprise that De Gaulle should see this institutional change as an excellent opportunity to get rid of his *bête noire*, Hallstein. A Franco-German agreement that followed the Merger Treaty meant that Hallstein would only be allowed to hold the Presidency of the unified Commission for a six-month period, hardly enough time for him to make any impression at all on the new structure. Rather than suffer this ignominy, Hallstein tendered his resignation. He left the Commission in the middle of 1967. As the last of the founding fathers of the Community still to hold formal office, his resignation clearly marked the end of a decade of Commission activism, and opened the door to new debates about the role that the institution would play in the future. Hallstein's vision of the Community had been spelt out clearly in a lecture in 1962, when he stated that:

> the European Community is not just a new power-bloc or a new coalition, although it has its pride, it is not a swollen version of 19th century nationalism, taking a continent rather than a country as its basis.

In fact, it is the concrete embodiment of a new approach to the relations between states. It is not merely international: it is not yet fully federal. But it is an attempt to build on the federal pattern a democratically constituted Europe – what I have called elsewhere a federation in the making.[37]

From being at first an accepted wisdom of European Community evolution, the sentiment contained within these lines was increasingly marginalised both by the actions of the member states, and by the changing constitutional make-up of the European institutions themselves. Hallstein's leadership was one of the main factors in ensuring the assertiveness and activism of the Commission in its first embodiment from 1958 to 1967. But Hallstein must also take much of the blame for the crisis that marked the beginning of a more reactive and cautious stage in the Commission's history.

A new era: Rey, Malfatti and Mansholt

The departure of Walter Hallstein led to a prolonged debate over the appointment of his replacement, the first president of the merged Commission. It was initially expected that the job would go to an Italian nominee, but the potential candidates, Emilio Colombo (then Minister of the Treasury) and Guido Carli (Governor of the Bank of Italy) both preferred to stay in the thick of Italian politics. Hallstein's eventual successor was an individual quite different in his style and approach from his predecessor. Jean Rey, a Belgian lawyer, was much more a technocrat than a politician. He had been appointed to the EEC Commission in 1958 with responsibility for external trade. His appointment to the presidency of the Commission was largely a reward for his successful completion of the Kennedy Round of GATT negotiations in 1967.

This was not an easy time to be President of the Commission. In the aftermath of the 1965–66 crisis, relations with the French were fragile. At the same time, confusion over staffing led to internal administrative problems, the consequence of some bad organisation at the time of the merger. And on top of all this, the British reapplication to join the Community also posed certain difficulties. At first sight, Rey gave the impression of being an assertive leader, coming down hard in favour of British membership and persuading all the commissioners to back the British application. However, although he openly stressed that the Commission should continue to play an independent role in Community affairs, there were criticisms that he played too much into the hands of the French. Statements made by Rey early in 1968 criticising the United States' economic policy suggested to some that the Commission was acting on behalf of French interests.[38]

Rey's three-year presidency has been characterised very broadly as one in which initiative was left largely to the member states, and in which the Commission at best played the role of mediator between national actors. This did not stop Rey from stressing, albeit rhetorically, the political and federalist ambitions of the Commission. But although a steady flow of proposals continued to be transmitted from Commission to Council via the EP, the Commission itself seemed less ambitious in its objectives, trimming back its initial proposals in line with what might or might not be acceptable to the Council. Clearly, the atmosphere within the Commission had changed, and for a variety of reasons. *The Economist* noted that:

> In 1962, the higher administrative ranks of the European Commission were largely a chapter house of European progressives in their 30s, intent on building a new superpower. Now they are a collection of clever people in their 40s, to some extent interested in a career structure and in not being given too much unnecessary bureaucratic work.[39]

Even the resignation of De Gaulle in 1969 did not provoke much speculation that the Commission would reassert itself.[40] Indeed, at the time, Rey wisely advised staff not to over-react to De Gaulle's demise, but told them that they should continue working on day-to-day policy management. It is not surprising therefore that the lack of leadership offered by the Commission was a matter of comment in the press.[41] As it turned out, European-level political leadership of a sort was to emerge over the next decade. However, it was to come not from the Commission, but from a new forum, the European Council, the summits of heads of state and government held two or three times a year. The European Council was not institutionalised until 1974, however. Until then, there was a political vacuum within the Community, a vacuum that led to a feeling of malaise amongst those working within the European institutions. Rey suffered from the fact that he was not only President in a period during which national governments had sought to challenge his authority, but that he had charge of the Commission just as the 'transition period' was coming to an end. The first set of specific treaty objectives and timetables had been completed, opening the door to a period of 'irresolution'. The stigma of being labelled a 'memorandum Commission' did not mean inactivity, however. One of the key documents of the decade, the Mansholt Plan, which introduced guidelines for the reform of agricultural structures within the Community, was issued in December 1968. But it was not until towards the end of Rey's term of office, in particular after the December 1969 Hague Conference, that member states and the central institutions alike became more optimistic about the future of the Community. There was a sense in which the 1967–70 Commission was an interim institution. Yet it is unfair to claim that the Commission was during this period 'recreated in a more traditional style of international bureaucracy'.[42] Rather, the external environment and the personality of the President did not allow for a proactive, assertive Commission role at this time.

Under the Merger Treaty, a new Commission was to be chosen to take up office in July 1970. The number of commissioners was to be reduced to nine, with the three largest countries (France, Germany and Italy) each having two commissioners and the others only one. Although the Belgian government was keen to see Rey reappointed for a second term, they agreed that it was rightly the turn of an Italian to hold the presidency. Once again, the Italians seemed unable to put forward a candidate, so that it looked as though Rey might be reappointed after all. But at the last moment, a candidate was found in the form of F. M. Malfatti, a young (forty-three year old) newcomer to the Commission.

He arrived with the reputation of a good manager, more likely to put emphasis on the effective running of the Commission, than on the implementation of any grandiose vision. However, the hope was that Malfatti would be able to inject a good deal more dynamism into the institution than Rey had before him. At the same time it was expected that Malfatti would focus on some of the internal organisational problems facing the Commission: namely the worrying procedural delays and backlogs, and the bureaucratic rigidities that had contributed to a slowing down of the decision-making process. At first sight the new Commission appeared to be taking a more proactive stance on certain issues. The issue of the Community's 'own resources' was a big issue at the time, as was the whole question of economic and monetary integration. In this sense, Malfatti's Commission was able to board the post-Hague bandwagon[43] which had led to the drafting of the Werner Plan (on EMU) in October 1970. With the Commission services given the task of drafting proposals for the first stage of EMU during 1971, there was some optimism that a new political energy could be found within the Commission. The monetary crisis of 1971 soon put an end to that thought.

The more assertive and high-profile members of the Rey Commission, Raymond Barre and Sicco Mansholt, for example, had stayed on under Malfatti, helping to provide the institution with some stability and continuity. In addition, the appointment of Ralf Dahrendorf as external relations commissioner gave the college a much needed boost. Expectations were too high, however, and the Malfatti Commission failed to deliver what it promised. In spite of outspoken criticism of Rey's tenure, the new Commission continued largely in the Rey tradition, taking a low-key approach to policy matters and to relations with the member state governments. Much of the Commission's time was taken up with preparations for the enlargement of the Community, which, after the resignation of De Gaulle, could proceed unhindered. It looked as though there would now be no barrier to Britain, Ireland, Denmark and Norway joining the EC as soon as negotiations could be concluded. To make sure, Malfatti had made it clear that he did not want to deter new members by introducing dramatic new policy initiatives over this period.

After only fifteen months in the job, Malfatti announced that he was resigning from his post in order to fight the Italian elections. For many working within the European institutions, involvement in domestic political life continued to be the number one priority. This was as true for the President of the Commission as it was for more lowly officials. As a stopgap until the new Commission could be nominated, Sicco Mansholt, the architect of the CAP and perhaps the best known of all the commissioners at the time, took over the post that had been denied to him while De Gaulle had remained in office.[44] Although he was only in the post for less than nine months until the start of 1973, he was able to stamp his strong personality on the Commission surprisingly quickly. With the enlargement treaties agreed in January 1972, Mansholt oversaw the ratification and, in October, the rejection of membership by the Norwegians. He also attended the October 1972 Paris Summit with its affirmation of support for European Union and EMU, confirming the Commission's right of initiative in these areas.

Mansholt was not without his critics, however. In the short time he was President, colleagues became especially uneasy over his out-spoken criticism of the bureaucratic image of the Commission, as well as of his dramatic gesturing in the few policy areas that came to dominate his thinking – ecology and development. Although his tendency to divide rather than unite the Commission was not always welcomed by other commissioners, it was said that: 'he did more in nine months as president to draw public attention on it [the Commission] and its doings than anyone since Mr Hallstein in the early 1960s'.[45] Nevertheless, the attention attracted was not always to the Commission's advantage.

The Ortoli presidency

By the end of 1972 the process of distributing portfolios in advance of the new 1973 Commission began to look, it was said, like a game of musical chairs, with almost all the nominated commissioners vying for the top jobs.[46] This time there had been a fairly early agree-ment that the post of Commission President would go to François-Xavier Ortoli, a French appointee. But this did not make the task of sharing out Commission jobs any easier. Wrangles over which com-missioner should get which job were only the first in a series of staffing and organisational difficulties that would plague the early months of Ortoli's office. However, disagreements over the alloca-tion of portfolios had to be settled before anything else could be done. A minor crisis occurred over the external affairs job, which Ortoli divided up between the second French commissioner, Deniau (development), and the British commissioner, Christopher Soames (external trade). This was not to Deniau's liking, however, and a subsequent raid of files and staff attached to Soames's office led to much consternation among the ranks of the commissioners. A second reorganisation, which involved the splitting up of the har-monisation law, banking, insurance and trade barriers department into three separate departments, also provoked bad feeling, prompting the resignation of the Director-General in disgust at what he felt was a political rather than an efficiency-oriented deci-sion.[47]

Most of the organisational problems faced by Ortoli in his first year as President were a direct result of the enlargement of the Community at the beginning of 1973. The accession of three new member states was to have a substantial impact. The appointment of sixty new directors (at A3 level – see section on hierarchy in the Commission, pp. 115–25) blew up a storm over who was going to make way for them. There were nationalistic outbursts on all sides. The situation became extremely tense, with (at all grades) between 300 and 350 officials having to make way for the new nationalities. However, commissioners were keen to make sure that the organisational errors that had occurred as a result of the merger of the executives, were not repeated. As a result of the creation of the unified Commission in 1967, some of the best and brightest staff had left their posts, encouraged by the offer of generous redundancy money.

Enlargement provoked a second administrative crisis within the Commission. With the introduction of English as an official and working language, the Commission's translators found it extremely difficult to cope with the extra workload. Documentation for meetings was often produced at the last minute, and communication between officials was at times difficult. Commission staff reacted by taking up English language classes in droves. Surprisingly perhaps, Ortoli came out of these staffing wrangles largely unscathed. Indeed, many thought he had accomplished a very difficult task with some political skill. Even so, morale among the ranks of the Commission staff clearly suffered as a knock-on effect of enlargement.

With administrative problems dominating Commission business, there was little time for the new commissioners to get to grips with their portfolios before being requested to draft policy proposals for the European Council meeting in Paris in December 1974. Although Ortoli pushed some deadlines back until after Easter, there was still very little time for any original thought. As a result, what emerged from the Commission was a rehash or reworking of papers already in circulation. It was due to the skill of Ortoli that he managed to present this hotchpotch of seven documents as a coherent whole. Praise from Ortoli's colleagues seemed unprecedented. For example, Ralf Dahrendorf did not mince his words when he spoke of Ortoli as follows: 'He dominates us by his intellectual grasp. He is a master of all our dossiers and the intellectual master of the commission as well'.[48] He certainly had a distinctive approach to Commission work, which was very much that of the technocrat rather than the politician. But he was not a public figure in the way that Hallstein had been. In fact, it was said at the time that he was a rather shy man who actually disliked speaking in public. The general line that he took was that it was not the Commission's job to impress or convince the general public, but rather to gain the respect of national civil servants. Aided by an excellent personal staff, his grasp of ideas and stamina in negotiations were notable. His strong belief in the merits of collegiality made for a stimulating atmosphere in which his colleagues could act. There was more communication between commissioners and attendance at Commission meetings was made compulsory, something that had been problematic during previous presidencies. His ability to hold his team together meant that the Commission was more coherent than it had been since the early 1960s.

However, this rather rosy picture of Ortoli's presidency presents only one side of the story. Though praised for his pleasant nature and his efficiency, Ortoli was at the same time criticised for being rather unexciting. He was not a fervent integrationist as Hallstein had been. His line was a cautious one, recommending incremental change rather than grand gestures. He was not considered an ideas man.[49] Even so, as the first two years of his presidency ended, Ortoli's strengths made arguments for his reappointment compelling, though he had lost his political base in Paris with the death of President Pompidou in 1974. Sir Christopher Soames, the British commissioner, had been suggested as a possible alternative, but this became too mixed up with the British government's renegotiation of the Accession Treaty, and the fact that the new British government was a Labour one (Soames was Conservative). Even so, as British commissioner, Soames did play the role of defender of the national interest during the renegotiation process, especially when the question of the budget contribution arose. Indeed the Commission was given some credit for keeping the negotiations going. Commission proposals made very early in 1975 had proved acceptable to the British Prime Minister, James Callaghan and, as such, the Labour government could subsequently recommend a yes vote in the referendum held in June of that year.[50]

Whilst internal administrative and organisational problems were initially very much on the minds of the commissioners and the Commission President, these soon faded into insignificance. Increasing inflation and unemployment and rising trade deficits, provoked largely by the oil crisis of late 1973–74, meant that any sense of international solidarity visible prior to 1973 was waning fast. The Commission was at a loss to react in any meaningful way to the economic crisis. The EC's political vacuum was filled only by the national governments trying to work together to overcome knee-jerk reactions to economic recession. This did not always produce results, but it did at least lead to steps that would help fill the Community's leadership deficit.

Although the EC was still considered to be the most useful forum in which the West Europeans could meet to deal with their common economic problems, there was strong opposition at national level to any enhancement of the role of the Commission in leading efforts to overcome those difficulties. Chancellor Schmidt and President Giscard preferred a pragmatic approach to co-operation that would operate through an institutionalisation of a system of European summitry. The new forum that was to emerge from the Paris summit of 1974, the European Council, was to be essentially intergovernmental, although Commission representatives did have the right to attend meetings. The European Council was to exist first and foremost as an arena in which international or global questions could be raised. As such, there was general agreement that the political identity of the Community should be emphasised through the creation of intergovernmental mechanisms that would allow for unified Community responses to international crises. This was to be based on proposals put forward by commissioner Etienne Davignon.[51]

Whereas there was a natural tendency among member states to turn inwards in times of recession, there was also a desire to present a common European line to non-Community countries. This was considered to be particularly important in terms of Europe's relationship with the United States. Tensions between the US and the West Europeans had been growing, in part as a result of a number of trade disputes and monetary uncertainty. A unilateral attempt by the US to improve relations by naming 1973 the *Year of Europe* was judged as patronising and only served to make the Europeans more suspicious of US intentions in Western Europe.[52] But while such matters concerned the heads of government, the Commission continued to spend much of its time at this important economic and political juncture staring (metaphorically) at its own administrative navel. Yet even here, Ortoli seemed unable to leave any permanent mark. Inefficiencies within the Commission continued to be the subject of criticism. On one occasion, for example, Ortoli sat silently through a formal dinner at which a barrage of abuse was thrown at the Commission by Chancellor Schmidt.

Reforms suggested did little to improve matters. A staff screening process in 1974 ended with only thirty staff being transferred from overstaffed to understaffed departments and low morale provoked a flood of departures from the Commission at all levels, continuing throughout 1974. This raised serious questions that touched on some of the big issues of European integration. Already by mid 1974, the Belgian prime minister, Leo Tindemans, had been asked to investigate how political union might be achieved. The Tindemans Report that eventually emerged at the start of 1976 made some cautious suggestions as to how the Commission might be reformed.[53] But even here the initiative had been taken by the European Council rather than by the Commission. On more substantive policy issues much the same story is retold. So although one or two novel ideas were advanced, these never really seemed to get off the ground. Indeed, the reputation of the Commission was at an all-time low.

The Jenkins Commission

The debate over a candidate to fill Ortoli's shoes in the next Commission began very early in 1976. It was generally agreed that it was the turn of the British to put forward a candidate, and initially it was expected that Christopher Soames would fill the post. However, the fact that Soames was not a Labour man continued to perturb James Callaghan, the British Foreign Secretary. An alternative candidate was sought, someone who would be high-profile enough to compete with Soames for the nomination. There were several names thrown around – George Thomson, Shirley Williams and Roy Jenkins, for example, but it seemed as though no one really wanted the job.

It took a long time for Roy Jenkins to be persuaded to accept the post. When he did, his nomination was openly welcomed in the Commission.[54] The appointment of a senior national politician could only serve to enhance the status of the Commission, though there were some who feared that he would be too distanced from the day-to-day administration of Community policy to be able to keep a check on what was going on. Otherwise, there were fears

that Jenkins would retain too close a link with the British government to be able to fulfil a Commission President's independent
vocation.

Once Jenkins had accepted the post, he was keen to do some solid
groundwork before the start of his presidency. He arranged a tour
of national capitals during October and November 1976, so as to
lobby governments over their choice of commissioners. Jenkins
understood the importance of gathering around him a team of high-
calibre colleagues. But his approach was not always tactful. This was
especially apparent in the case of Wilhelm Haferkamp, a German
nominated commissioner whom Jenkins had tried to dissuade
Helmut Schmidt from appointing. When Haferkamp did eventually
take up his post in the Commission, it is hardly surprising that relations were awkward between the two men. Other commissioners
also suffered the stigma of having been initially rejected by Jenkins.[55]

The appointments were confirmed at the Hague European Council meeting early in December 1976. Of the thirteen commissioners,
six had been part of the Ortoli team: Ortoli himself, Claude
Cheysson, Guido Brunner, Finn Gundelach and Raymond Vouel.
The first meeting of the new Commission was held informally at
Jenkins's cottage in Ditchley, Oxfordshire, in late December. It was
here that the portfolios were divided up. As ever, this process was a
rather acrimonious one. Jenkins had a lot to live up to. The press
had made much of the leadership he would offer the Commission,
though on first sight his team was not particularly impressive. After
raising expectations of Jenkins's likely impact on the Commission,
the first six months of 1977 were a great disappointment. His
speeches did not go down well. It was noted for example that after
his inaugural speech to the EP he received only seventeen seconds
of applause. Neither were the Commission press conferences any
better, with journalists soon becoming disillusioned with Jenkins's
reticence on his intended policy approach. The media hype was
taking its toll and Jenkins himself very quickly became disillusioned
and depressed by the barrage of negative commentary on his first
months in post. Contrary to earlier fears, the new President seemed
to be spending too much time on the minutiae of daily management,
rather than focusing on the big issues.

Generally speaking, though, Jenkins's management of Commission business was competent, even though his style was considered

to be rather dry. His presidency was to develop a distinctive character to it in that Jenkins soon gathered round him an inner cabinet of three or so commissioners, a sort of inner circle, made up of Ortoli, Davignon and Gundelach, each of whom had a good reputation in European political circles. A second notable characteristic of his style of management was the *think-ins* he held at various resorts in the Ardennes and on the Belgian coast. At these lengthy meetings, some of the most crucial broader aspects of his presidency were discussed. In some ways this seemed an attempt to instil some sort of collegiate spirit amongst the commissioners, otherwise absent from the Jenkins Commission.

In spite of some very negative first impressions, Jenkins was to prove himself capable of rising to the challenge of the post, using his position as Commission President to push forward a pathbreaking initiative on monetary policy, the setting up of a European Monetary System (EMS). Outside of this policy field, there were other less dramatic success stories. But these tended to be based on reaction to external and often national circumstances rather than on any Commission initiative. The main concerns for Jenkins included the role of the Commission in international arenas; the enlargement of the Community to include first Greece and then Spain and Portugal; institutional reform; and direct elections to the EP.

Jenkins was particularly concerned that the Commission, that is, the President, should be represented at international summits, where issues concerning Commission competences were to be discussed.[56] This led to a great deal of friction, particularly between Jenkins and the French President. Giscard resisted what he saw as an elevation of the Commission President's role. After all, this was a request that De Gaulle had refused Walter Hallstein back in 1967. But in spite of Giscard's opposition, a compromise was eventually reached. At the Western Economic Summit held in London in May 1977 Jenkins was allowed to attend some sessions, though he was excluded from those on energy and world trade for which the Commission had indisputable responsibility in some areas. Jenkins found humiliating and petty his treatment outside the meeting room, however. For example, he was prevented from sitting at the same dinner table as the heads of state and government. And at the final press conference he found that he had been given no microphone![57] Nevertheless the very fact that his attendance at summits was permitted was a step towards greater recognition for the Commission, though it was not clear then whether all this time and effort would actually establish a precedent.

Plans for Greek accession to the EC were well under way before Jenkins took up his post. He had not been particularly enthusiastic about Greek membership, although he was sympathetic to the political arguments for a speedy accession. Although this was to be of importance for the future of the Community, the Jenkins Commission did not play a major role in the accession, nor in the setting up of negotiations between the Community and Spain and Portugal.[58] Likewise, there was little progress made on the question of institutional reform although this was on the agenda. There were some good appointments made to the higher administrative grades early on in the term, but this did nothing to alter and improve structures. In September 1978, a decision was taken to set up a committee, led by Dirk Spierenberg, to look into staffing and organisation in the Commission, with the aim of developing proposals for improvement. It should come as no great surprise that there was little done to implement the recommendations that were eventually made.[59]

The only dramatic institutional change that took place during the Jenkins presidency had been initiated much earlier. The commitment to hold direct elections to the EP had been around since the enactment of the Treaty of Rome in 1957. Although it was hoped that by raising the profile of the EP the image of the Commission would also benefit, there was little evidence of how this would work in practice. Indeed 1979 was characterised by an unprecedented onslaught of criticism over the wastefulness and bureaucratic inefficiency of the Commission after the damning Court of Auditor's Report. A big issue at the time concerned the huge expenses and perks available to commissioners. Although there was clearly some measure of misreporting over these, there was also substantial evidence that account was not being taken of funds spent on travel and entertainment. The unnecessary use of air taxis by commissioners was especially condemned and Jenkins could do little but concur with the criticism, encouraging commissioners to take extra care in future.

What marks out the Jenkins presidency from the list of 1970s and early 1980s Commissions relates very much to the role that Jenkins himself played in proposing and seeking a compromise on the creation of a zone of monetary stability in Western Europe. This was Jenkins's own brainchild. He first proposed the idea in the middle of 1977 and the initial reaction from the national capitals was not encouraging. By the time he was able to convince Helmut Schmidt and Giscard d'Estaing of the viability of his proposal in mid 1978, Jenkins's reputation as an effective Commission President was largely assured. Jenkins's grasp of complex economic issues impressed the national leaders. His never-ending round of meetings with prime ministers and presidents made conciliation between the member states much easier, preventing unnecessary friction in the Council of Ministers and in the European Council. The EMS itself differed greatly from Jenkins's initial idea, however. It is worthy of note that the idea was never advanced as a Commission proposal but as a more informal and personal project of the President.[60]

Overall, Jenkins's success as Commission President involved enhancing and manipulating the Commission's role as *go-between* amongst national governments. In the case of the EMS idea, this amounted to much more that just an effective use of his consensus-building armoury, but also involved an expansion of the Commission's right of initiative. In other policy areas there was less evidence of an activist approach, though. There were several proposals put forward by the Commission over this period, but few were accepted. And although one might fairly criticise Jenkins for focusing too narrowly on his EMS plans, and on the question of his attendance at international summits, this is perhaps unfair. It is clear that the recessionary environment of the time was not conducive to a burgeoning political-initiative role for the Commission. When Jenkins did try to raise the profile of the Commission, this provoked vitriolic attacks at the highest of national levels. Helmut Schmidt was especially critical of the Commission and its political presumptions. In spite of more than ten years of caution and timidity, the gaullist anti-Commission rhetoric of the mid 1960s was alive and well a decade and a half after the Luxembourg Compromise.

The Thorn presidency

Given an alternative economic scenario the story told about Roy Jenkins's presidency might have read very differently. Although one might consider him as an activist President, it seemed as though it was now increasingly difficult for the Commission to take steps to drive forward integrative policies without the groundwork having largely been completed by the member states. The Franco-German axis and in particular the relationship between Helmut Schmidt and Valéry Giscard d'Estaing had been pivotal in this respect.[61] But with the ending of Jenkins's term of office, the Schmidt–Giscard tandem was also soon to end.[62] There was little to suggest that the new Commission President would be able to fill the political vacuum that would remain. The proposal at the Venice European Council of June 1980 that Gaston Thorn, the Prime Minister of Luxembourg, should replace Jenkins, was not universally supported. Giscard initially opposed Thorn's candidature on the grounds that he was too much of a federalist, but conceded that he should be given the post after pressure was placed on him by the governments of the five smaller EC states.

Of the new Commission, only six of the fourteen appointed were newcomers, with the President himself included among that number. The allocation of portfolios is never a simple matter and the inclusion of one more commissioner, the new Greek member, did not help matters. Likewise, the fact that Etienne Davignon was given two portfolios, industry and energy, when it was clear that there were few enough jobs to go around, was a source of real friction amongst hard-done-by commissioners. One of the British commissioners, Christopher Tugendhat, felt particularly aggrieved that part of his budgetary portfolio had been transferred to the Irish commissioner, Michael O'Kennedy. This provoked a rather nasty telephone call from Mrs Thatcher in support of *her* appointee. The intervention of the British Prime Minister has long been remembered within the Commission as a blatant example of national interference at the highest level, interference which did not succeed in getting Tugendhat all that he wanted, but which managed to cause the commissioner a fair amount of embarrassment.

It took a while for the Thorn Commission to make any headway at all in policy matters. But this was not simply due to a lack of leadership and the modest goals of the new President. The 1981 Commission was plagued by resignations and deaths. Indeed the death of the Danish agriculture commissioner, Finn Gundelach, only a couple of weeks into the new Commission, began a serious row over who should have his portfolio. After much wrangling, Thorn decided that Gundelach's replacement, Poul Dalsager, should take over. The departure of Claude Cheysson in May 1981 did not provoke much argument, but the whole period was largely taken up with a pay dispute in which Commission officials resisted attempts to remove a formula which provided a mechanism for increasing salaries. Staffing problems of a more headline-grabbing sort also plagued Thorn's own presidential office, with the head of his personal staff leaving after a matter of weeks, and his replacement, Fernand Spaak, murdered in July of the same year.

In spite of disorientation over the first few months, the Commission was forced to cope with a number of pressing issues, notably those involving the implications of the Greek accession at the start of the year. With the new PASOK (Greek Socialist Party) government committed to a renegotiation of the terms of entry and possibly even withdrawal from the Community, the Commission was put under pressure to find a package of proposals which would allow the Greek government to back down whilst at the same time saving face.

Nevertheless, it is clear that over this period the Commission was largely sidelined by national leaders.[63] Thorn himself did not help matters. Although, unlike his two predecessors, he was at his best on public occasions, the President seemed unwilling or unable to advance new initiatives, and was often criticised for being too reliant on his officials. In his internal management of Commission business, he seemed generally well liked by his colleagues, although there was little evidence of teamwork or collegiality. Indeed, there seemed an increasing tendency for national interests to dominate the often interminable discussions that took place during Commission meetings. These regularly ended inconclusively, an indictment of Thorn's role as chairman. Although Thorn did not surround himself with a favoured inner circle of colleagues, there was still scope for individuals to make their mark. The strongest commissioners were given the freedom to drive through their own personal programmes of action. But there was little sign of an overall Commission strategy.[64]

High-profile and assertive commissioners such as Ortoli, Natali and Davignon ran the show to a large extent. Davignon, in particular, as the most experienced member of the Commission, was able to consolidate the position he had held under the Jenkins Commission. He was usually able to get his way with his fellow commissioners, even in those policy areas not directly under his control. And in some ways he seemed to hold the reins of the Commission more tightly than the President himself. His specific interest, the encouragement of cross-border industrial collaboration such as the ESPRIT programme (European Strategic Programme for Research and Development in Information Technology), went some way towards preparing European industry for the single market proposals to come and turned industrial competitiveness into a number one Commission priority.[65] However, although the role he played in developing proposals for the restructuring of the European budget in 1981 was crucial, it was in fact Thorn who was able to find a solution, albeit temporary, to British demands for a budget rebate. Mrs Thatcher's attempt to link the budget rebate to the annual farm price review, and her insistence on the use of a unanimous vote on the issue in the Council, was rejected by Thorn, who claimed categorically that a majority vote on farm prices would suffice. However, even here, it is clear that no solution would have been possible without the groundwork done by the French presidency early in 1984. This was part of the new French strategy to encourage European political union after the failure of Mitterrand's 1981–83 socialist programme.

Gaston Thorn seemed unable to overcome the obstacles placed in the way of an EC revival, falling foul of them to an even greater extent than Jenkins had done before him. There was little evidence of strong leadership and a great deal of evidence of frustration within the Commission. Where there were achievements, they were often based on deals done at national level, rather than on initiatives taken at the centre. The Commission's position within the European policy process seemed at an all-time low. The European Council continued to dominate in agenda-setting terms, while the Commission was noted for its timidity. This was in spite of Davignon's efforts on the industrial policy front and growing signs that a consensus on the need to revive the internal market plans was emerging not just within the Commission, but also beyond.[66] Still, the Thorn Commission served to play down the more political or high-profile functions of the Commission whilst at the same time failing to take advantage of its mediative capacity. The 1982 clash with the British Prime Minister seemed to be the only example of activism on the part of the Commission President, and even this was a reaction to events outside his control. Although there were some concrete policy successes: the creation of a common fisheries policy after a fourteen-year wait; Greek acceptance of a renegotiated accession deal; and the containment of the US–EC trade dispute, most of the positive attributes of the 1981–84 Commission involved 'treading water', with few new ideas emerging.

Conclusion

In this 'story' of the evolution of the Commission, individual actors and particularly presidents clearly take centre-stage. Hence, conclusions drawn at this stage reflect a bias towards leadership dynamics within the institution. There is no denying that individuals are important, therefore. Yet it would be foolish to imagine that leadership was anything more than one factor determining the internal and external dynamics of the European Commission. Nevertheless, it is often the activism of Commission presidents or commissioners, or at least the scope and substance of their reactions, that have shaped the institution's role within the wider Community system.

The most troubling difficulties facing Commission presidents are regularly those exogenous to the institution: economic recession, recalcitrant national governments and a general hostility towards the Commission itself. Roy Jenkins, for example, recognising the limits placed on the Community in times of recession, was determined to extend the profile of the Commission, making good use of its acknowledged functions and his own personal skills as a mediator to that end. Thorn, it seems, arrived in Brussels with more modest objectives. It is not surprising that little was achieved by the Commission during his term of office. External circumstances do not just impact upon the Commission presidents, but also on the very choice of presidents. It is often stated, with little more than superficial evidence, that the choice of a Commission president is shaped by the activism or inactivism of the previous occupant of the post. In other words, a strong proactive president will tend to make national leaders cautious in their nomination, whilst a lacklustre leader will encourage heads of state and government to be bolder. Although this may appear to be little more than common sense, there is in fact no concrete evidence to back up this view. Indeed, it seems to suggest that national leaders can see into the future. The argument loses its weight when we consider that Jacques Delors was appointed with the help of Mrs Thatcher – as a *compromise* candidate!

Structural problems have plagued all Commissions since Hallstein's. On no occasion has any president made headway in resolving the most important organisational questions of his day. But even if this has not determined the fate of Commission presidents, it has provided a serious constraint on their capacity to operationalise their policy objectives. Nevertheless, the adaptability and malleability of the Commission is quite remarkable. There is ample evidence here of how different functions or policy approaches can come to the fore at different periods. As a prerequisite for the survival of the institution, this is crucial. If the Commission is to be able to cope with external and internal pressures, it must be flexible.

Finally, little has been said explicitly up to now about the nature of cultural or symbolic change within the Commission. From the very start, symbolism and idealism were at the heart of the European integration project, a project that underpinned the establishment and early development of the Commission. Gradually, however, the visionaries were replaced by pragmatists, and the general consensus on the creation of a European Union was undermined by the need to focus on the internal management (and creation) of policy. If a cultural perspective implies a shared vision or set of beliefs, this seemed much less important in 1984 than it did in 1958 – though this is not to say that it disappeared entirely. Beliefs and values are influenced and moulded by a multitude of different elements – structural contexts, external conditions, as well as the professional background and socialisation of individuals. If the leadership qualities of Commission presidents are important, so too are the beliefs and ideas they bring with them into the institution.

Notes

1 The word 'commission' really only means 'committee' in French.

2 Of the High Authority, Henderson (1962) noted that it normally met once a week, in private. It acted as the executive organ of the ECSC, though with some legislative functions and it was responsible only to the Common Assembly. While some of its powers were exercised alone, others were used in conjunction with those of the Council of Ministers, though it did have the right of initiative. There were nine members originally, eight of whom were appointed by national governments and one of whom was co-opted. Jean Monnet was the President. It was independent of its member countries, and its nine members were not to take instruction from national or any other source. The High Authority was, in addition, staffed by full-time salaried officials, and was independently resourced (from contributions made by the coal and steel industry). See Henderson (1962, pp. 146 and 162). Holt (1967, p. 27) notes that neither the Common Assembly of the ECSC nor the Council of Ministers was foreseen in the Schuman Plan and that it was intended originally that the High Authority should govern alone.

3 There were three 'commissions' at this stage, one for each of the three Communities, the EEC, the ECSC and EURATOM (the atomic energy community).

4 Jean Monnet was the first President of the European Coal and Steel Community, and is now considered to be one of the founding fathers (if not 'the' founding father) of the European integration process.

5 The Belgian government wanted Brussels as the European capital, while Luxembourg did not want to give up the European Coal and Steel Community which had been located in the city since earlier in the decade.

6 *The Economist*, 11 January 1958.

7 Quoted in *The Economist*, 18 October 1958, from a speech given by Hallstein to the International Press Institute in Luxembourg.

8 Quoted in *The Economist*, 2 December 1961.

9 Emile Noël was said to be responsible for much of the organisation of the Commission in the early years. He remained as Secretary-General until 1987.

10 Ludlow (1991, p. 89).

11 See, for example, *The Economist*, 19 July 1961, for an assessment of the 'European spirit' of the new Commission officials. This is something that is also pointed out by Coombes (1970).

12 Willis (1983, p. 11).

13 Care was taken to avoid duplication of tasks that could so easily be the consequence of the existing three often overlapping executives. Periodic meetings of the presidents of the three Commissions, inter-executive groups in which officials in specific policy areas could meet, and a committee that would involve all three institutions as a means of keeping a check on policies initiated and decisions taken, were all ways in which the co-ordination could be ensured. It was also planned to develop co-operative channels between services (DGs) as a means of avoiding duplication. This was not necessary, however, for the Legal Service, Statistical Service and the Information Service which were from the start to be common to all institutions. See Commission (1958), *First General Report on the Activities of the Communities*, Luxembourg, pp. 30–2.

14 Sasse (1977a, p. 185).

15 *Ibid.* goes on to comment on the 'self-effacing' nature of the Commission between 1958 and 1962. One definition of 'institution' includes reference to the capacity for the body to act autonomously and cohesively. In defining the Commission instrumentally at this stage, we may therefore prefer to describe it as an 'organisation'.

16 *The Economist*, 1 December 1962.

17 See for example, Swann (1983).

18 In fact it came about by mid 1968.

19 George (1991).

20   *The Economist*, 21 February 1959.

21   EFTA is the European Free Trade Association. See Wallace (1991) for details.

22   Commission (1964), *Sixth General Report on the Activities of the Communities*, Luxembourg.

23   Commission (1966), *Eighth General Report on the Activities of the Communities*, Luxembourg.

24   This was taken from a speech given by Walter Hallstein in London in March 1960, reported in *The Economist*, 5 March 1960.

25   On competition policy, see McLachlan and Swann (1967).

26   The European Parliament was not directly elected until 1979.

27   Sampson (1971) labelled the two men, 'the Pope and the Emperor'.

28   See, for example, Henig (1980, p. 40) and Urwin (1991, p. 103) where this is mentioned.

29   This was reported in Sampson (1971, p. 62).

30   See Commission (1967), *Ninth General Report on the Activities of the Communities*, Luxembourg, p. 30).

31   On De Gaulle's distinctive vision of Europe, see, for example, De Gaulle (1970).

32   Sampson (1971, p. 64).

33   Sampson (1971, p. 64).

34   The EEC, the ECSC and EURATOM.

35   To be reduced to nine in 1970.

36   See, for example, the Commission (1965), *Seventh General Report on the Activities of the Communities*, Luxembourg, p. 293, on the merger and the Merger Treaty.

37   This was quoted in Weigall and Stirk (1992).

38   See *The Economist*, 5 February 1968.

39   *The Economist*, 16 May 1970.

40   Sasse (1977a, p. 196) argued, however, that activity did speed up after this date.

41   *The Economist* wrote on 3 May 1969 that Europe 'will require a new vision and a new political commitment. It is not obvious from Brussels from what quarter it will come – the Commission has no such grandiose ambitions'.

42   Taylor (1975, p. 348).

43   The optimism of the period after the Hague summit of 1969 has since been talked of as the 'Hague spirit'.

44   De Gaulle had disliked Mansholt intensely.

45   *The Economist*, 6 January 1973.

46   *The Economist*, 9 December 1972.

47   *The Economist*, 27 January 1973.

48   Quoted in *The Economist*, 9 June 1973.

49   *The Economist*, 9 June 1973.

50   The negotiation process ended with few changes made to the deal done initially by Edward Heath. What had changed in the meantime was the Labour Party's position on Europe.

51   The mechanisms which were put in place came to be known as European Political Co-operation (EPC). See, for example, Nutall (1992).

52   See Urwin (1991, p. 100).

53   The Tindemans Report, Bull-EC, (S) 1.76. See chapter seven on institutional reform and the Santer Commission.

54   See in particular, Jenkins (1989).

55   *The Economist*, 20 November 1976.

56   Note that this is discussed at length in Jenkins (1989).

57   *The Economist*, 14 May 1977.

58   Dinan (1994, p. 102).

59   See chapter seven on institutional reform.

60   Compare this with the approach often taken by Jacques Delors. See chapters three and six.

61   The Franco-German axis is considered still to be the centrepiece of the European integration process, with the original deal over the pooling of coal and steel and on the creation of a broader common market done between the Germans and the French.

62   Helmut Schmidt was voted out of office in 1982 and Giscard in 1981.

63   This was the time of the Genscher-Colombo initiative and the Solemn Declaration on European Union by the heads of state and government. The external relations of the Community was particularly important given the heightening of tension between the US and the Soviet Union, and strained relations within the Atlantic partnership, especially over the building of a gas pipeline from Siberia to West Germany.

64   George Ross (1995, p. 28) noted for example that at this time 'the body as a whole was stuck'.

65   See for example, Steinberg (1990); Sharp and Shearman (1987); and Sharp *et al.* (1991).

66   Dinan (1994, pp. 118–19).

3

'Leadership by ideas':[1] the external role of the Commission, 1985–1994

1985 was a crossroads for the European Commission.[2] The fluctuating fortunes of the European institutions had demonstrated the extent to which supranational political actors were seemingly subject to the whim of national governments and conducive external environments. But in the period following Jacques Delors's appointment to the Commission, something changed. It seemed that the new Commission President was capable of offering to the Community a form of European leadership unheard of since the Hallstein decade. 'He was ... political leader of both the Commission, through the ideas, working methods and vision that he applied to the institution and its task, and of the Community more generally, by virtue of personifying – by default – the European entity.'[3] It is this latter role that provides the focus of this chapter.[4]

Delors's vision and strategy

When Jacques Delors took office in 1985 there was little to suggest that a new phase in the history of the EC was about to begin. Delors's experience of French domestic politics had already given him ample opportunity to demonstrate his European credentials. Yet his only direct involvement in European-level politics had been short-lived. In 1979 he had briefly been a member of the first directly elected European Parliament, before moving speedily back into French politics to become Finance Minister after the Socialist Party won the 1981 general election. Delors's appointment to the European Commission meant that he was able to put into practice much of his earlier thinking on social and economic policy, without the constraints of elected office upon him.

Such an approach would not have been possible without the support of national leaders; so that before Delors officially took up his post in Brussels, he was sure to spend a fair amount of time travelling between national capitals talking to politicians about their European policies and the part that the Commission might play within them. By the time Delors started his new job, his European strategy was already well on the way to being formulated. His approach was simple: instead of introducing new European-level policies, emphasis would instead be placed on resolving matters already agreed upon (in principle at least) by the member states. There were many Community policies that remained to be implemented. And it was clear to Delors that national governments would find it rather difficult to resist action in areas on which agreement had already been reached. By the time of his first address to the EP on 14 January 1985, the new President was already confident enough of the route he was about to take to spell out to MEPs (Members of the European Parliament) certain aspects of this approach. Considering Delors's early experience working for the Banque de France, it is hardly surprising that his initial plan revolved around the revival of the economic and monetary union idea. This had been proposed and agreed upon in 1970, in the so-called Werner Plan, but had been shelved with the onset of monetary instabilities and then recession early in the 1970s. However, Delors was quick to recognise that there would be little hope of consensus on the issue of reviving EMU at this stage.

Also on the Delors list of unfinished Community business was the European common market goal, first proposed in the 1957 Treaty of Rome, though never completed.[5] Here there was potential for agreement amongst the member states. Indeed, the issue was already a live one, with an Internal Market Council of Ministers having been established three years earlier; the principle of 'mutual recognition' agreed in 1979;[6] and a speeding up of legislative activity in the field under the previous Commission. Delors was attracted to the idea as it seemed to provide answers to questions he had already been posing in a French context, about the lack of European industrial competitiveness. As such, in his address to the EP, he was able to guarantee that the issue of the single or common market would be investigated, with a report promised for the meeting of the June 1985 European Council.

To claim that the single market goal was simply a means of achieving a federal Europe would be to underestimate and simplify the delorist vision. As far as Delors was concerned, there was little contradiction between ends and means here. Although the single market could provide a series of stepping-stones that might one day lead to European political union, the creation of one enormous European market was also very much in tune with Delors's commitment towards the use of market mechanisms as a foundation for European economic growth and for the improvement of living and working conditions that would surely follow.[7] Indeed, Delors came fervently to believe that the economic future of Western Europe would depend upon the success of this project. There was nothing neo-liberal in delorist motives, however. Whilst Delors was convinced that the single market was a necessary element in the economic revival of Western Europe, he would argue with just as much conviction that it could in no way be a *sufficient* route to European competitiveness. This was very much in tune with the Commission President's own political views that fell on the middle ground between social and christian democracy. Although Delors was frequently labelled a socialist, he was far from associating himself with policies normally defined as such. His faith in market mechanisms existed alongside a recognition of market imperfections, on both an economic and a moral level. These were part and parcel of Delors's political pedigree and of his 'personalist' vision of the world.

The underpinning of Delors's philosophical approach was derived largely from his reading of the works of Emmanuel Mounier, whose personalist philosophy rejected both individualistic society and the collectivism often considered the only alternative to selfish utilitarianism.[8] Although individuals are considered to be important, they are so within the context of interdependent social groups. As such, solidarity is central to the personalist vision, though the only role for the politician to play is that of facilitating relationships between these groups. The state should not dominate these relationships; but neither should there be a complete withdrawal from the lives of individuals. On a practical level, these views were translated by Delors into a belief that the only way to achieve acceptable political solutions to social and economic problems was to encourage social groups to enter into dialogue with one another. Delors's vision of a 'European model of society' was crucial to what he considered to be his end goal, 'a humane social order based upon a mixed economy, civilised industrial relations, the welfare state, and a commitment to basic social justice'.[9] As such, it was logical to Delors that the single market should lead to the application of such a model.

How this vision became part of a commitment to a federal Europe rests with a recognition that such an approach was no longer either feasible or desirable at the national level alone. Delors's European strategy was therefore not intended to end with the creation of a unified European market, free of unfair barriers to trade. Nevertheless, there was some ambivalence about how the move from single market to political union would actually occur. Clearly, market-building was to be the first stage in the process. This stage would itself incorporate some elements of positive integration, such as the creation of common policies and institutional reform. The intention was that these flanking policies would help to create an ongoing logic in favour of further integration, a logic that has been explained by means of a 'Russian dolls' metaphor.

> Social and economic cohesion was needed to promote economic convergence and prevent disruptive social dumping. At the same time, it embodies new commitments to interstate regional solidarity to serve as a precedent for breaking with earlier EC member state egoisms. Economically, the social dimension was a way of regulating the consequences of the Single Market to prevent the emergence of unfair trade in the labor market. It was also an avenue to greater dialogue and negotiation between employers and workers on European level (*sic*), a way to counteract market-based tendencies undercutting industrial relations systems on national levels. The CAP needed more reform because of the waste and trade distortion which it promoted. But it also needed to be changed because of the centrality of rural development and the unique contributions of farmers to European society and ecology. New Community initiatives in research and development and environmental regulation were needed to enhance competitiveness. But they were also to reinforce specifically European co-operation in industry.[10]

Thus a logic emerged that linked, for strategic gain, one discrete policy domain with another, in ways not unlike those envisaged by functionalist theorists decades earlier.[11] There may indeed be much of the 'Monnet method' of integration in Delors's approach.[12] As such, the emphasis was on the pulling (or dragging) of member states into further integration through what were, to all intents and purposes, the unintended consequences of their own actions.

In spite of the 'Russian doll' logic of the single market, there were clearly going to be difficulties in making the great leap of faith from the construction of a huge European market-place to that of a political union. There was no consensus at national level on the merits of European unification as the ultimate aim of the integration process, and it was this that made a successful and speedy transition rather unlikely. National elites were not unaware of Delors's political objectives, even though the British Government did not seem fully to comprehend the non-deregulatory (or re-regulatory) aspects of the SEA. The conventional tensions between those envisaging a more intergovernmentalist or confederal Europe, as against those whose ultimate objectives involved political union, possibly of a federal kind, were not going to disappear. It would have been naive to believe that national governments could be forced into taking such a step against their will. Even for those who wanted to see the initiation of a 'state-building' project, there were differences of opinion over the form that integration should take and the speed at which it ought to develop. Extremely sensitive political policy priorities were at issue here.

It was clear that the move to a commitment on political union would have repercussions not only for national elites, but also for national electorates. Public opinion was ambivalent about (or just plain uninterested in) the process of creating a single market. Although complex, the arguments in favour could be advanced in simple terms, and were often emphasised from the point of the view of national interest. But all in all, there was little national debate over the '1992' programme in the way that there would later be over the Maastricht process. Once the move to European state-building became public property, a fundamental flaw in the Delors vision was exposed – that the process leading to change was essentially an undemocratic one.

Delors was not unaware of the issues of democracy, accountability and legitimacy that were going to be raised by plans to create a political union. But a decision had to be made as to whether the democratic reform of the institutional environment should precede any further attempts at European integration, or whether the democratisation of the Community would merely delay a revitalisation of the EC.[13] As it seemed to Delors that a window of opportunity had opened with the growing consensus on the need for a single

European market, there seemed no time for delay if this opportunity was not to be missed. Delors eased his democratic conscience by seeking to involve in this process as many outside interests as possible,[14] whilst at the same time making efforts to keep the general public informed of developments, although this had little impact on public perceptions, it seems.[15]

This was not the end of the matter. The 'democratic deficit' issue raised fundamental questions about how the EC should evolve. Delors proposed a left-of-centre vision of a Europe which played down the importance of national policy instruments in favour of European-level ones, as a means of coping with the problems associated with the creation of a global economy and declining European competitiveness. Delors's belief was that a European model of society could only be created at a European level: that part of that process would involve economic liberalisation, but that this liberalisation process would be tempered by European-level regulation, redistribution and common policies. The story that follows demonstrates the extent to which the delorist vision of a European model of society was used as a pathway to further European integration. The aim here is not to provide a comprehensive treatment of all events that took place between 1985 and 1994, but to focus on the broader Commission role in the integration process during a period of intense policy activism.

1992 and the Single European Act

Although the most urgent matter to be resolved at the time of Delors's arrival at the Commission seemed the imminent enlargement of the Community to include Spain and Portugal, the issue of market integration immediately took priority over all other policy concerns. But the rather vague objective of completing the European single market had to be transformed into a concrete and workable set of policy proposals. Otherwise, the '1992' programme would have become little more than the inflated rhetoric of a new Commission President. '1992' was as much about the creation of a self-fulfilling prophecy as it was about policy formulation and implementation within and by the Commission. As such, the members of the Commission, and in particular the internal market commissioner, Lord Cockfield, spent a great deal of time and effort organising meetings with industrial leaders, government departments and with the financial press, so as to convince as many key actors as possible of the merits of the programme.[16] A research project on the effects of the single market, which was to look into the 'costs of non-Europe' was also set in motion, though this was undertaken largely on a contract basis using experts from outside the Commission.[17]

Lord Cockfield, the British commissioner responsible, was left very much to his own devices during the first half of 1985. During this time he oversaw the drafting of the White Paper, 'Completing the Internal Market',[18] which listed the legislation that would be necessary before unfair barriers to trade between the EC member states could be removed. The Commission President made a personal contribution to the White Paper in the fields of VAT (Value Added Tax) harmonisation and company law.[19] Delors was adamant, however, that these Commission proposals should take the form of a treaty revision, and that this should require the extension of qualified majority voting in the Council. This was imperative if the December 1992 deadline was to be met.

With no consensus emerging on the question of revising the Treaty of Rome at the time, the Council presidency made do with initiating an Intergovernmental Conference (IGC), which could be set up with only the majority agreement of the member states.[20] Formally, the Commission's role was minimal. Delors was nevertheless allowed to attend meetings of the member states' foreign ministers. And more importantly, the Commission President and his personal staff, along with the Secretary-General, Emile Noël, personally took charge of the Commission's written contribution to the Conference. This submission to the IGC was crucial in shaping the discussion that was to take place. The first contribution comprised a draft chapter on the internal market, which placed the 1992 programme at the centre of a proposed treaty revision. Subsequent submissions on subjects such as environment, research and 'cohesion', and on the decision-making role of the EP, were also used as the basis for intergovernmental debate. Although Delors's later claim that his officials wrote 85 per cent of the treaty[21] is perhaps something of an exaggeration, it is clear that the Commission's input was none the less substantial. Commission proposals were taken on board either in one form or another. In the case of economic and monetary union in particular, certain member states (notably the British, Germans and Dutch) rejected the Commission's draft chapter as unrealistic. This was seriously disappointing for the Commission President.

> Despite mention of EMU, the new treaty fell far short of Delors's federalist hopes. The morning after the summit, at a meeting of foreign ministers, Delors harangued them for failing to rise to the challenge of doing something for Europe, and for having given birth to a 'monstrosity'. He tried to reopen the text on the arcane subject of 'comitology', which he – but no one else – considered of the utmost importance. Delors wanted the treaty to specify that the commission rather than national officials should control the committees which managed the single market. The ministers ignored him.[22]

All the same, Delors came to recognise the importance of the new treaty as a stepping-stone towards his vision of a more integrated Europe. In spite of Delors's discontent with certain aspects of the treaty, the SEA clearly helped to consolidate and even extend the role that the Commission played in the Community policy process. The introduction of new policy areas in which the Commission could use its right of initiative, and the introduction of qualified majority voting in the Council of Ministers when single market legislation was being agreed, would clearly give the Commission more of a role in the decision-making process.

The extension of the Commission's policy competences as a direct result of the SEA meant that there was an urgent need to extend the scope and size of the Community budget. This was something of a political minefield for the member states. One of the main reasons why this was such a sensitive issue was that it was tied closely to the high level of spending under the CAP. At the end of 1986 Delors was asked by the British presidency to consider a range of budgetary problems, including CAP funding, regional aid and the overall size of the Community budget. By February of the following year, Delors had come up with a set of proposals under the heading of *Réussir L'Acte Unique* (Making the Single Act work). This came to be known as the Delors Package and later on as 'Delors I'. These proposals sought to establish limits for certain categories of expenditure over a period of five years. This would mean that the financial wrangles that had previously taken place on a yearly basis would no longer serve to act as a continuous source of contention.

But this was not the only objective of the Delors Package. The thinking behind it arose from a need to compensate the poorer member states for the potentially detrimental effects of the single market programme, at least in the short term. Delors believed that without some redistributive commitment, support for the creation of an internal market would be short-lived in those countries less in a position to benefit from a more competitive industrial environment. As such, over the first five-year period, expenditure on the structural funds would be doubled and Britain would be allowed to keep its budget rebate.

Gaining the national governments' acceptance of the Package was far from an easy job. The Germans in particular were reluctant to foot the bill. At the Brussels summit at the start of 1988, the whole Package came close to being rejected. Delors, however, was 'on peak negotiating form, scurrying from one delegation to another and showing himself sensitive to the priorities of each'.[23] A deal was finally struck at three o'clock in the morning of the last day of the summit and came to be considered as a major personal success on his part, thus helping to enhance his reputation at national level.

The story of the SEA is one in which the Commission played a pivotal role. In understanding its impact in terms of Commission activism, four elements are especially important. Firstly, the Commission's contribution to the setting of the SEA agenda, and more specifically, to the intergovernmental discussion that took place within the IGCs, gave the institution a notable input into the substantive content of the new treaty. Treaty revision remains an intergovernmental prerogative. Here was the Commission making its mark in this way for the first time. Secondly, the participation of Delors in the intergovernmental process reawakened memories of Roy Jenkins's involvement in intergovernmental summits. This helped to enhance the role of the Commission presidency, illuminating at the same time the profile of the Commission as a whole. Thirdly, the legislative impact of the SEA, in extending majority voting, would soon help to make Commission input into the European decision-making process more effective. The Commission would also benefit indirectly from the increasing powers endowed in the EP. And finally, the knock-on effect of the treaty was to become crucial, in that it increased the Commission's competence in a number of substantial policy fields. With the Commission *more* involved in a larger number of policies, it was increasingly difficult for member state governments to ignore it. Generally, then, the Commission was able to assert itself very effectively in the task of

vices (and in particular by DG XIX – budgets (see Figure 2)). The outcome was the publication in February 1992 of *From Single Act to Maastricht and Beyond: The Means to Match our Ambitions.* The aim was to continue the reformist efforts of the first package by emphasising the need to institutionalise budgetary procedures, whilst also demonstrating a commitment to the 'cohesion' principle. What this amounted to in practice was a second five-year programme which included further plans to reform the Structural Funds, alongside a five-year provision for the CAP. To achieve the objectives set out in the package, the EC budget would have to be increased. The Lisbon summit in the middle of 1992 resolved little, although it became clear that British demands for Delors II to be stretched over a seven-year period looked likely to be taken seriously.

The reform of the CAP was an important element in the discussions over the budgetary implications of the Maastricht Treaty. It was at the same time tied extremely tightly to the ongoing GATT negotiations. When the agriculture commissioner, Ray MacSharry, came close to a deal with the Americans on the controversial question of oilseeds in November 1992, tensions over CAP reform became apparent within the Commission. Delors threatened to block the agreement, as he claimed it went beyond the Council's mandate. This led to the resignation of Ray MacSharry as GATT negotiator. With Delors outvoted on the issue of CAP reform in the Commission, MacSharry rescinded his resignation and went on to conclude the agreement with the Americans at Blair House on 20 November 1992. As such, the linking together of the GATT negotiations and CAP reform produced results, but not without further friction amongst the commissioners.

The enlargement of the EU was another priority area for the Commission. With a favourable opinion on Austrian accession having been issued in 1991, the Commission went on to react in a positive manner to the applications from Sweden and Finland. Over the course of 1992, work also began in response to the applications from Norway, Cyprus, Switzerland and Malta. The European Council that was held in Edinburgh at the end of 1992 agreed that negotiations for the accession of Austria, Sweden and Finland would begin early in 1993, with the Norwegian negotiation process to start as soon as the Commission had issued its 'avis' or opinion. At Edinburgh, the relationship between the EU and the East and Central Europeans was also given some consideration. Indeed, the

Edinburgh summit became in this and other respects something of a post-Maastricht landmark. As well as having to face the implications of the ERM crisis of September 1992, the member states had to come to some agreement over Delors II. British pressure to reduce the expenditure commitment did lead to some compromise, and by the end of the European Council agreement had been reached. The European Council also revived the theme of competitiveness, in response to growing economic recession, through the so-called Edinburgh Growth Initiative. Over the course of 1993 and 1994, this was to form the basis of the last burst of activity from the Commission.

The new Commission that took office in January 1993 knew that it would only hold office for an interim period of two years. The low-key cautious approach of 1992 carried on into this new Commission, with work on the implementation of the Maastricht Treaty, the first wave of new members, and on relations with Eastern and Central Europe taking precedence over all other policy matters. There was one exception, however. Building on the Edinburgh Growth Initiative, Delors revived his interest in the problems associated with European competitiveness. Prompted by a European Council request, Commission staff set to work on an analysis of the economic situation in the Union, considering at the same time potential solutions to the difficult questions that would shape the industrial future of the EU. At the European Council in Copenhagen in June 1993, Delors presented his economic analysis and was asked by the Council to deliver a further paper on the subject to the Brussels summit which was to be held in December of that year. As such, this 'one last sprint',[48] ended Delors's decade in office in much the same way as it began, with the publication of a White Paper, intended to solve some of the most pressing of Europe's economic, industrial and social problems.

The White Paper drew together many of Delors's ideas on social democracy.[49] Questions of employment and competitiveness provided the focus. Entitled *Growth, Competitiveness, Employment: The Challenges and Ways Forward into the Twenty-first Century*, the paper suggested a variety of ways in which investment and job creation could be encouraged through gains in productivity. This would involve the creation of a more flexible and cheaper labour market alongside an unequivocal commitment to education and training. In spelling out options from which governments would be

able to pick and choose, and by setting the paper out in the form of
non-binding recommendations, the Commission was able to restore
some of its lost credibility without being accused of being power-
hungry. To the extent that the White Paper was favourably received,
Delors left office with a flourish.[50] However, it is clear that the last
three years of his presidency was a period of consolidation after the
exertion and exhaustion of the pre-Maastricht build-up. Hostility
towards the Commission made it difficult, if not impossible, for the
President to adopt any controversial high-profile strategies without
further threatening the position of the Commission. As such, the
White Paper revived questions about how, in a period not conducive
to an assertive Commission role, the Commission might be able to
legitimise and consolidate its position within the EU. It also helped
to set the agenda for future Commissions. The emphasis placed on
job creation and industrial growth was a sensible one. But in an
institution where success has so often been defined in terms of legislative output, it would be difficult to counter criticism that the
Commission was once again reverting to a sort of pre-1985 inertia
and that the 1985–91 period was nothing more than an 'aberra-
tion'.[51]

Conclusion

The argument that the leadership of Delors marked merely a temporary and exceptional phase in the evolution of the European
Commission is too simplistic a conclusion to draw from this chapter. Clearly, however, certain lessons can be learnt from the Delors
years, lessons that point to the importance of leadership in turning
a weak and ineffectual institution into an activist and assertive political actor – at least in terms of popular perception. But other elements in this story are also worthy of note. Firstly, it is once again
clear that the institutional fortunes of the Commission are in many
ways synonymous with those of the Commission President.
Although this might not always be the case, it certainly seems true
of Delors's decade in office. Secondly, the focus of this chapter has
largely been the political tier of the Commission (the college of
commissioners and the President), with little mention of the specific
work done by the Commission staff. This does not mean that the
work done by officials was unimportant. Rather, it seeks to stress
that innovation and leadership during this period emanated largely

from the presidency, the commissioners and from their personal staffs. Thirdly, this chapter draws out the importance and implications of the Commission's various functions. This is crucial when exogenous circumstances alter and the external environment becomes less conducive to activism by the Commission. The ascendancy of some Commission functions at the expense of others is crucial as it demonstrates how the Commission can continue to play an important political role even when it ceases to provide visionary leadership.

Finally, though, it should be remembered that even if the change of pace of integration after 1985 has focused our attention on the commissioners and their President, much of the Commission's most important work is unsung. It is even possible to argue that it is the unglamorous daily administrative grind that makes the Commission an effective, or an ineffective, institution. It is the work of the officials that sustains the Commission and its leadership. As such, in the chapters that follow, attention is much less on the broad narrative of European integration, and much more on the organisation, procedures and conditions that shape the work of the Commission's services.

Notes

1   Drake (1995b, pp. 23–4).

2   This point was made by Wessels (1985, p. 11).

3   This quotation is taken from Helen Drake's paper on the political leadership of Jacques Delors (1995b, p. 3).

4   The internal leadership role performed by Delors within the Commission is dealt with in chapter six.

5   Although tariffs and quotas had been done away with and a customs union established in 1968, there had been no subsequent move to a truly common market which would have involved the removal of non-tariff barriers to trade between the member states of the Community.

6   The mutual recognition principle was established in the *Cassis de Dijon* court judgement (1979). It established an important principle of free movement, that was to underpin the entire single market programme.

7   Delors's strategy appealed to both free marketeers and to interventionists, in what *The Economist* (25 June 1994) called 'a clever mix'.

8   See for example, Hellman (1981).

9   Ross (1995, p. 46).

10   Ross (1995, pp. 46–7).

11 The neo-functionalists, for example, talked of the spillover effect. See the works of Haas (1968) for example, for details.

12 Ross (1995, p. 230).

13 This question will be pursued further in chapter six below.

14 Delors developed a network of external contacts at a high level, including those organised into the European Round Table of industrialists. It was noted by Middlemas (1995, p. 224) that industry was by this stage saying that the Commission was fighting *its* corner.

15 Drake (1995b, p. 11) says that when he arrived in Brussels, Delors had no disciples as such; no ready-made audience, though he sought out audiences receptive to the European message and created them where they did not exist.

16 Note that the 1985 Commission was considered a strong team, especially commissioners Cockfield, Natali and Sutherland. See Middlemas (1995, p. 221).

17 See Cecchini (1988). This is a summary of a more comprehensive set of reports on a sector-by-sector basis.

18 'Completing the Internal Market. White paper from the Commission to the European Council', Commission of the EC, June 1995.

19 Grant (1994, p. 69).

20 Article 236 (EEC).

21 Middlemas (1995) noted that Delors's deputy *chef de cabinet*, François Lamoureux, wrote much of the SEA himself.

22 Grant (1994, p. 74). See chapter five on comitology. Note that Delors's reaction to the SEA was similar to his reaction to the Maastricht Treaty in 1992.

23 Grant (1994, p. 80).

24 Whilst negative integration implies the removal of obstacles to European integration, positive integration suggests the more concrete construction of common policies and institutional structures at a supranational level. See, for example, Pinder (1968) and W. Wallace (1991).

25 On EMU, see Padoa-Schioppa (1987); and Thygesen (1989).

26 Ross (1995, p. 81).

27 See chapter six for details of how Delors and his cabinet were able to evade formal hierarchical structures in this way.

28 Ross (1995, pp. 81–2).

29 *The Economist*, 22 April 1989.

30 The Delors Report would later become the basis of the EMU element of the Maastricht Treaty.

31 *The Economist*, 24 February 1990.

32 On the EFTA countries and the EEA, see H. Wallace (1991).

33 Grant (1994, pp. 136–7).

34 Ross (1995, p. 90).

35 This was on 1 November 1990.
36 Ross (1995, p. 90).
37 Grant (1994, p. 200).
38 Ross (1995, p. 189).
39 This account is taken from *ibid.*
40 See, for example, Grant (1994, p. 210).
41 Dinan (1994, p. 181).
42 See, for example, *The Economist*, 24 February 1990.
43 See George (1995, p. 1).
44 Middlemas (1995, p. 216) talks of his 'skill of retreat and defence' from the 'dark period' of 1992–94. He also talks of the revival of the Commission's 'benign image' during this period (p. 236). See also George (1995, p. 1) on the 'black clouds over the Breydel'.
45 On the ratification process, see Duff (1994b).
46 The results of the referendums held over 1992 and 1993 were as follows: Denmark (49.2 per cent in favour; 50.7 per cent against in first referendum: 56.8 per cent in favour; 43.2 per cent against in the second); Ireland (69.05 per cent in favour; 30.95 per cent against); France (51.05 per cent in favour; 48.95 per cent against).
47 Indeed, during the 1989 and the 1993 Commissions, the college of commissioners was divided on many issues. Some strong and forceful characters (Brittan, Andriessen and Bangemann, for example) who would regularly stand up to Delors, meant that arguments and dissent were commonplace.
48 Ross (1995, p. 221).
49 The White Paper was drafted by Delors with the help of the Cellule de Prospective (the Commission think-tank, the Forward Studies Unit). Many of the ideas in the White Paper can be found in the writings of Delors, according to Drake (1995b, p. 28). Drake called the paper a 'punch in the stomach' for the member states.
50 The member states did not accept all elements of the White Paper. Substantial borrowing powers that the Commission had requested for the purpose of funding public works were not viewed at all favourably.
51 This point is made by Middlemas (1995, p. 238). See also George (1995, p. 2).

II

Organisation, process and management

4

Organisation, structures and staffing in the European Commission

On one level, an assessment of the formal, tangible components of organisational life will give us only a superficial impression of how the European Commission operates in practice. But organisational perspectives need not exclude more intangible elements, and may even help us to establish a framework within which the more informal Commission dynamics can be exposed. Yet, without an initial understanding of formal structures and legal procedures, more profound (and more accurate) conclusions drawn about the Commission are likely to be ill-founded. The word *Commission* is itself a useful starting-point for explaining organisational characteristics.[1] Rather confusingly, the word can be used in two entirely different senses. On one hand, the *Commission* is the collegiate Commission, a meeting of the twenty commissioners (or members of the Commission). This narrow definition suggests a focus on the decision-taking organ, the political cap on a bureaucratic body. On the other hand, the *Commission* is also a word used much more broadly to describe not only the commissioners and their personal staffs, but also the officials, linguists and researchers who work within the directorates-general and services, as well as those officials located within the Commission's national representations and within the Commission-funded research institutes.[2] Here, the use of the word *Commission* is much more generic, with emphasis placed on the institution as a whole (including the administrative units), and on the dynamics that exist between its component parts. As the focus of this chapter is largely upon such internal dynamics, the latter definition seems more appropriate for our purposes.

The Commission services

Most groups and individuals who have dealings with the European Commission will have made contact with one or more directorates-general, known colloquially as 'DGs' (Figure 2). These DGs are very roughly comparable to government departments, although in terms of size they are mere shadows of national ministries. There are at present twenty-four DGs,[3] each one of which has responsibility for a specific policy area or administrative function. DGs are known by both their names and numbers, and it is quite common for them to be talked of in numerical shorthand: for example, DG VI (six) deals with agricultural policy; DG IX (nine) with personnel policy and so on. At first sight, the logic of organising the Commission's administrative departments in this way is not obvious. Functions invariably overlap and, where at national level responsibility would lie with one department, it is not uncommon for several DGs to share control of a policy field. In addition, there is no correlation between the Commission's organisation and that of the EP's committee structure. It has to be said that in many cases, there really is no logic at all to this functional pigeon-holing of jobs. Indeed, it is not even clear whether the work of the DGs actually relates to the job that needs to be achieved.[4] Through historical accident, political necessity and layer upon layer of minor reform and reorganisation, the Commission has ended up with what many consider to be a number of DGs far in excess of what is required.

As well as the twenty-four DGs and a number of often temporary Task Forces and special units, there are also five horizontal services.[5] These are administrative departments whose responsibilities cut across the largely vertical policy concerns of the DGs allowing them to perform a co-ordinating or general across-the-board role on behalf of the Commission. The most important of these services is undoubtedly the Secretariat-General (SG). Of all the Commission services, this body has perhaps the most overtly political role to play. The SG manages the co-ordination of all aspects of Commission life and its relationships with the outside world, and is under the direct supervision of the Commission President. Its main purpose is to provide for the Commission a unified institutional identity, to present and, where necessary, to manufacture a common Commission voice. This is not an easy task. One of its main responsibilities is that of co-ordinating relations between the Commission, other EU institutions and the member states, and as such it often represents the Commission in meetings with outside bodies. Much of its work involves the selling of Commission proposals to policy actors involved in the EU decision-making process.

Secretariat-General	
Legal Service	
Spokesman's Service	
Joint Interpreting and Conference Service	
Statistical Office	
Forward Studies Group	
Security Office	
DG I	External relations
DG IA	External relations
DG II	Economic and financial affairs
DG III	Internal market and industrial affairs
DG IV	Competition
DG V	Employment, industry relations, social affairs
DG VI	Agriculture
DG VII	Transport
DG VIII	Development
DG IX	Personnel and administration
DG X	Audio-visual; Info., Communication and culture
DG XI	Environment, nuclear safety
DG XII	Science, R&D; Joint Research Centre
DG XIII	Telecoms, IT and innovation
DG XIV	Fisheries
DG XV	Financial institutions/company law
DG XVI	Regional policies
DG XVII	Energy
DG XVIII	Credit and investments
DG XIX	Budgets
DG XX	Financial control
DG XXI	Customs union and indirect taxation
DG XXII	Co-ordination of structural funds
DG XXIII	Enterprise, distributive trade, tourism
DG XXIV	Consumer affairs

Figure 2 The services of the European Commission

The SG also performs a crucial internal function. It seeks to obtain the maximum amount of consistency and unity of approach amongst the DGs. This is particularly important where there is a potential overlap between the responsibilities of two or more services. As such, the SG at times ends up playing the unenviable role of procedural watchdog: scanning timetables and deadlines, making sure that procedural safeguards are applied satisfactorily and checking that the DGs have consulted effectively over draft proposals. More routinely, the SG also organises the meetings of the college of commissioners, preparing documentation, writing up minutes and publishing agreed decisions and recommendations.[6]

For a long period the SG was considered to be the real powerhouse of the Commission. This was largely due to the influence of the man who held the post of Secretary-General for almost thirty years, from 1958 to 1987, Emile Noël. The fact that Noël was in post for far longer than any other commissioner allowed him to develop a power-brokerage role for himself within the Commission. On his retirement he was replaced by a former British civil servant, David Williamson. This led to a dramatic change in the function and style of co-ordination performed by the Secretariat-General, with a much more low-key and cautious approach replacing the high-profile leadership of Noël.[7] Nowadays, however, the glory years of the SG seem to be over, with the service playing a role much closer to that of 'letterbox' of the Commission,[8] although the proximity of the SG to the presidency means that its profile will now tend to mirror that of the President.[9]

Another very important horizontal Commission service offering an across-the-board facility to all DGs is the Legal Service (LS). All documentation drafted inside the Commission, intended for external consumption, must come under the scrutiny of the LS lawyers. This allows them to check whether Commission proposals are likely to contradict or go beyond what is acceptable to the European Court. Their at times cautious approach, in that they are what may be termed a 'people of the book',[10] is perhaps understandable. If the Commission is taken to the European Court for a breach of Community law, it is the LS that must defend Commission action. As such LS lawyers clearly want to minimise the risk of losing cases at a later stage in the policy process.

The other cross-cutting Commission services are the Translation Service, the Spokesman's Service and the Statistical Office. The functions they perform are largely self-explanatory. By contrast, jobs attributed to the DGs tend to be much more functionally specific, with the tasks performed closely linked to the initiation, execution and implementation of policy, depending on the competence of the Commission in that particular field. DGs vary greatly in size, but usually have around 200 to 400 staff. There are a few exceptions however. DG IX, dealing with personnel matters, has over 2,600 officials working within it, and DG VI (agriculture) has over 800. DG XII (research) also has over 2,000 staff, though this includes scientific personnel not located in Brussels (Table 1). Based on instructions laid down in the Commission's internal rules of procedure, each DG is divided into three or four directorates headed by directors; and each directorate is divided into three or four divisions, in turn capped by a *chef de service* or a head of unit (*chef d'unité*). This model varies considerably, however. It has been noted, for example, that while DG I has nine directorates and twenty-four divisions, DG XXIII has only two directorates and no divisions.[11] With an increase in the responsibilities of the Commission came also an increase in the number of DGs, from an original nine, to twenty-four in 1995. Since constraints on expenditure for staffing were laid down in the mid 1980s, staff for new posts in the newly formed DGs have largely come from existing departments, although numbers are still increased annually by a small amount.[12]

Table 1   Staff numbers by policy function

Internal market	1969
Social affairs	610
Flanking policies	1432
Economic development	1141
Common policies	678
External relations	2242
Admin/data	2538
Co-ordination	1160
Financial control	501
Linguists	2230
Cabinets	310

Source: Commission, *Budget* (1995)

The illusion of an enormous Commission bureaucracy is misleading, therefore, given the diminutive size of many of Commission
services. Of a total of around 26,400 EU administrative staff, only
around 16,000 actually work for the Commission. Indeed, the 1995
budget allows for 15,568 full-time, permanent and temporary staff
(excluding researchers who themselves total 3,487 staff; and 612
staff who work in various bodies attached to the Commission).[13]
The total number of staff now compares favourably (per head of
population) with the total of 5,234 in 1970, given that the EC grew
from six states in 1958 to fifteen in 1995. This is all the more
remarkable given the ever-increasing workload and widening policy
competences of the institution. One might assume that either the
Commission has become more efficient, or that its job has become
much more difficult in recent years. Both are of course true. The
issue of Commission overload[14] is a matter of some seriousness that
has inevitable implications for the effective running of the institution.

The college of commissioners

The decision-making hub of the Commission is the meeting of the
twenty commissioners who, as a collegiate body, give or withhold
their approval from or to draft proposals before they enter the
public domain. As such, the commissioners are the most important
channel through which the Commission's image is projected on to
the outside world. The role played by the college of commissioners
reflects, to a large extent, the role of the Commission as a whole.[15]
The commissioners may indeed be viewed as a sort of government
or cabinet (in the British sense), performing functions at the European level that are conventionally (in a national context) attributable to ministers. This is accurate to the extent that when
commissioners are appointed, they are given responsibility for specific portfolios, and like ministers they are often thrown in at the
deep end, with no one to guide them through the often byzantine
procedures and practices that are part and parcel of Commission
life. Until recently, only justice and home affairs departments did
not have their equivalents in the Commission. Since 1995, however,
these too are covered by Commission portfolios.[16] However, the
governmental analogy can only be taken so far, even if there are parallels to be found. And analogies drawn between senior national

civil servants and commissioners are also problematic, with the functions performed by the latter being much more overtly political.

The commissioners' responsibilities are set out in Articles 155–163 of the Rome Treaty. Here, the functions of the Commission are listed alongside matters affecting the college's appointment, its independence, its replacement, as well as some matters of procedure. Until the end of 1994 there were seventeen commissioners, each appointed for a period of four years. The larger of the member states, France, Germany, Britain, Italy and Spain each had two posts, while the smaller states (Netherlands, Belgium, Luxembourg, Greece, Denmark, Ireland and Portugal) could nominate only one commissioner. Since the accession of Austria, Finland and Sweden at the beginning of 1995 and the swearing in of a new Commission at the same time, an additional three commissioners have been appointed, each now nominated for a five-year period – bringing the total number to twenty. This change to the rules was brought about, as required, by treaty revision, with the unanimous support of all member states. The problem of an ever-increasing number of commissioners provoked some debate, though not for the first time, during the political union Intergovernmental Conference (IGC) of 1991, in the run up to the Maastricht summit. At the time, the matter was linked to the question of the college's efficiency as a decision-taking body. Although the prospect of further EU enlargement has made a decision on the number of commissioners imperative, the bigger member states who presently hold two posts in the college are reluctant to allow their influence to be reduced. The UK has consistently been the exception here, with Mrs Thatcher first proposing a reduction in the number of commissioners in the mid 1980s.

Convention has dictated that when a member state nominates two commissioners, the first is appointed from the party of government or from the leading coalition party, with the second coming from the opposition or second coalition party. For the British, this has meant that the first commissioner, currently Sir Leon Brittan, has tended to have links with the Conservative Party, whilst the second has had associations with Labour, as is the case with Neil Kinnock's appointment to the 1995 Commission. The larger states do their best to ensure that their first commissioner is given control over one of the prestigious high-profile portfolios such as external relations or the internal market. As such, the second commissioner often has to make do with what is considered a lesser role.

Reducing the number of commissioners to one per country would seem a logical, if temporary, solution to concerns about the size of the body. It is clear, however, that the entire manner of the college's appointment is controversial, as it raises important questions about the legitimacy of Commission decision-taking. In principle, commissioners are appointed by the 'common accord' of the member states. In practice, however, in what has been called 'a useful piece of political patronage',[17] each commissioner effectively has an electoral college of one, namely the Prime Minister or President of his or her country of origin, even though the appointment must be formally approved by the Council of Ministers and the EP. There is no doubt that the appointment process is arcane. On the whole, decisions are taken behind the scenes, even if there is often a great deal of press speculation and national lobbying starting as much as a year before a new Commission is sworn in (and sometimes earlier). It is not surprising that the secrecy involved in this procedure has led to calls for commissioners to be directly elected.[18] But such demands have largely fallen on the deaf ears of the national governments. Governments are obviously keen to retain as much influence as possible over the Commission. But even taking this into consideration, it seems that the very idea of electing commissioners is straying from the point somewhat. At least in its original conception the Commission reflected the political realities of West European domestic politics. The weighted system within the college mirrored demographic and nationalistic biases and the requirements of political credibility. Indeed, one might even go so far as to argue that the fact that the Commission is unelected is 'in the nature of its existence'.[19]

But what sort of people tend to get themselves nominated? The answer to this question is not obvious, as there is little evidence of a commissioner 'type'.[20] While some appointees have held high office at national level, others were previously civil servants or technocrats. There is, in addition, nothing preventing the reappointment of former commissioners time and time again, as was the case with Frans Andriessen who held posts within the college continuously between 1981 and 1992.[21] There is clearly some correlation between the perceived importance of the Commission and the stature of commissioners nominated by their national governments. As such, the type of nominee is likely to alter over time. For example, in the Hallstein decade, many of the first commissioners were figures with well-established political reputations. Such appointments were less evident during the 1970s when the European integration process appeared to be slowing down, and when the Commission seemed to become a less prestigious place to work. In the mid 1980s, when the single market programme began to suggest the growing importance of the Commission, national governments soon came to recognise the importance of appointing more high-profile individuals, so as to ensure a stronger national voice within the college. Of the seventeen commissioners appointed in 1993, thirteen had previously held ministerial office.[22] Indeed, in a 1994 study of the college, it was noted that nearly 80 per cent of all appointees had held some form of elected office before coming to the Commission. This, the authors of the study claimed, demonstrated the inherently political nature of the post.[23]

National wrangling over the appointment of the Commission President has also reflected the waxing and waning of the Commission's political status. The President's nomination continues to be subject to intense bargaining between national governments. Here, there really does need to be 'common accord' between the member states before a decision can be made.[24] The President of the Commission is the 'first amongst equals' within the college, with few powers over and above those of the other nineteen commissioners.[25] But the role of President is very much for the making, with strong assertive individuals dominating college business, and more consensual figures tending to work more closely within the collegiate structure. However, over the last decade, the collegiality principle has sat uncomfortably alongside the strong presidential-style leadership of Jacques Delors. Some have suggested that the principle of collegiality ought to be done away with entirely,[26] though the implications of such a change would certainly affect the way in which the Commission works, and it might imply further structural fragmentation. It has long been unclear where the balance lies between the commissioners' capacity for autonomy within their own policy sphere, and the need for a more collective approach to decision-making,[27] which would ensure at least the perception of consistency in policy outputs.[28]

Commissioners may define themselves both as part of the college, the decision-making organ of the Commission, and, as situated at the top of a hierarchical chain of command that involves the Commission's administrative units, though this Commission-DG relationship exists *de facto* rather than *de jure*, as neither the commissioners nor their personal staffs are formally part of what may be termed the 'European public service'. They are certainly not officials of the European Commission. There may be, then, a certain ambivalence in the relationship that commissioners have with *their* DGs, as although they are linked through their portfolios, they are clearly not of the DGs. On the surface, one can easily make a distinction between the political cap and the Commission body (the services) below. Indeed, the very fact that the commissioners are often found far from the DGs they supposedly oversee, in the Breydel building, suggests a psychological as well as a physical distance between the two.[29]

There has long been criticism of the manner in which portfolios are divided up, especially since a political, rather than legal or administrative logic, has tended to prevail.[30] It is clear that governments do try to influence the distribution process. As a result, in some cases DGs are split between two commissioners, often causing a great deal of confusion. Even where this does not happen, work is rarely distributed evenly. While some commissioners shadow the work of a number of DGs, others seem to have few responsibilities at all. Some DGs seem neglected, for what appear to be rather spurious reasons. And on top of this, common sense frequently takes second place to political considerations as commissioners are appointed to oversee policy areas about which they have little knowledge or interest. This is important as commissioners can have a fair amount of autonomy in managing their portfolios.

The independence of the commissioners is also an issue when we come to look at their relationship with national governments. It is written into the treaties that members of the Commission must act as independent agents, that is, that they must not follow instructions given to them by their sponsoring government. It is in this sense that it is accurate to say that 'Commissioners are not commissioned by anyone to do anything in particular'.[31] Indeed, before a new Commission begins its work, commissioners take an oath in the European Court of Justice, part of which stresses the autonomy of their position *vis-à-vis* the member states. However, this does not mean that all ties to national governments or national political parties are severed – far from it. It is clearly to the Commission's advantage if the networks of contacts that exist between the commissioners and their domestic constituencies continue to be used to the full. One might even argue that commissioners have a responsibility to ensure that national viewpoints gain a hearing within the Commission. Even so, there is a fine line between taking heed of domestic concerns on one hand, and playing at national politics on the other.[32] And for those commissioners who hope to return to the domestic political arena after the end of their time in Brussels, adopting more of a representational line may be crucial to their future career prospects, though they will find their time in Brussels rather difficult if they take such a blatantly partisan approach. Overt nationalism is just 'not the done thing'.[33] Still, should the Commission only take a broad-ranging Europe-wide perspective, draft proposals would, more often than not, be heavily criticised once received by the Council of Ministers' working groups. It is therefore right and proper that national interests be taken into consideration at the earliest of stages. Not only does this mean that the Commission will have greater success in influencing legislative outcomes; it also helps commissioners to sell their policies back home.

The college of commissioners exists to provide leadership and decision-making capacity both within the Commission and, potentially, for the broader Union. Leadership from the top of the hierarchy is crucial if the Commission is to make a meaningful contribution to the European polity. Without it, the institution would be little more than a secretariat, working at best for the good of member states' sectional interests. The external face of the Commission is therefore closely allied to the effectiveness of the college in the tasks that it performs. Yet, its collegiate nature, the ever-growing number of commissioners, the secretive appointments procedure, and the limits placed on parliamentary scrutiny, can all be seen as persistent organisational irrationalities. Indeed, tensions, horizontally, between the collegiality principle and the autonomy of members of the Commission, and vertically, between the system of quasi-ministerial portfolios and the organisational structure of the services, continue to provoke discontent amongst those who work within the institution.

The growth of the cabinets

The notion that each commissioner should have the support of a small personally appointed staff was initially proposed by the first

Secretary-General, Emile Noël, as a general aid to both horizontal and vertical co-ordination within the Commission. This was very much in the French tradition of a personal ministerial office, and indeed the French word *cabinet* is used to identify the personal appointees of the commissioner.[34] The process by which cabinet staff are selected varies dramatically from country to country. This means that the commissioner does not always have a completely free hand in the choice. Nevertheless, cabinets are likely to vary in terms of the backgrounds and calibre of their staff depending both on the personal choice of the commissioner and on their nationality. All, however, are employed on a temporary basis, without security of tenure. In some cases they may be national civil servants perhaps known already to the new commissioner. Otherwise, internal Commission staff, party officials, academics and managers from the private sector are all potential candidates. Generally speaking, cabinet members are high-fliers in mid-career who already have something of a proven record. Where a cabinet member has earned a good reputation in post, he may be requested to stay on when a commissioner's term of office ends, thus providing an element of continuity between colleges.

The cabinet's role is an ambivalent one and, as such, there has, since the 1960s, been some discontent over the position they have come to adopt within the Commission. The size and importance of the cabinet was contentious as far back as the 1970s when it was acknowledged that the growing influence of cabinet members reflected the increasing importance of nationality and national allegiance within the Commission. Although there is a convention that at least one cabinet member should come from a member state other than that of the commissioner, cabinets still retain their distinctive national identities. Indeed, they are often identified by their national labels – as the 'British' or the 'German' cabinet, for example. In terms of size, when the EEC Commission was first set up commissioners were allowed only two personal staff. But by the late 1970s, the number of people employed within the commissioners' personal offices had increased from an average of four in 1968 to fourteen in 1972, though only six of these would be at a high administrative grade.[35] By 1995 the average number of people at the highest grade was nine (though only six of these were actually financed from the Commission budget), with the total number of cabinet staff reaching on occasion as many as seventeen. In total, funding from the Community budget for 1995 allows for 310 staff for twenty cabinets. As well as the six A grade staff, this also gives cabinets a budget for, on average, one or two B grades, seven or eight C grades, and a share of a total of seven D grades.[36] This number is far too large, this being one area within the Commission where there is indeed 'surplus fat'.[37]

The growth of the cabinets in size and status has resulted from an ever-increasing workload imposed upon commissioners. A negative consequence of this has been the emergence of tensions between cabinet members and director-generals, the officials who head the DGs and services, who very often feel that before their very eyes their powers are being usurped. Relationships at this level can be particularly sensitive as cabinet members increasingly dip their fingers into the technical or administrative matters that directors-general see as their own responsibility. Indeed, one of the most important functions of the cabinet is to act as an intermediary between the Commission and the DG. As such, it is clear that cabinets lie 'at a juncture where political and technical considerations must be confronted'.[38]

But even where the relationship between cabinet and DG is drawn rather more tightly, problems of a different sort may emerge. Where DG staff focus on the more technical questions, the cabinet members are much more conscious of the broader political environment into which proposals are sent. It is clear, then, that the 'potential for conflict exists between cabinets and DGs because of their relative positions in the hierarchy, and their tendency to have somewhat different points of view'.[39] However, where DG and cabinet work well together (and this often involves close liaison between the assistant director-generals and the cabinet members) there lies the potential for a mutually beneficial synergy between these two branches of the institution. The demarcation between the political and technical aspects of the policy process is in practice rarely visible.

Tensions, then, tend to emerge where there is confusion within hierarchical relationships between the responsibilities of the cabinet and those of the more senior of the DG staff. Cabinet members are often graded at a lower level than the top DG officials. This causes difficulties amongst rank-conscious staff when they find themselves having to take orders from what they consider to be 'inferior' cabinet members. But, in addition, cabinet staff may also be setting their sights on some of the top jobs in the DG as the end of their term of office approaches, thus restricting promotion opportunities for ambitious officials. The sense of frustration that results from these frictions may be compounded by policy differences that are a consequence of different national perspectives.

Intentionally, director-generals are rarely of the same nationality as cabinet members. And as such, commissioners and cabinet members may apply different working practices and norms of behaviour within their offices. In some cases, especially where relations are bad between the director-general's office and the cabinet, cabinet members will prefer to deal directly with middle-ranking officials, thus failing to respect the usual hierarchical chain of command. Managing the relationship between the DG and the commissioner and acting as a buffer in that relationship is not the only task of the cabinet, however. Their job depends largely on the style and approach of the commissioner. But in general the cabinet's priority is to assist the commissioner with his or her portfolio. Here the cabinet does much of the groundwork before Commission meetings: dealing with non-controversial policy matters, often taking decisions in these areas through powers delegated from the college of commissioners; and acting as political advisers to the commissioner. The cabinet must also look beyond the specifics of a particular portfolio to make sure that the commissioner is kept abreast of general developments within both the Commission and the Union.[40] This is crucial, as collegiality requires that commissioners speak with one voice on behalf of the Commission, though of course there are occasions when internal disagreement becomes public property. Part of the cabinets' job involves maintaining open channels of communication with other European institutions and with interest groups. The cabinet also has an important role to play in ensuring a constant flow of information between national governments and the Commission. Increasingly, however, cabinets have come under fire for adopting additional roles. Personnel management is one aspect of Commission life not formally under the scrutiny of cabinet staff. Involvement, or even interference in promotions and the appointment of staff often along nationally defined lines, has meant that Commission officials will often see cabinets as lobbyists for a certain nationality. As such, there can be a substantial amount of pressure placed on cabinet staff by Commission officials – even when those staff have nothing to do with the DG or service to which the official belongs.

Cabinets lie outside the formal, hierarchical structure of the Commission. As such, their growth can be seen as a challenge to the notion that the Commission was more about the construction of a European public service than it was about flexible and informal organisation. It is perhaps ironic that the latter is much more in line with what Jean Monnet envisaged for the Commission. The cabinet itself was originally created to emphasise the political role that the Commission was to play in the creation of European political union. However, the attachment of a cabinet to a commissioner means that the loyalty of cabinet members has often tended to lie with the individual or the member state rather than with the Commission or with any notion of European public service. As such, there is a danger that the cabinet system promotes a sort of parallel bureaucracy within the Commission. Indeed, '*Cabinets* are increasingly instrumental in building policy majorities and package deals across Community institutions and with the Member States'.[41] But, while the functions of the cabinet altered somewhat over the 1970s and early 1980s to focus much more on planning and co-ordination, since the mid 1980s attention has focused on the cabinets for different reasons. These have much to do with the style of leadership brought into the Commission by Jacques Delors. In his attempts to forge coherence and consistency within the institution, the cabinets have had a vital role to play in a process of centralisation that was exemplified in its most extreme form by the cabinet of the Commission President himself.[42]

Hierarchy, flexibility and working conditions

The staffing policy of the European Commission is overseen by DG IX, the directorate-general in charge of personnel and administration. Individual DGs, however, have been eager to gain as much autonomy as possible in the taking of personnel decisions. This has been allowed increasingly at the lower grades, and where national experts or consultants are appointed on a fairly informal basis. DG IX, by contrast, seeks to retain control of personnel decisions at the centre in order to make some contribution towards the creation of a European public service devoid of excessive national influence. It is also hoped that this would avoid exacerbating the division of the Commission into individual personnel 'fiefdoms', each with their own norms, working practices and, indeed, staffing policies.[43]

Staffing matters are also conditioned by the 'Statute', the rules and regulations which govern the rights and responsibilities of staff employed not just within the Commission's services, but also in the EU administration generally.[44] Thus, the input into Commission personnel policy comes from a variety of levels that makes for a complex and often opaque working environment for officials.

Hierarchy in the Commission

The Commission is essentially a hierarchical institution. Its formal structures tend towards rigidity even though the scope for a more flexible approach does exist within the Commission's operating procedures. Yet the extent to which the hierarchical model is actually implemented is left largely to the discretion of senior officials within specific directorates or units.[45] So while some are willing to delegate authority to their middle ranking staff, others prefer to control tightly from the centre.

The grading of staff roughly follows a French administrative model. There are four discrete streams: 'A' grade officials 'are the administrative elite entrusted with what is referred to in French as *conception*, a concept that is perhaps best translated as "creative thinking"'.[46] 'B' graded officials, by contrast, concern themselves rather more with routine administrative tasks. Secretarial and clerical workers are graded 'C', while service workers – cleaners and chauffeurs – fill the 'D' grades. The 'A' graded officials are those that are of most interest to this study, as it is the A grade officials who are most involved with the formulation and management of policy. At the lower end of the grade, the A8s, the assistant administrators, provide entry points for new graduates. The A7s and A6s, the administrators, undertake basic policy and administrative tasks, while the more middle-ranking officials at grade A5 and A4, the principal administrators, tend to have a great deal more responsibility. These officials are the mainstay of the Commission services, with the majority of staff found in these middle-ranking posts. As such, the pyramidal structure often found within formal hierarchies does not accurately equate with the structure of the Commission, as there are more middle-grade than lower-grade officials. From grade A3 up, posts become more politicised, with A3s often acting as head of division, and A1s and A2s, director-generals, assistant director-generals, or directors. This is somewhat misleading, however, as there is no necessary link between responsibility and grade. What this means in practice is that the post of head of division, for example, will not be reserved for an official of any particular grade (Table 2).

Table 2   Administrative (A grade) staff (1995)

A1	A2	A3	A4	A5	A6	A7	A8
27	166	483	1204	1108	770	748	42

Source: Commission, *Budget* (1995)

The question of hierarchy is inseparable from the question of national administrative culture and the effect that the coexistence of a multitude of administrative and management styles has on the Commission. Suggestions that national background and culture can affect the content of Commission proposals is perhaps worrying, as it suggests that a national bias may be evident in legislative output in spite of the multinational character of the institution. It has often been argued, however, that there is no one style of administration that could be characterised as a European style. This is accurate up to a point. However, styles of administration raise questions that concern national culture, questions that relate to the institutional autonomy of DGs and services. There is evidently a blurring here. So while DGs that may be labelled as 'German', like DG III (industry) or 'French', like DG VIII (development) demonstrate certain characteristics in the way that procedures are operated, these may well outlive the leadership of a particular nationality at the top. It is still possible to identify Commission approaches to management, nevertheless, even though there may be a plethora of exceptions to the rule. This sees a high level of informal responsibility with little formal delegation. As such, it is often to be expected that drafts will only be signed at the highest level, having passed through intermediate levels within a DG. Files will be held by a particular official charged with overseeing a specific piece of work, with officials tending to work on their own rather than as part of a team.[47] Naturally, this is only one approach to management and organisation within the Commission. There will be many others within the Commission too.

Aside from the variation in management styles that comes with the influence of differing administrative cultures, there is another reason why formal hierarchical structures are not always used in practice. 'In management terms, it is interesting to note that the normal hierarchy is in practice significantly shortened because at any one time some officials will be away on business trips or in all day meetings.'[48] In other words, practical management requires that in certain circumstances steps in the hierarchy may be skipped. The chain of command is not always what it seems on paper. To some extent, this cannot be helped. More notable perhaps is the manner in which hierarchical chains are evaded through the creation of alternative structures. This may involve the appointment of external and temporary staff who are not subject to the rules that apply to statutory staff. The creation of alternative channels of communication is an informal process and is often very difficult to detect. However, the creation of new positions outside the formal framework of the Commission's hierarchy presents tangible evidence that formal hierarchies are not always perceived as an efficient form of managerial structure. This was certainly the case with the creation of the post of assistant director-general in the 1970s. This was partly a means of dealing with the Commission's increased workload, but it also sought to tackle the sensitive matter of the balancing of nationalities in the upper echelons of the Commission's services. Likewise, the post of *conseiller* (or adviser) to the director-general is often created when a senior official cannot be found an alternative position.[49] As such, one might usefully make a distinction within the Commission between 'staff', who are outside the normal chain of command, and 'line of command categories of officials'.[50]

Recruitment of established staff

The competition for appointment to statutory established posts is tough, with only around 500–600 people recruited each year in all grades and for all nationalities. The process by which appointments are made is lengthy and arduous. In some cases, recruitment can take as long as five years,[51] although this is now the exception rather than the rule. The usual channel for entry into the Commission is through the open competition, the *concours*. This involves an open examination held on a regular basis in all member states. The only restriction placed on applicants for 'A' graded posts is that they must be university graduates and must be under thirty-two years of age.[52]

The competition involves three stages, that is, two written tests and an interview. At each stage in the process, a large number of candidates are eliminated. At the interview the selection board comprises three to five individuals, one of whom has been nominated by the Staff Committee representing employee interests. Successful candidates are placed on reserve lists which are supposed to hold twice as many names as posts to be filled. However, there is no guarantee that a position will be offered to a successful candidate within any space of time. It is for the individual DGs to choose their preferred candidates from the reserve list which is circulated when a vacancy arises, suggesting that this process might lead to the recruitment of teams of staff within DGs with similar backgrounds.[53] The success of applicants at this stage is as much the consequence of effective lobbying as it is the effect of suitable skills and experience or other objective factors. In 1993 the A7/A8 *concours* recruited around 250 people, from a group of 58,000 who took the first qualifying test.[54]

In recent years the Commission has made a concerted effort to cut down the waiting time on reserve lists to around one and a half years. This is intended to benefit the Commission as much as the candidates, especially given that the recruitment procedure is an especially complex and costly one. In 1987, for example, almost £1,700 was spent for each successful candidate recruited.[55] Competition is tough, for at the end of the process lies a lucrative and permanent post within one of the Commission's services. The recruitment process has been compared to that of a classical (weberian) model,[56] in which standards are normative, and in which there is no prejudging of candidates based on subjective criteria. Although this is perhaps an ideal to which the Commission might wish to aspire, it bears little resemblance to the way in which vacancies are really filled. The formal route to employment within the Commission is subject to lobbying and to personal contacts as much as it is to objective criteria. Indeed, once on the reserve list, finding an interesting job depends much more on who you know than what you know.

It is at the A2/A3 grade and above that the appointments procedure become particularly controversial, in a process known as *parachutage*.[57] A2 officials have occasionally been brought into the Commission on temporary contracts, and after taking an internal *concours* for which there is no age limit, have been established as permanent officials. Rumours of fixed competitions have abounded, even though in recent years there have been fewer 'outsiders' appointed to senior Commission jobs. However, there is still a tendency for senior officials to be *parachuted* into DGs from cabinets at the end of their term of office. The experience former cabinet staff bring with them can be extremely useful to a DG, although this appointment practice can cause bad feeling and frustration for potential candidates within the department concerned. Where these develop into legal disputes, grievances may be brought to the European Court of Justice on appeal. But although the Court can cancel an appointment, it can under no circumstance act as surrogate recruiter of staff.

Temporary appointments

A permanent post within the Commission is quite often coveted by those who are employed only on a temporary basis. Officially around a quarter of all staff hold either external or non-statutory posts, though unofficially the figure is likely to be higher. This is because the number of temporary agents who are on Commission contracts and who are subject to the same rules as permanent officials do not include staff appointed by individual services and DGs.[58] These individuals are often on secondment as national experts or consultants, usually for a maximum period of three years. Likewise, so-called auxiliary staff who are appointed for a maximum of one year are not considered as part of the statutory service. As they are not subject to the same rules as established staff, the advantages to the individuals filling these posts are less in terms of social benefits, pay and other perks of the job. It is not surprising therefore that these temporary officials are desperate to join the permanent staff. Here, contacts (or *piston*) is crucial. There *are* routes into permanent employment via these temporary positions, but inevitably there are more applicants than places – and by far. With the right contacts it seems that it is possible to find underground (or *soumarin*) fast tracks from temporary or seconded to statutory posts. But this avenue is only available for those who are '*destined* to join the staff'.[59] There is, as such, a fair amount of sponsorship of outsiders for internal posts. This can clearly undermine morale within the institution, as those without good contacts feel the entire appointment process to be unfair.

In the 1950s and 1960s, the French government had made a strong case for the Commission to be comprised solely of temporary officials seconded from national administrations. Rejecting the notion of a European public service, it was clear that what the French wanted to see was a fluid, non-permanent Commission whose staff would owe their allegiance to national governments rather that to some European ideal, institution or embryonic state. As such, the Commission would be as nationally-oriented an institution as the Council of Ministers. Although the staff that made up the ECSC's High Authority were first composed of seconded national staff, this was only the case until 1956 when the notion of a European public service was introduced in line with the supranational ethos that had led to the foundation of the ECSC in the first place. In practice a balance has since been struck between the permanent established officials and the temporary national staff. And although the national affiliations of temporary staff should not be overstated, it is clear that there are implications here for the way in which the Commission works. It may even be apt to talk of the existence of a 'parallel administration'.[60]

The Commission is heavily dependent on the expertise brought in from outside the institution. Having a facility for co-opting national officials and other temporary staff is, then, crucial. Temporary staff also inject an element of flexibility into the institution, an additional means of sidelining often rigid and stultified organisational structures. Furthermore, the appointment of temporary staff encourages an intermingling of national and European administrators which itself has the potential to provoke a sort of process of europeanisation at the national and subnational levels. This notion was a component of early theories of international integration, something that came to be known as *engrenage*.[61] It is clearly in following this kind of logic, alongside the more pragmatic logic of flexibility and effective information retrieval, that the use of national officials and other national experts within the Commission is justified and will continue to shape the institution.

Pay and working conditions

Morale is affected by much more than pay and conditions. Nevertheless, salaries and the environment within which staff work do have an impact upon the way in which Commission officials perceive themselves and their functions. It is clear that the Commission originally faced a great deal of criticism for paying its officials well. This initially served to attract well-qualified staff away from

national administrations, maximising the effectiveness of the institution. More recently, the gap between the pay of Commission officials and of national officials has diminished, especially for those
coming from countries where both salaries and standards of living
are high.[62] Yet even if it is no longer true that pay for an 'A' grade
official coming from Greece or Portugal is around ten times that of
a national official, there are still financial advantages to be had from
joining the Commission staff, even in spite of the high cost of living
in Brussels.

Salaries are based on a complicated formula, known as *la méth-
ode*. They are decided by the Council of Ministers based on a proposal from the Commission. This allows for pay to be reviewed
annually in order to account for changes in exchange rates and pur-
chasing power in all member states. For each grade of staff there are
a series of salary steps (*échelons*), and officials move up a step every
two years. Salaries are supplemented by a tax regime which means
that Commission officials pay tax to the Community's own budget
rather than to their own national exchequers or to the Belgian government. The tax rates vary between 10 per cent and a top rate of
45 per cent, though most pay between 20 and 25 per cent. VAT
exemptions are also part of the perks of working for the Commission. Other inducements exist explicitly to attract 'quality' staff
away from their home countries. These include child allowances, an
expatriation subsidy and relocation expenses. It is not clear whether
such inducements really do attract the best staff, however.

The conditions under which Commission staff work are laid
down in the Staff Regulations. These set out the rights and duties
involved in working for the Commission, and spell out career structure, pay scales, social benefits and pension schemes. The Regulations were first developed in 1962 to be used as the foundation for
a European civil service mirroring those at national level. They are
updated and amended in a continuous process of revision. Two features clearly distinguish the Commission administration from that
of the British civil service. Firstly, there is no equivalent of the Official Secrets Act. In other words, there is a remarkable openness
amongst Commission officials other than where confidentiality is
essential (namely, in some competition policy matters). And secondly, Commission officials are entitled to leave their posts temporarily in order to stand in elections and even hold office, knowing
that their posts will be held open for them. Officials are employed

in the Commission for a period of thirty-five years, or until they are sixty (or sixty-five, should they wish to continue working). There were, towards the end of the 1980s, rumours that staff were taking even earlier retirement, invaliding themselves out of the Commission in order to claim the generous invalidity pensions provided. Such allegations were vehemently rejected by the then personnel director-general, Richard Hay.

After two years in a post, an official may apply to be promoted. Promotion prospects in the Commission are very much coloured by the same criteria as recruitment, with personal contacts and the 'right' nationality seeming to be more helpful than ability and hard work. There is nevertheless a fair amount of mobility between jobs, though there is still room for improvement. Most staff will move within their DGs and many between DGs, some even moving to different Community institutions. Around 20 per cent of 'B' and 'C' graded staff are recruited from lower grades, though this is lower for the 'A' grades.[63] Promotion Committees, involving administrative and staff representatives oversee the promotion procedure – up to grade A3, after which staff representatives are excluded. Conditions within the Commission are generally considered to be good. Yet staff morale is fickle and fluid. In 1989 the personnel director-general claimed that:

> The staff of the Commission are highly motivated by their role in the construction of the Community. They are aware of the Commission's overall objectives, believe that their work is useful and that they are called on to assume significant responsibilities. They like their working environment, relations with supervisors and colleagues, and the confidence which is placed in them.[64]

This rose-tinted account of life as a Commission official certainly has to be tempered by certain recurrent areas of contention. It is clear that job satisfaction is to some extent linked to the particular task at hand, and will therefore be higher in some parts of the Commission than others. It is not surprising that there tends to be a greater degree of grumbling emanating from DGs that are not in the political limelight and whose powers are rather weak.[65]

Complaints from officials tend to focus on the lack of decentralisation within the Commission; the fact that some parts of the Commission are overworked, whilst others have little to occupy themselves; the routine nature of much of the work; and on the lack of potential for mobility and career development, especially when a certain stage in one's career is reached. The bottleneck of staff at around A4 level is a source of grievance to many ambitious middle-aged, middle-grade staff, who see little prospect of promotion.[66] Just as merit seems on many occasions to be devalued, laziness and serious errors at work rarely provoke disciplinary measures. The impact on morale and for motivation in one's work can be damaging. Although the unions are involved in many aspects of a Commission official's life, informal networks are much more likely to be the way that real change is made. More joy is to be gained therefore by a quiet word in a cabinet member's ear (usually of one's own nationality) than by making a formal complaint.

Staff representatives are nevertheless involved in a wide range of internal Commission activities, such as recruitment. The relationship between the administration and the staff representatives is not always a happy one, but it is aided by the existence of a *mediator*, a neutral and impartial appointee whose job it is to ensure that difficult staff problems are seriously looked into. The idea is that staff who are in trouble have someone to whom they can go and air their grievances in confidence. The majority of problems that come to the attention of the mediator are related to a lack of information, misunderstandings that arise as a result of different national working practices, cultures and expectations.[67]

Generally speaking, however, questions of internal management have not been considered as a particular priority within the Commission until very recently. It is only in the past decade or so that matters such as the balance of male to female officials has been seriously raised. A special committee was established in 1982 to study the extent to which this was an issue; an equal opportunities clause was introduced into the Staff Regulations in 1992 and a special Commission group was set up early in 1995, but there has still been little real action on this front. Emphasis placed on improving management techniques came with the so-called 'modernisation drive' of the mid 1980s.[68] This did not really amount to much, however. A series of seminars and workshops on interpersonal relations is hardly likely to be enough to alter what are often deeply ingrained working practices. Financial problems, too, have also had an effect on staff management policy with a total of 965 posts left vacant in 1993.

A multinational, multilingual set of institutions

In spite of the non-nationalistic vision of European Union propounded by Jean Monnet and the other founders of the European Commission, national affiliation remains a fundamental characteristic of internal Commission affairs. Far from seeing a fall in the importance of national identity amongst Commission officials, there seems by contrast to have been a heightening of national consciousness as the institution evolved. National stereotyping also continued unabated. Indeed, from the very start there was recognition that some sort of balance between nationalities needed to be struck.[69] Initially, this balance was based on national budget contributions.

Cleavages based on nationality are to be expected within the college of commissioners where appointments are made by national governments, though perhaps less so within the Commission's services. One element of importance here has to be the increasing influx of seconded national officials. But this is not the only cause of the ever-growing process of 'nationalisation' within the Commission. To some extent it is in the Commission's interest to ensure that strong links remain between Commission officials (whether temporary or permanent) and national administrations. This means that there will be a broad cross-section of officials with a wide knowledge of national procedures and systems of administration, and that national administrators will feel comfortable dealing with the Commission services.

As is the case with the commissioners and their cabinets, it is clear that effective communication between the national and the European levels has as much to do with informal personal contacts, often between individuals of the same nationality, as it has with formal institutionalised channels. From the point of view of the national authorities, it is certainly useful to have access to one's own national contacts within the Commission. More broadly still, the knowledge that there is a substantial number of one's own nationality within the institution is likely to make it seem less alien, and perhaps even more legitimate in the eyes of those who have to deal with its officials.

It is not surprising then that there has been a concerted effort, especially in the upper echelons of the Commission, to make sure that all nationalities are fairly represented. The proportional representation of nationalities within the Commission has become increasingly important for national governments too. Although a formal quota system exits only at the highest administrative grades, a rougher, more informal balance of nationalities has also been sought throughout middle management. In the British case, for example, there was for a long time a serious underrepresentation of UK officials within the Commission. There have been some attempts to rectify this situation recently, with the introduction of a 'European Fast Stream' in the British civil service.[70]

The matter of balancing nationalities has not been without its problems, however (Table 3). Especially at the very top of the hierarchy it tends to mean that posts are filled more on the basis of nationality than on merit. As such, senior officials often owe their position more to their nationality than to any other objective criterion. It is hardly surprising that the relationship between the official and their country of origin is likely to be enhanced by this process of selection. It is really only at grade A3 and above, though, that the quota system really takes hold of the promotion process. The fact that there is a massive overrepresentation of Belgians in the low 'B' grades, and in the 'C' and 'D' grades (due to the location of most of the Commission offices) does not concern national governments too much, as these grades have little, if any, influence on policy. As such, the total figures of national employees tells us little.[71]

It is at the top of the 'A' grades that appointments really become politically significant. As such, a stage is reached at which specific posts really do seem to 'belong' to a specific country. This often leads to external recruitment even if suitable candidates are available internally. However, the effect of quotas also reaches the middle grades, with promotion prospects for some nationals barred because of an overrepresentation of a particular nationality. This can be highly demoralising for the individuals concerned. Likewise the importance of nationality is demonstrated in the difficulties found in disciplining or sacking staff. It is often repeated that in the Commission one cannot discipline an individual official, only a particular national. There are other potential problems too. Loyalty to the institution and to the EU may conflict with national loyalties; an informal internal structure based on nationality may well mean that the organisational performance of the Commission suffers; and informal barriers to communication within the institution as a whole may also be drawn up along linguistic lines.

Table 3 Personnel numbers by nationality (before the accession of Sweden, Austria and Finland)

Member state	1993	1994
Belgium	3,795	4,008
Denmark	486	516
Germany	1,554	1,617
Greece	690	753
Spain	1,127	1,251
France	1,636	1,799
Ireland	399	459
Italy	1,985	2,105
Luxembourg	445	433
Netherlands	634	676
Portugal	586	648
UK	1,159	1,281

Source: Cassidy (1995)

Generally, the nationality issue merely reflects the broader process of integration within the EU. With the focus of action still on national governments and on the member states more broadly, it comes as no surprise that this is reflected within the central institutions of the Union. It only serves to illuminate the importance of national actors at the European level. In constraining any move towards a real European public service based on merit much more than on nationality, national governments are ensuring that their national interests (rather than – or as well as – a broader European interest) continue to be heard within the Commission. This becomes more relevant as the competences of the Commission expand. It is far from being a straightforward matter, however. The independence of the Commission may be threatened, but 'In spite of this, national balance serves a positive function, and, paradoxically, may be seen as a means to ensure the Commission's independence'.[72] Independence in this sense implies freedom from member state control, rather than 'national neutrality'.[73] There may in fact be dangers associated with attempts to europeanise officials to the extent that they lose all sense of nationality – if indeed this is even a slim possibility.

The identification of the Commission as a multinational organisation is of course closely allied to recognition that the Commission is also multilingual. The linguistic diversity found within the institution is something all international organisations must come to terms with. The now eleven official languages mean that there are 110 possible language combinations, creating a logistical problem of immense scale. All official documentation must be published in all official languages. And although there are a large number of linguists within the Commission, delays are endemic. The linguists are located within the Joint Interpretation and Conference Service and the Translation Service of the Commission. There are more than 450 interpreters (plus a couple of hundred employed freelance) and 1,200 translators employed within the LA (linguist) grades, with a support staff of about 650. The work of the Translation Service is particularly taxing, with immense pressure on staff to provide quick but fluent and accurate translation. This is all the more difficult given the legislative weight of much of the documentation. For more routine translations, the Commission officials will often see this as part and parcel of their own workload, and will tend not to bother with the Translation Service at all. This means that the author can ensure the technical accuracy of the text, even if the translation itself may leave a lot to be desired. The often not too happy alternative is to hand the translation over to someone skilled in the language but not in the subject matter. Doing one's own translation is of course impossible when final drafts of legislation are to be produced. Here the translators must tackle extremely difficult linguistic subtleties and technicalities in order to produce legally enforceable versions of legislation in all the official languages. In 1988, 900,000 pages of translation were produced.[74] The costs involved are of course substantial, something the media often point to as proving the inefficiency of the European institutions. Although only around 2 per cent of the total budget is spent on language services, this amounts to around one-third of the total administration budget. However, only a quarter of this is actually Commission expenditure.

The 'working' languages are those that are used in Commission meetings. Generally, French and English (and to a lesser extent German) dominate (and at times a mixture of languages). Commission officials without at least some knowledge of all working languages may feel rather vulnerable as a result. There has been a notable increase in the use of English within the Commission, something that is likely to expand further as the officials of the newest member states are more likely to have English as a second language. However, there has quite recently been a campaign by the German government to encourage greater use of German within the Commission. It is unlikely that this will have much effect, even with the prospect of the East European enlargements. The implications of having two or three working languages is clear. Most Commission officials will not be working on a daily basis in their mother tongue. Indeed, while 33.3 per cent of staff have French as a first language, only 11.5 per cent have English, and 11.4 per cent German. This means that, at the very least, 44 per cent of Commission staff have to work in a language other than their mother tongue. This is clearly going to provide scope for misinterpretation and misunderstanding, if only due to differences in style. It also means that meetings will take longer and workload is likely to be affected, with clear repercussions on the efficiency of the institution as a whole. The use of language amongst Commission staff is an expression of culture, and as already noted, 'cultural differences affect management styles'.[75] Even so, this should not force us to ignore the benefits that can accrue to an institution as a result of cultural richness and diversity.

The Commission may well be better understood if one divides it up along national or linguistic lines, but this is far from being the only useful perspective to adopt. Bureaucratic politics models have recently been applied to the European level, as a way of throwing light on the supranational policy process and, more specifically, on decision-making within the Commission.[76] This is an important consideration, as it implies 'a world where the *outcomes* of decision-making processes *reflect balances internal to the bureaucracy* rather than any public preferences'.[77] Commission DGs and services are thus seen as quasi-autonomous actors, possessing their own organisational and policy objectives. These objectives will often conflict with other Commission goals, leading to territorial and demarcation disputes between services. The broad implication is that policy-making within the institution becomes increasingly fragmented. The dangers inherent in the compartmentalisation of the Commission have been highlighted at least since the late 1970s when a process of 'diversification' between DGs, in terms of organisational structure, relations with external actors, leadership and internal dynamism was noted. This rehearsed Ernst Haas's own critique of the concept of neo-functionalist spillover by highlighting the existence of autonomous functional contexts within the Commission. However, it has been suggested that the source of this fragmentation may well be the deliberate manufacture of 'creative tension' by elites within the Commission.[78]

A possible alternative approach might consider the effect of national cultures on bureaucratic cleavages. But this goes well beyond the notion that national cultures determine institutional fragmentation within the Commission and that administrative units managing discrete policy areas develop their own line on the policy (perhaps through a process of capture, or for rather arcane historical reasons). The argument here is that the Commission's services possess their own administrative cultures, closely linked to the policies they oversee, but affected by a multitude of other factors, such as professional background and socialisation processes, as well as nationality. Different management styles can therefore be attributed to different cultures, but these cultures need not only be nationally determined. DGs certainly differ from one another. As such, we have a problem. If the individual components that make up the Commission are in fact quasi-autonomous institutions, how is it possible to draw general conclusions about the organisation, function, policy and internal dynamism of the Commission in any broad sense? The logic is therefore that it should be the individual services that are the focus of study, rather than the Commission as a whole.[79]

This would be a valid point to make. Yet, there is nevertheless an organisational framework which is *the Commission* (in the broadest of its definitions). There are common features of the DGs and services, common rules and procedures that apply to all staff within the Commission, and co-ordinating, horizontal services whose function exists only in relation to the more vertical DGs. There are also basic principles and processes that apply to all staff, even if variety and differentiation remain the rule. To cap it all, there is the college of commissioners and the cabinets, defining themselves not only in terms of the policy portfolios they control, but also in relation to each other, as the political 'hat' that tops the administrative units. The justification for examining the Commission as a whole is as valid therefore as the justification for examining its component parts.

To stress both the component parts and the whole, Cram's definition of the Commission as a 'multi-organisation' is useful. This accepts that the Commission is not a monolithic unit. 'There is a variety of ways in which the Commission might influence the policy process. Yet the constraints upon, and opportunities for, Commission action vary between policy sectors.'[80] Most commentaries that deal with the increasing compartmentalisation of the Commission consider this to be a negative development, and seek to answer the question: how do we reverse this trend, and encourage greater co-ordination between DGs and greater coherence between policy areas? Indeed, this was what Jacques Delors himself came to see as a necessary prerequisite for an effective Commission role. One reason why institutional cohesion and policy coherence are so important is that the Commission is not the only institutional policy actor on the European stage. It is therefore to the inter-institutional context that we now turn.

The inter-institutional triangle

The Commission defines itself and the functions it performs partly through the relationships it is able to forge with its partner institutions. This institutional triangle of Commission, Parliament and Council is at the centre of a broader, more confusing network of relationships that include interest groups, government departments and agencies, firms and individuals.

The Commission and the Council
The relationship between the Commission and the Council is at the centre of the European decision-making process. There is little that can be achieved, in terms of legislation at least, without the consent of both institutions. Mutual dependence between the two bodies is an ever-present theme, although it is clear that the two institutions are also in competition with each other.[81] Indeed, 'the Commission is in a monopoly position *vis-à-vis* the Council since the latter is unable to take any decisions without having received proposals from the Commission'.[82] Yet the Commission is similarly dependent upon the Council if it wishes to see its proposals adopted as legislation.

The relationship between the two institutions has altered substantially since the EEC was established. The institutionalisation of the European Council, the increasing use of qualified majority voting in the Council, as well as the emergent political role of the Council secretariat, have all contributed to this change. One might argue that in order to understand the relationship between Commission and Council, it is necessary to understand the processes at work within the EU as a whole. Rejecting simplistic technocratic, federal and intergovernmental interpretations, it is perhaps helpful to see the Commission as playing the role of 'promotional broker' *vis-à-vis* the Council.[83] This suggests that the Commission-Council relationship is far from being a zero-sum game; rather, it appears more accurately to rest on notions of co-operative federalism and of two-level games in which both the EC and the member states are legitimate policy actors. As such, the Commission becomes a player that has certain procedural rights within the policy process. 'Its specific power would be based on its ability to use these rights in the complex bargaining central to a multi-level system.'[84]

The extremely close contacts that exist between officials in the Commission and national officials have been encouraged through what has been labelled a 'strategy of involvement',[85] and a process of 'bureaucratic interpenetration'[86] adopted consciously by the Commission from early on. Through blatant attempts to attract member state (as well as interest group) involvement in the policy process, the Commission has been keen to legitimise its own position through the setting up of a variety of committees.[87] This is very much part of the process of *engrenage* which to some extent at least, acted as a surrogate for the mobilisation of popular support in the early days of the Community. As noted above, this has involved the co-opting of national officials and 'the intermingling of national and international bureaucrats in various working groups and committees in the policy-making context of the EEC'.[88] It is clear that this process has led on occasion to a sort of partnership developing, which may emerge at the expense of both the national and European political elites.

The European Council-Commission relationship is equally one of mutual dependence, although one might imagine that in terms of 'power', the Commission would find itself in a vulnerable position.[89] Both institutions clearly gain from the relationship, however. On the Commission side, there is some measure of legitimacy to be had from working closely with the heads of state and government. The role they play in guiding Commission policy agendas does not necessarily mean that the Commission's role in the policy process is weakened. The Commission is well able to use the European Council as a forum for the elaboration of its own objectives, whilst the

European Council is dependent on the Commission if it wants to see its grand policy proposals turned into workable draft legislation. The same largely goes for the member state holding the Council Presidency. It must make sure that its programme of action is not at odds with the annual programme of the Commission. Indeed, the practical involvement of the Commission President in European Councils can equally be seen to have increased the profile of the Commission through 'the personalisation of hitherto "technocratic" power'.[90]

Perhaps surprisingly, there is much more ambivalence about the developing relationship between the Commission administration and the Council's secretariat than there is about the more high-profile Council-Commission links. On one hand, there have been increasing contacts between the SG of the Commission and the Council secretariat since the late 1970s, with, in the case of Jacques Delors and Niels Ersbøll, the Secretary-General of the Council, liaison on the highest of levels taking place almost daily. However, the Commission has not been happy about what it sees as the increasingly political role being adopted by the Council administration. There has even been a fear that national governments (especially those opposed to what they see as the increasing politicisation of the Commission) have intentionally sought to raise the profile of the Council Secretariat at the Commission's expense. This does not necessarily imply that the secretariat is any more or less 'political' than the Commission, but the former does tend to follow more of an intergovernmentalist line. As such, although the relationship between the Commission and Council may well have been strengthened in an administrative or organisational sense, this may have occurred at a political cost to the Commission.

The Commission and the Parliament

The relationship between the Commission and the European Parliament has undergone a metamorphosis based largely on the emergence of the new decision-making procedures of co-operation and co-decision.[91] But these shifts in the relationship between the two supranational institutions of the Union rest upon much more than simply a juridical logic. Well before the direct elections of 1979, the Commission viewed the EP as an ally within the Community system. This allegiance was a reaction to the dominant position of the member state governments in the Council, and was linked to the notion that the European-level policy process comprised two sets of actors, the national and the European. Legally speaking, the relationship between the Commission and the Parliament is one which is constitutionally defined. However, there was little in the treaties to dictate how the two institutions should relate to one another. As ever, there is a rather sketchy framework, defining boundaries rather than substance, although the Parliament's supervisory powers (under Article 137) and the ways in which the Commission is accountable to the EP is spelt out, though this does not help to explain how both co-operative and combative elements in the relationship have emerged. Constitutionally, the original treaty provisions have been expanded upon through treaty amendments, joint declarations, European Council statements, inter-institutional agreements and other such political and administrative undertakings. Much of the fleshing out process has been of an informal nature, however, and a large proportion of the working practice of the EP-Commission relationship rests upon convention. There has as such been a steady drip of informally-based custom translated into a much more formal context, as Parliament has sought to extend the range and depth of its powers. The process has essentially been a political one, in the sense that it has been concerned with questions of inter-institutional power and influence.

The Commission has often found itself in a difficult position *vis-à-vis* the Parliament. The need for co-operation between the two institutions is crucial, and ever more so since the Single European Act and the Treaty on European Union extended the role that the EP plays in decision-making. The Commission itself has a vested institutional interest in the extension of the Parliament's powers. This is clear not only in the sense that there should be honour amongst hard-done-by supranational bodies, but also from a more constitutional point of view, as the Commission sees the EP as a source of legitimacy for its own actions and for the policies of the Union as a whole.

There should be no presumption, however, that the relationship between Commission and Parliament is an entirely harmonious one. Neither should there be any presumption that the Commission inevitably feeds off the increasing powers of the Parliament, and that the Commission can only gain from pushing forward the objectives of the EP. This may well be the case on occasion, but there are times when the Parliament's gains are more likely to be at the expense of the Commission. With many national governments keen to respond to criticism that the EU is subject to a democratic deficit, enhancing parliamentary powers has been a natural starting-point for improving the situation. At the same time, however, national governments who often consider the transfer of sovereignty to be a zero-sum game have not been keen to see the EP role enhanced at what they believe to be their own decision-making cost. As such, democratisation, such as it is, has often been restricted in all but marginal cases to increased scrutiny over the Commission. It is hardly surprising then that there should be, in the inter-institutional relationship, a fundamental contradiction, to the extent that it is based on an '"adversarial" relationship compromised by the two institutions' *de facto* need to co-operate and collaborate, even as the Parliament's independence and powers grow'.[92]

The Commission has demonstrated its commitment towards co-operation by setting up numerous forums in which EP business can be discussed. The most important of these is the *Groupe des Affaires Parlementaires*, which was created in 1979 after the first EP elections.[93] But it is a department within the SG that deals with all links between the two institutions. At the level of the college, however, it is the budgets commissioner and the commissioner in charge of Commission-EP relations who have most contact with the Parliament, though the President, too, can have a great deal of input. This was certainly the case with Jacques Delors, who went out of his way to stress the importance of the Commission-EP relationship to the Union as a whole. At the weekly meeting of the college there is always a separate item on the agenda on relations with the Parliament, when amongst other matters the minutes of the GAP are considered. And when the plenary session is held (in Strasbourg), the commissioners follow suit and head for France. The EP too has helped to consolidate a new type of inter-institutional relationship with the Commission through the creation of a variety of forums within which consultation and general discussion can take place. Perhaps the most important is the Neunreither Group, the inter-institutional co-ordination group.[94] More formally, the Commission is also represented at the Conference of Presidents.[95]

These institutionalised contacts are symbolic of a relationship which goes much deeper and which is more political than might appear from any description of structural linkages. We may even assume that the drafters of the Treaty of Rome foresaw in the development of Commission-Parliament interaction the emergence of a classic executive-assembly type relationship,[96] though the drawing of tight parallels between West European liberal-democratic political systems and the EU is not always helpful. However, the differences between Commission and Parliament – with the Commission collegiate and unelected and the EP pluralistic and representative – do suggest a certain complementarity between the two bodies. This is in the nature of the system itself. Even though the division of responsibilities between the European institutions is not always clear, differentiation between institutional roles remains all-important. The fact that the Parliament is unlike the Commission, and that both are very different from the Council is what allows for the checks and balances inherent in the European policy process. This occurs in spite of criticism that the system is itself flawed and undemocratic.

The apparent paradox of a Commission arguing for more EP powers that would potentially constrain its own role must be viewed in this context of the Commission's quest for legitimacy. The Commission's lack of direct legitimacy means that it looks to the Parliament 'for popular legitimation of its policy proposals and administrative actions'.[97] The most fundamental power the EP has in this regard is the as yet unused power of censure over the college. There has always been disagreement about how useful this power is, given that it has been compared to a 'nuclear weapon whose consequences are so terrible as to be almost unthinkable'.[98] Some, however, prefer to emphasise its deterrent effect upon the Commission. The argument that the censured Commission could simply be reinstated by the member states misses the point somewhat. The impact of the political crisis that would ensue as a result of such a breakdown in inter-institutional relations would be hard to predict, but would certainly damage the Union. In any case, more often than not it is the Council that the EP would wish to censure, not the Commission.

Even so, the potential for the individual censure of Commission members has also been raised on occasion, although there would be implications here for the collegiality of the Commission. The absence of an effective and believable weapon against the actions of individual commissioners has certainly weakened the Parliament's position. As a result, there has been some talk of making more use of *motions de blame*, which are a sort of parliamentary reprimand of an individual commissioner, though without real consequence for the individual concerned. But even this has run up against the collegiality argument, that is, that it is not the commissioner but the college that must take responsibility for any individual member's words or deeds. In any case, too much emphasis on how and when to criticise, reprimand or censure the Commission does not work to either institution's advantage when what is most important is the cultivation of a co-operative mutually beneficial inter-institutional environment for both bodies.

Parliamentary Questions (PQs), both written and oral, are a more positive form of scrutiny over the Commission. Commissioners are also held to account both in parliamentary committees and in plenary. Indeed, the EP does its best to keep a watchful eye on all aspects of the work of the Commission, especially in areas where formally it has little or no role to play (such as in external relations), though the usefulness of PQs has been challenged.[99] The Maastricht Treaty really only served to formalise a Commission-EP relationship that already existed *de facto* beforehand. For example, in 1985 Jacques Delors (a former MEP) waited for a parliamentary vote of approval before he and his newly appointed colleagues took their oath in the European Court. But the very fact that this was the Commission President's prerogative and could not be demanded as a right by the EP demonstrates the difference between *de facto* and *de jure* scrutiny. When the Commission is willing to open itself up as a means of legitimising itself, the benefits, not surprisingly, would seem to accrue to the Commission more than to the Parliament. 'Rather than the European Parliament acting to check the Commission, the reality is the potential use of the Parliament by the Commission as an instrument in order to assert its independent policy-making role.'[100] Not until the post-Maastricht period has it been a right of the EP to demand that the nominated President and members of the Commission come before the Parliament to be interrogated on all matters pertinent to their future positions. By a simple majority, government nominations can be blocked. The process has been made easier since the commissioners' period of office has become coterminous with that of the parliamentarians (a five-year term for both, that is). While the EP is elected in June, the Commission takes up its position in the following January, giving the new Parliament time to consider fully the nominations put forward by member governments. For many, however, this does not go far enough. Yet the argument that the EP should elect the President of the Commission, or that the commissioners should be drawn from amongst the MEPs are ideas too federalist for most governments to entertain. Even so, the effect of the new investiture procedure and of the coterminous office of Commission and Parliament will be important, if only in terms of institutional prestige.[101]

Notes

1   The Commission is often talked of familiarly as 'the House' or '*la Maison*', by those who work within it.

2   These officials are often known, sometimes disparagingly, as 'eurocrats'.

3   See Middlemas (1995, p. 214). The number increased from twenty-three to twenty-four at the start of 1995 with the addition of consumer affairs.

4   A. Smith (1995, p. 445).

5   The five horizontal services are the Secretariat-General, the Legal Service, the Spokesman's Service, the Translation Service and the Statistical Office.

6   Commission (1993), 'Rules of procedure' OJ L230/15 of 17 February 1993.

7   See also chapter six below on the changing role of the Secretariat-General under Delors.

8   A. Smith (1995).

9   Middlemas (1995, p. 222), says that the SG was stronger in 1994 than it was in 1984, as it now chairs the external affairs triumvirate, for example. However, there is much to be said for the view that the SG was living in Delors's reflected glory over this period.

10   Ludlow (1991, p. 95). The 'book' in this case is the Treaty of Rome.

11   Nugent (1991).

12   Enlargements also lead to increasing staff numbers of course, though not necessarily to a proportionate increase.

13   See the Commission's *Budget* (1995).

14   The French word *lourdeur* is often used to denote overload of work within the Commission.

15   See chapter one on the functions performed by the Commission.

16   The justice and home affairs portfolio is currently held by Emma Bonnino (under the 1995 Commission).

17   Donnelly and Richie (1994, pp. 32–4).

18   Note that Ludlow (1991, p. 123) has called the current appoint-

for economic and monetary union. The parallelism that came to exist between the IGC on EMU and the second IGC on political integration largely resulted from this need to respond to German demands for institutional change within the EC. And although there was some reluctance at national level, a pivotal element in this approach was to make it clear to the Germans that East Germany would be treated as a special case when it came to dealing with its incorporation into the Community. As such, there would be no demand that the East Germans go through the formal accession process. With the Delors line on German unification winning the day at the special Dublin summit in April 1990, there was some criticism that the Commission President was beginning to act more like a head of state than as an unelected head of a European body. Whilst Delors had made a friend of Helmut Kohl, there was talk in other governmental quarters that the Commission President needed to be taken down a peg or two.[33]

Plans for the IGCs were being put together over the course of 1990. Crucial here was the deal that was struck between France and Germany in April 1990 on the issues to be discussed under the heading of political union. It was eventually agreed that four elements ought to be included, concerning (i) the democratic legitimacy of the EC; (ii) institutional reform; (iii) the coherence of political, economic and monetary elements of the Union; and (iv) the matter of foreign and security policy.[34] A fifth element, that of European citizenship, was proposed by the Spanish Prime Minister at a later stage. But whilst plans for EMU had been tightly controlled by the Commission and by Delors personally, it was clear that the Commission President was unable to influence the political union discussions to the same degree. Increasingly, discussions seemed to take a confederal path, suggesting that the supranational institutions would end up losing out as a result of compromise solutions reached through the IGC process. The lack of preparatory work being done on the political union side was also a source of concern. There seemed no way for the Commission to reinsert itself into the debate without offering itself up for further criticism. Indeed, as the year went on Delors became increasingly alarmed that the British and the French were seeking to use the political union IGC as a way of undermining the role of the Commission.

The Commission's formal opinion to the political union IGC, much of which was written by Delors himself, was published in

October 1990. It proposed that a single unified Community should be retained, as should the existing balance between the European institutions. It went on to foresee the European Council deciding on areas to be dealt with under a common foreign and security policy, with the Council of Ministers voting on these areas by qualified majority voting. The Commission, it was argued, should keep the right of initiative, with the EP having a say over legislation (though the Council would still have the last word, using qualified majority voting at all times). There were, perhaps surprisingly, few suggested extensions to the areas of competence to be covered by the Community, other than under the social policy umbrella. This was because Delors had come to accept that there was enough already being dealt with, policy-wise, at the European level.

So even before the IGCs had opened, things were beginning to look bleak for the Commission. Even Delors's cherished plans for EMU, which had already been spelt out in an opinion for the IGC in August, were being torn apart by the Bundesbank governor. The resignation of Mrs Thatcher was no cause for jubilation as far as Delors was concerned, especially as attacks in the British press were reaching an all-time high, with the 'Up Yours Delors' headline appearing on the front of *The Sun* newspaper on the very day that the British Foreign Minister, Geoffrey Howe, made his memorable resignation speech in the House of Commons.[35] Even at this point, there was a sense that control of the integration process was slipping from the grasp of the Commission. What this would mean for the outcome of the IGC was not difficult to imagine. With national priorities now the starting-point for considerations under the political union banner, it was not hard to envisage the extent to which the intergovernmental conference would lead to intergovernmental policy responses. Increasingly, the Commission seemed overcome by a *lourdeur* or overload that resulted from an ever-expanding set of policy priorities and from the growing need to focus on the implementation of the single market and its flanking policies. Indeed, it was increasingly apparent that the Commission was becoming a victim of its own success.

The 1991 IGCs: the Commission role

Intergovernmental Conferences (IGCs) are essentially a set of meetings between government ministers and their representatives. While

Delors had played a substantial role in the IGC which led to the SEA in the mid 1980s, there was no willingness on the part of the member states in 1991 to see this state of affairs repeated. In part, this was the consequence of the rather poor relationship that developed between the Commission staff and the Luxembourg presidency during the first six months of the IGCs. In addition, the Commission staff became increasingly concerned about the role that the rather cautiously intergovernmental Council Secretariat and Niels Ersbøll, the Council Secretary-General in particular, appeared to be playing in the drafting process.

During the IGCs, Delors had decided to adopt a maximalist line on behalf of the Commission in the hope that the watering-down that was the inevitable result of intergovernmental negotiation would still mean satisfactory progress. But rather than working in the Commission's favour, the effect of this strategy was the discrediting of the Commission line, so that to many government representatives the Commission position, at least on political union, was considered too outlandish to be taken seriously. Indeed, the political union IGC started in something of a shambolic manner. The member states, preoccupied with events in the Gulf and in Yugoslavia, spent a lot of their early meetings wrangling over defence and security issues in a rather vague and abstract fashion. Delors's position was that these crises could be used as an impetus to push forward action on a common foreign and security policy. However, there were limits to what Delors himself could do, given an increasingly bad press in several member states.

Delors's commitment to a single Community framework which had been spelt out in the Commission's opinion did not stand up well within the IGC. In general, Commission participation in the process was poor, with the Commission representatives finding themselves on the defensive from the very beginning. Part of the problem was that the Commission had only been able to submit its draft treaty to the IGC in March 1991, three months *after* the Conference had begun. Many of the key issues had already been discussed by that stage, so that the Commission draft became just another working paper alongside a plethora of others. Indeed, 'serious Commission agenda-setting for the second IGC was not possible: nothing comparable to the Delors Report on EMU had set out the parameters of the talks'.[36] But this did not prevent a small team of Commission officials from churning out documentation on polit-

ical union throughout the rest of the year.

The first draft of the Treaty produced by the Luxembourg presidency in April 1991 proposed a 'polarisation' process which would institutionalise co-operation on foreign policy and home affairs questions outside the formal structures of the Community. This seemed to suggest that the Commission and the EP would be excluded from these policy areas. Delors did what he could to undermine the pillar approach of the Luxembourg draft of the treaty, whilst continuing to stress that all Community affairs should be dealt with under one institutional roof. This meant some serious lobbying at national level. The second Luxembourg draft produced a compromise to which Delors was slightly more amenable. Whilst retaining the pillar idea, the treaty at the same time placed the pillars under one roof (*or chapeau*). Delors's original metaphor of an organic Community tree was not adopted, however. Instead, the image of a 'temple' (with pillars) was seen to satisfy all parties. Yet particularly pleasing for Delors was the fact that the second Luxembourg draft mentioned the federal vocation of the treaty and restored the Commission's role where it had previously been undermined.

When the Dutch took over the presidency in July 1991, they almost immediately scrapped the Luxembourg version, replacing it with a draft treaty closely resembling the proposals that had been advanced by Delors in the Commission's own draft. There was an almost unanimous outcry by the other member states. The Dutch draft was subsequently binned and the IGC in effect delayed for about two months. The influence of the Commission papers on the Dutch representation was clear, although there has since been some disagreement over the extent to which Commission officials actually played a role in the drafting of the Dutch version. There was at the very least some encouragement from Brussels on this score. The last draft of the Treaty, produced by the Dutch in October 1991, reverted back to the pillar/temple approach adopted in the second Luxembourg draft.

Delors was critical of much of this. In particular, under the new co-decision procedure, he was keen to make sure that the Commission would retain the right to withdraw a law that had been amended in a way not approved of by the Commission; and he did not want the EP to have the right to propose legislation. Moreover, Delors was critical of the fact that the IGC was doing little to tackle

the democratic deficit. By increasing the accountability of the EP only at the expense of the Commission, the respective influence of the supranational and the intergovernmental institutions would continue to tip in the latter's favour. It was for this reason that Delors believed the extension of co-decision to be so important. This was a way of expanding the powers of the Parliament *vis-à-vis* the Council of Ministers, that is, the member states. National governments were, not surprisingly, reluctant to take this new procedure too far. Earlier in the IGC, the Commission had proposed the introduction of a 'hierarchy of norms' which had sought to make a distinction between framework 'laws' and regulatory acts. The Commission proposed that the 'laws' (that is, the framework legislation) would be subject to the co-decision procedure, after which they would be 'filled out' and applied either by the Commission or by national parliaments by means of regulatory acts. After some difficulty getting this idea through the Commission, the member states rejected the proposal out of hand.

By the autumn of 1991 there was little that the Commission could do to influence the direction of the political union IGC. A process of intergovernmental bargaining and consensus-building had taken over from the initial agenda-setting of the first half of the year. Delors nevertheless continued to pursue a hard line, and fairly late in the proceedings was able to win a substantial victory on the inclusion of provisions on the social dialogue in the final Dutch draft. Just before the Maastricht summit was due to begin, the Commission published its final position on the negotiations. It was not surprising that joint action on foreign and security policy took pride of place here, with the Commission still critical of the pillar approach. The line generally taken was that the Commission was looking to the European Council to agree a treaty that took an 'evolutive' approach to political union. This seemed to suggest that the Commission realised that the treaty itself would not establish political union, but that procedures would be agreed within it that could lead to developments in that direction (that is, an evolution) in the future.

By contrast, Delors's influence on the EMU IGC was considerable. Much of the Commission's work in this area had already been done before the IGCs began, with the aforementioned Delors Report, and a draft treaty published in December 1990. The issues that remained to be resolved revolved around the 'British problem'

– the fact that the British government could not commit a future Parliament to the move to the third stage of EMU. There were also difficulties over the sticky question of the convergence criteria that would be required before a move to the 'third stage' would be permitted. Delors lost some of what he had wanted here. He did not manage to secure agreement on the setting up of the ECB at Stage Two of the EMU process which he felt would prevent reluctant member states from prevaricating over moving to the third and final stage. He did, however, win his argument on the need for a clearly defined timetable for entry to Stages Two and Three.

So, while the Maastricht European Council, on 9–10 December 1991, began with most of the EMU matters resolved, the same was certainly not true for political union. Delors attended the European Council meeting along with one other adviser (this was all that was allowed). For most of the summit his role was one of providing summaries of the discussion to date.[37] In all, thirty Commission staff were present in Maastricht during the summit, very few compared to the huge national delegations.[38] They arrived laden with draft texts that might be of use as compromise documents over the course of the meeting. Delors was usually accompanied in the meeting room by David Williamson, Frans Andriessen or Henning Christophersen. The role of Pascal Lamy, Delors's second-in-command, was one of co-ordination, outside in the corridor.[39] The Commission team was, as ever, highly organised. Lamy later boasted that they had been miles ahead of the national delegations in their understanding of the deliberations that were taking place. As such, there were few surprises for the Commission. The most contentious area remained the social chapter, mainly because of the refusal of the British to agree to any extension of EC competence in this field. Delors's presence at this stage in the process proved invaluable, as he worked hard to find a satisfactory solution to the deadlock that seemed inevitable. Although the obvious solution to the social chapter dilemma was to have an opt-out for the British on social policy, the British delegation refused to be treated as a special case. The suggestion that the social chapter should be turned into the social protocol and placed outside the Treaty proper, to be signed by eleven of the twelve member states came from Pascal Lamy, although others have claimed responsibility for this outcome.[40] Delors's team had already prepared documentation along these lines, so that when the suggestion was made and John Major seemed

amenable, a text was ready for perusal on the spot. After some revision the Treaty could be approved.

Delors was clearly not happy with the outcome of the Maastricht summit. As the negotiations had progressed, his position had gradually been undermined until his hopes for the Treaty diminished dramatically. Nevertheless, he was prepared to defend it, albeit weakly, in order to ensure its eventual implementation. However, 'One of the many ironies of the subsequent ratification crisis was that, by default, Delors defended a treaty that benefited the Commission little but that the public perceived as having greatly enhanced the Commission's power.'[41] There are, in any case, many question marks hanging over Delors's participation in the IGC process, especially with regard to political union. Was the Commission's weakness here attributable to Delors having lost his grip on the EC policy agenda? Or was the failure of the Commission merely the result of a concerted sidelining undertaken intentionally by the member states who were only too aware of the extent to which the Commission had determined the Single Act agenda? Increased workload accounts for some of the feeling of *lourdeur* that characterised the Commission at this time. But this is not the whole story. In taking an overtly maximalist line on political union, Delors played into the hands of the member states' anti-EC and anti-Commission domestic constituencies. In many of Delors's public statements, he clearly does give the impression that his concern is first and foremost the role that the Commission should play in the post-Maastricht Union.[42] The self-aggrandisement that the Commission and that Delors himself had been accused of was confirmed by the tone and content of the Commission line in the run up to and during the IGCs. In this sense, Delors had made a serious tactical error which continued throughout the entire IGC process.

Winding down

The three years that followed the Maastricht summit were something of an anti-climax for the Commission. Whilst national political elites could claim victory in having achieved an agreement of sorts at the end of the IGC process, there was little upon which Delors and the Commission could congratulate themselves. Indeed, although the Commission had not come out of the Maastricht process as badly as some governments had hoped, the tide of popu-

lar opinion was at a particularly low ebb.[43] With the Commission and its President playing out the role of scapegoat, it is hardly surprising that Delors tried over the course of the post-Maastricht period, to keep a much lower profile than he had done prior to the IGC. These years, at the end of the second Delors Commission (1992) and over the course of his third Commission (1993 and 1994), were marked by a more cautious, behind-the-scenes Commission style.[44]

At this stage, Delors was particularly keen to demonstrate the Commission's commitment to the subsidiarity principle. This was increasingly important as and when difficulties with the ratification process became apparent.[45] Delors could do little in response to the 'no' vote in the Danish referendum, though when it came to the turn of the French electorate, he did play a more active role in the 'yes' campaign, stating that he would resign as Commission President if the French people rejected the Treaty.[46] Over this period, Delors's efforts at keeping his commissioners in check, encouraging them not to rock national governments' boats too much were not always successful. There was clear and often well-publicised friction, one of the most notable disputes being that between Delors and Ripa de Meana, his activist and often outspoken environment commissioner, as Ripa tried to call non-compliant national governments to account over their failure to implement environment legislation – much to the irritation of the Commission President.[47]

But there were still a large number of policy matters to be resolved. Externally, the main priorities involved drawing the Uruguay Round of the GATT to a conclusion as quickly and effectively as possible; and dealing with the enlargement questions that had been put on hold until after the ratification of the new treaty. And as had been the case in the aftermath of the SEA, the Maastricht Treaty brought important budgetary issues to the fore. 'Delors II', as it came to be known, sought to do for the Maastricht Treaty what 'Delors I' had done for the SEA. It sought to provide a multi-annual financial package which would allow the requirements of the treaty to be fulfilled. Times had changed, however, and the European economies were about to enter a period of recession. Although Delors could easily remember the difficulties involved in getting through his first budgetary package, there was no doubt that things would be more onerous this time round. His cabinet set to work on first drafts which were subsequently refined by the Commission ser-

ments process simply 'inappropriate'.

19   Neville-Jones (1985, p. 180).

20   The conditions under which commissioners work are usually good and because of this, senior figures may be attracted to the post. They have security of tenure, which is specifically designed to contribute to stability and continuity within the Commission. It is in fact very difficult to remove a commissioner once in post. It is only as a result of 'serious misconduct' that this is possible. So far, this has never been used. In practice, only death or retirement will curtail a commissioner's term of office.

21   Donnelly and Richie (1994, p. 32).

22   *Ibid.*

23   Page and Wouters (1994).

24   See chapter seven on the 1994 'common accord' and the process leading to the appointment of Jacques Santer as the new Commission President.

25   Middlemas (1995) talks of the Commission President as being at the 'centre of the centre'.

26   Ludlow (1991, p. 124) makes this suggestion, for example.

27   It is indicative of this ambivalence that the President of the Commission is assisted by two vice-presidents. Before 1995, the commissioners nominated five vice-presidents from the seventeen-strong college. More recently, the number has been reduced to two.

28   Whether this denotes a move in favour of collegiality, or away from it, is unclear. Note that a convention seems to have emerged which suggests that if the senior vice-president comes from a right-of-centre party, the second should come from the left.

29   Bellier (1994, p. 53). The Breydel building is the glass-fronted building, close to Rond-Point Schumann in Brussels, that is now home to the commissioners, their personal staffs and to the Spokesman's Service.

30   Henig (1980, p. 41), for example.

31   Page and Wouters (1994, p. 449).

32   In specific policy areas, such as those that concern the Commission scrutiny over the granting of national state aids, national colours are most frequently exposed.

33   Middlemas (1995, p. 234).

34   See Suleiman (1984, pp. 119–23) on the role of personal cabinets in France.

35   Sasse (1977, p. 163).

36   See p. 116 for an explanation of the grading system within the Commission.

37   Ludlow (1991, p. 93).

38   Michelmann (1978a, p. 17).

39   *Ibid.* (p. 18).

40 Middlemas (1995, p. 34). Middlemas notes the importance of 'corridor gossip' in providing information of this sort for cabinet staff.

41 Donnelly and Richie (1994, p. 47).

42 See chapter six for details of the Delors cabinet.

43 Peterson (1972, p. 129) commented that: 'DG IX is a force for the increased bureaucratisation of personnel decision-making and for the limitation of any form of national influence'. It seems that the DG has, over the past two decades, been fighting a losing battle.

44 This includes the EP's secretariat, the Council secretariat, and the secretariats of other EU bodies.

45 Spence (1994b, p. 68).

46 Michelmann (1978a, p. 23).

47 A further account of the dossier approach to working in the Commission is given in chapter five below.

48 Hay (1989, p. 28).

49 A. Smith (1995, p. 484).

50 Such a distinction was made by Sasse (1977, p. 152).

51 Tutt (1989, p. 20).

52 In certain cases, where formal exceptions are made, the upper age limit is in effect thirty-five years of age.

53 A. Smith (1995, p. 472). The implications of this are that distinctive characteristics or even cultures may develop, based around these appointees.

54 Spence (1994b, p. 62).

55 Tutt (1989, p. 29).

56 Weber's definition of bureaucracy, although now considered flawed in many respects, remains seminal. See Weber (1978).

57 That is, the parachuting of top officials into the Commission from senior posts outside.

58 Middlemas notes that when DG XIII moved offices, the personnel DG discovered that there were 200 more bodies than they had expected.

59 Spence (1994b, p. 74). Author's italics.

60 This point is made in *ibid.*

61 The French word *engrenage* suggests the effective meshing or engaging of cogs in a machine.

62 Middlemas notes that salaries were fixed in ecus before the 1992–93 ERM crisis which meant that they depreciated 15 per cent against the DMark at that time.

63 Lopès (1990, p. 501).

64 Hay (1989, p. 40).

65 Willis (1983, p. 65).

66 See chapter seven on questions of institutional reform within the Commission.

67 Hay (1989, p. 29).

68 See chapter six on the question of organisational reform and the modernisation drive under Delors.

69 See Page (1995).

70 Cassidy (1995).

71 The fact that in 1994 (before the 1995 enlargement) 26.6 per cent of Commission staff were Belgian should not be shocking. Other percentages for the Commission as a whole are perhaps more representative: the French had 11 per cent; the Germans 10.5 per cent; the UK 8 per cent; the Italians 13.8 per cent; the Spanish 8.7 per cent; the Netherlands 4.3 per cent; the Greeks 4.7 per cent; the Portuguese 4.1 per cent; the Danes 3.2 per cent; the Irish 2.6 per cent and Luxembourg 2.5 per cent. The percentages of 'A' grades by nationality are much more telling: UK 11.4 per cent; Germany 13.8 per cent; France 16.5 per cent; Italy 13.1 per cent; Spain 10.5 per cent; Netherlands 5.5 per cent; Belgium 12 per cent; Portugal 4.1 per cent; Greece 5.4 per cent; Denmark 2.9 per cent; Ireland 3.4 per cent; Luxembourg 1 per cent. See Spence (1994b, p. 79).

72 Peterson (1972, p. 121).

73 Middlemas (1995, p. 232) notes that key members of the college have 'to balance weight (measured by portfolio repercussions) against numbers. The requirement to act together itself becomes a guarantee against national excess or personal and departmental rivalry'.

74 Hay (1989).

75 *Ibid.* (p. 27).

76 See for example, Peters (1991, p. 16).

77 Page and Wouters (1994, p. 447).

78 A. Smith (1995, p. 444) suggested this.

79 Michelmann's (1978a) study looked at five DGs in depth and examined the comparative effectiveness of each.

80 Cram (1994).

81 Middlemas (1995, p. 210) talks of a 'primordial tension' between the two institutions.

82 Sasse (1977, p. 192).

83 Rometsch and Wessels (1994) use this term to characterise the role played by the Commission.

84 *Ibid.* (p. 210).

85 Peterson (1972, p. 74) and Sasse (1977).

86 Scheinman (1966).

87 The committee networks within the Commission are dealt with in chapter five below.

88 Scheinman (1966, p. 751). See also chapter five below.

89 Indeed, a power struggle over control of the GATT negotiations was played out by the two bodies in the early 1990s.

90   Ludlow (1991, p. 114).

91   Nugent (1994).

92   Westlake (1994a, p. 1.2)

93   The GAP is made up of cabinet members, one from each of the commissioners' cabinets, together with a Legal Service representative. The cabinet officials hold the position of parliamentary attaché, which gives them responsibility for liaison with EP committees and political groups and for keeping themselves, 'their' services and their commissioners well informed about goings-on in the Parliament. The GAP secretariat is in the Secretariat-General, with meetings taking place three times a month, chaired by a representative of the cabinet responsible for EP-Commission relations. The main function of this committee is to make preparations for the coming parliamentary session, which means sorting out such matters as which commissioner will attend which plenary session, and what progress is being made on the replies to parliamentary questions.

94   This committee deals with all matters on the agenda of the plenary and meets once a month just before the full meeting of the Parliament takes place.

95   This is a body which was set up in September 1993 as part of the implementation of the Maastricht Treaty. It deals with management matters, which were previously dealt with by the Enlarged Bureau in the EP.

96   Westlake (1994a).

97   *Ibid.* (p. 1.1).

98   *Ibid.* (p. 3.1).

99   Ludlow (1991, p. 125), for one, notes that they are often 'anodyne', while questions in plenary or committee are little better.

100   Vibert (1989, p. 5).

101   Duff (1994a, p. 152). The Maastricht Treaty also instituted a process, again already a *de facto* role of the Parliament, to scrutinise the annual legislative programme and the indicative legislative timetable of the Commission. This was confirmed by the December 1992 Edinburgh European Council meeting which stated that the Commission should make sure that its programme was ready in the October before the year of implementation so as to allow the Parliament more time to consider its implications. The Edinburgh European Council also encouraged the Commission to consult with both EP and Council before proposals are drafted by means of pre-legislative Green Papers where possible. This should also be considered in the context of the EP's new right to request initiatives from the Commission.

5

Process and procedure: decision-making and the Commission

In order to understand Commission involvement in the European policy process, it is important to come to terms with policy-making not just within the boundaries of the Commission, but also in other EU arenas, notably the EP and the Council of Ministers. The strategic position of the Commission within this policy process allows us a special standpoint from which we can begin to survey the informal workings of the Union, whether on a day-to-day basis, or in terms of the grander projects developed and functions performed. Yet to understand fully the character of European policy-making, such generalisations are merely a starting-point. This chapter cannot compete with the many excellent in-depth case studies of EU decision-making that focus on specific policy sectors, departments or even on individual pieces of legislation. However, in providing an overview of decision-making from the point of view of the Commission, it is certain that we can learn more about the institution at the centre of this process.

Uncertainty and agenda-setting

Policy issues are, more often than not, social and political constructs. The why and how of what has been termed the 'issue attention cycle', that is, why particular issues reach the attention of policy actors at a particular time, and how those issues emerge, are created, manipulated and transformed, is a fascinating area of public policy research beyond, however, the scope of this chapter. Nevertheless, to consider the Commission as a 'policy entrepreneur'[1] is to make some connection between its role in the formulation of European-level policy, and its control over the ideas, knowledge and, indeed, the issues that underpin it. For the task which is often assumed by political parties at national level – the presentation of competing policy conceptualisations – is, within the EU, a task for the Commission.

So, as far as the Commission is concerned, the agenda-setting phase is the most creative of all stages in the European policy process. Opportunities for the Commission to establish the parameters within which future discussion takes place, and thus to influence final outcomes, are substantial. This may involve attempts to upgrade the common interest, that is, to raise the stakes of European policy and to broaden the policy debate. It is clear, however, that the Commission is not the only player in this policy formulation game. As such, although it is the sole initiator of legislation, it would be misleading to overemphasise its unique role in establishing the EU policy agenda. No one institution really has an exclusive monopoly on policy initiation. Policy ideas emerge from a variety of sources: from the formal requests of the European Council or the European Parliament; from national governments individually or jointly; from international organisations or interest groups; or from commitments made in existing legislation or treaties. Thus, although 'There appears at first glance to be a clear political domination by the Commission in the policy process of the Community, ... in reality there are multiple avenues of potential influence, even within the Commission'.[2] For outsiders, this makes the European policy agenda notoriously difficult to predict, and poses a serious challenge for all actors who are in the business of trying to do just that. Indeed, 'the market for policy ideas within the EC policy process is much more dynamic than in any one national policy system. This is no doubt beneficial in terms of policy innovation, but the ensuing process is more difficult for everyone – including groups – to manage'.[3] This 'agenda uncertainty' makes involvement in the EU policy process a risky and often unsatisfying business. There is no science of lobbying; each case is unique, involving a different set of inputs, influences and pressures upon the Commission. Nevertheless, interests have consistently sought to influence the broader strands and substance of EU policy content, as well as focusing on more specific instances of legislative activity. Of course, this is not something that all interests are able to do; nor do all think it important. Yet it is clear that this is where the European-level umbrella groups, the so-called Euro-groups, come into their own.

This situation is as uncertain for the Commission officials involved as it is for those attempting to influence European legislation from outside the institution. 'The process of agreeing legislation in the Community usually includes some degree of confusion on all sides as to the effect of various often contradictory pressures on those involved in key negotiating decisions.'[4] What we seem to be talking about here is a rather pluralistic process of 'competitive agenda-setting', in which entrepreneurial agenda-setters take advantage of the multiple channels available to push forward their particular perspective or conceptualisation of an issue, creating as they go, 'quasi-markets' for policy ideas. Thus, competition would often seem to be at the heart of the process; competition not only amongst actors outside the Commission, but also amongst the DGs and Commission actors themselves. One must be careful in making too many generalisations of this sort, however. Whilst in some policy areas this is certainly an accurate characterisation of the agenda-setting process, in other cases, the reality will be quite different.[5]

It would be wrong, though, to assume that the Commission merely acts as a filter for policy ideas emerging from other institutions and actors. Activist commissioners have certainly been able to project their own policy vision or their own personal hobby-horses on to the European agenda. And as we have already seen, Commission presidents are particularly well placed when it comes to putting their ideas into practice, though not all have been able to take advantage of this potential for influence. Indeed, even though this might be a rarer occurrence, policy initiatives can even emerge from within the Commission's own services. This is more likely, though, when the DG concerned finds itself stepping in to fill a policy vacuum, or, perhaps, if it is known that the leadership is in the process of mobilising support for a particular policy. Examples of this sort of DG activity have been provided, for example, in the fields of European information technology and social policy.[6] But even where there is no policy vacuum, Commission officials may well have ideas of their own. 'Access to cross-national data places the Commission in the position of being able to identify common problems and thus potential areas conducive to future regulation.'[7] It is this capacity for overview and synthesis that places the Commission in a powerful position *vis-à-vis* other actors in the European policy process. In any case, it is in the Commission's interest to make full use of its initiative and promotional functions as it seeks to emphasise its own usefulness as a reservoir of independent thought and as a well-informed think-tank. It is in this sense that the Commission's role may be defined as both goal-seeking and goal-setting.[8]

There are a number of ways in which the Commission can influence policy. Although some of these rely upon the institution's ability to initiate legally enforceable regulations, directives and decisions, one should not forget the importance of non-binding recommendations and opinions. Although these may in practice be little more than think-papers, when taken alongside other forms of Commission documentation such as policy statements often found in annual reports, and speeches and newspaper articles written by commissioners and director-generals, it is often possible to identify from them the Commission's line in a particular policy area. Whilst in many cases, statements of this sort will simply summarise a policy position which is already well known, they still provide useful insights into Commission thinking. The increasing use of Green Papers is interesting in this respect as it formalises this agenda-setting function. In so doing, it, at one and the same time, consolidates the Commission's involvement at this stage in the process, whilst serving to reduce some of the aforementioned uncertainty that has plagued European policy formulation.

As such, it is clear that non-binding non-legislative policy tools at the Commission's disposal can compel change within a particular policy environment as much as any legally-enforceable instrument can. As those affected by Commission policy adjust their expectations and their behaviour in line with general policy statements, the Commission is effectively rewriting the rules of the game for these actors. It has to be said, however, that this form of policy discretion is found more often during the implementation stage, than at the genesis of an entirely new European-level policy. Nevertheless, its impact on policy actors outside the Commission is phenomenal.

Interest groups and policy formulation

Although there are a multitude of influences upon the Commission, the drafting of legislation continues to take place in a rather arcane fashion. Attempts to open up the formulation process have not really helped to explain the informal stages through which draft legislation passes before it enters the public domain. Every example looked at will be different of course, as the many case studies of EU policy-making have demonstrated. But it is nevertheless helpful to make some general points about the input into the policy process both from Commission officials and from the interests they consult at this stage.

Once it has been decided to draft a piece of legislation, the first step in this process will be pivotal. It is at this initial draft stage that a large proportion of the final Commission proposal is put down on paper. And as majority voting becomes ever more prevalent within the Council of Ministers, it is even more likely that the ultimate outcome will be closer to the Commission's original proposal. It is hardly surprising that those opposed to any increase in the Commission's influence over policy-making also tend to reject the extension of majority voting in the Council. Indeed, the final proposal adopted by the Council contains at least 80 per cent of the original Commission draft.[9]

The drafting process itself is usually the job of an official in one of the middle 'A' grades, possibly an A4 or A5 principal administrator. He or she has the responsibility of being the *rapporteur*, the drafter (literally the reporter), of a particular proposal. Officials will be responsible for the proposal even after it leaves the college. As such, they often continue to represent the Commission later in the decision-making process, for example, in Council working groups. The image often conjured up is that of the lone Commission official, sitting in front of a blank sheet of paper, wondering what to write on it. This presents a potent if somewhat exaggerated picture. It is more than likely that the main political and technical parameters for the draft will have been established earlier. The *rapporteur*'s job is, then, to explore ways in which these prior considerations and prerequisites can be taken into account, whilst avoiding as many of the potential loopholes and unintended consequences as possible.

Not surprisingly, the involvement of interests is vital for the *rapporteur* at this initial stage. The responsible official will normally consult widely with interest groups of all types. Depending on the policy area under consideration, these may include governmental representatives, academics, sectional and promotional groups, firms, and regional and local authority representatives – amongst others. For interest groups, the importance of getting in on the act as early as possible cannot be overstated. One senior official's already much quoted recommendation is that groups should make contact when 'legislation is little more than a gleam in an official's eye'.[10] And as such, knowledge about *when* proposals are to be formulated becomes as important as knowledge about *who* is to make them.

Lobbying is not just the preserve of private interest groups and consultants, however. National governments and their representatives are also keen to have an ongoing dialogue with the Commission. The staff of the UK Permanent Representation (UKREP) in Brussels have, for example, fairly fixed contacts with their opposite numbers in the Commission, and as such act as a sort of permanent lobby.[11] They do this in the hope of influencing Commission thinking at as early a stage as is possible. This sort of semi-permanent relationship also means that national governments can get an early warning of the content of new proposals before they enter the more formal policy channels.

To assist in this interest aggregation process, the Commission has at its disposal a large network of advisory committees.[12] Committees of this sort that have a role to play in policy formulation exist only to *advise*. There is as such no constraint placed upon the Commission. Advisory committees come in many shapes and forms. So-called 'Group 1' committees, often called expert committees, tend to comprise national officials and national experts, individuals whose names are put forward by government departments. In spite of this, these nominees rarely act blatantly as official representatives. The set-up is rather informal and the status of these committees varies enormously. Some are fairly long-standing with stable memberships, whilst others are set up on a more *ad hoc* basis to perform a specific function. Generally, it is compulsory for the Commission to consult expert committees during the policy formulation process, although there is no requirement that the Commission should take on board any of the advice proffered. Whether the advice is accepted or not, these committees are extremely useful to the Commission, providing staff with a valuable insight into relevant policy thinking at national levels. While members of expert committees are nationally nominated, members of 'Group 2' committees, sometimes labelled consultative committees, represent sectoral interests. Officials from Euro-groups and other interest associations make up most of their membership, with a large proportion of these committees concerned specifically with agricultural matters. Consultative committees tend on the whole to be considered less important and less helpful than expert committees, in part as they meet less frequently.[13]

The *raison d'être* of the advisory committees is to give the Commission an opportunity to sound out potential opposition to a policy proposal, whilst at the same time supplementing its own knowledge and expertise in the area under consideration. It is not surprising therefore that while some DGs want, indeed depend upon, more assistance from outside advice, others have less need for this kind of advisory structure. Of course the same applies to DG contacts that are less formally structured, a method of achieving the same ends which is preferred by some departments. This need for information may indeed be characteristic of an 'adolescent bureaucracy', but it can all the same place the Commission in a rather vulnerable position. Dependence upon interest group involvement may even be dangerous if it appears to instil a lack of institutional confidence amongst officials. Likewise, there are also potential dangers should officials forget the inherently political nature of the advice they are receiving. It may well be that the Commission *thinks* it controls the game at this stage, but this should not be taken for granted.

Interest groups hoping to pursue their objectives through a more informal route have been advised to keep in touch with the *rapporteur* of a proposal. This can be done through visits and meetings, letters and telephone calls. However, although it is wise for interests to target the *rapporteur*, this official might in fact be less willing to open up to interest groups than would a more senior official. Indeed, there may be as few as two officials who really know the detail of a proposal well: the senior official who gives the policy advice, and the more junior official who knows it all.[14] This sort of specialisation has both advantages and disadvantages. On one hand, it means that the authors and those responsible for draft proposals are easily identifiable. On the other hand, however, it has certain implications for the work of the Commission officials. It tends to imply that officials' expertise is at the expense of any knowledge of policy matters outside the area for which they are responsible. This may mean that while officials become immersed in the technical detail of their proposal, they are less aware of political constraints likely to make the legislation or its implementation unworkable.

And for the officials themselves, it is likely to have a restrictive effect on their own potential for mobility within the institution.

The omnipresence of interest groups at the policy formulation stage has led to accusations that a form of 'agency capture' exists within the Commission.[15] This suggests that while the Commission claims to be impartial and objective, it is in fact acting as a voice for sectional interests. It is certainly clear that some outside actors have developed close relationships with their counterparts in the Commission. As such, there tends to be something of a gap between those interests with preferential insider-type access, and those largely excluded from the formulation process. This may even occur contrary to the best intentions of the officials concerned. 'Almost against their will it seems, Commission officials are in danger of being drawn into quasi-clientelistic relationships with the limited number of groups which are really able to keep pace and respond to Commission proposals.'[16] And even though there is a distinction to be made between 'capture', on one hand, and a close 'symbiotic' relationship, on the other, there are dangers inherent even in the latter.

> [For interest groups] … there are relatively high returns through the possibility of developing symbiotic, power-dependence relations with parts of the Commission. This can lead to bureaucratic advocacy, such as in the case with DG XII/E – I/II and biotechnology, or more generally with DG III, regarded within the Commission as the spokesman for industrial interests.[17]

Interest groups rarely see themselves in this light, however. They frequently complain that the Commission deals with too many groups, and that this has threatened to undermine all interest group influence. If Commission officials become incapable of handling relations with relevant interest groups *en masse*, it is possible that Commission efforts to listen more generally to interests might wane. To resolve some of these potential problems, the Commission has in recent years sought gradually to develop a more systematised form of consultation, one which is outside the advisory committee system, but which would nevertheless enable officials to 'manage' the consultation process more effectively. This involves the creation of a register of interest groups and a code of conduct which would govern their relationship with the Commission. Some of the guiding principles have already been set out in a Commission publication.[18]

Such subtle attempts to alter the nature of the relationship between interest groups and the Commission must be considered in the context of the Commission's avowed commitment to greater openness and procedural transparency. This was an issue raised at the December 1992 (post-Maastricht) Edinburgh European Council. It was agreed in this forum that member states should be given more advanced notice of Commission initiatives and that the Commission should consider widening their fact-finding exercises in some specified cases (those cases being spelt out in advance). This could be achieved through a more widespread use of Green Papers and (to a lesser extent) White Papers, and might even include some form of notification procedure published in the Union's official journal. This makes some sense, as it suggests that opposition to proposals later in the policy process could be preempted at this stage. However, it also raises important questions about the autonomy of the Commission in the decision-making process. The more difficult questions could be phrased as follows: is it the Commission's responsibility to build consensus with actors *outside* the Commission at *this* stage in the policy process?; or should the Commission only perform that function later, once it has taken *its* decision? It certainly seems sensible to assume that the Commission ought to be proposing legislation that has the most chance of success in the Council, in order to avoid delay and time-wasting.[19] However, it is also clear that the requirement that the Commission consult more widely with all interests (including national governments) suggests an attack on the Commission's monopoly of initiative beyond that already confirmed at Maastricht. It implies that even at this early stage the Commission is acting as a consensus-builder rather than as an agenda-setting policy initiator.

Consultation and co-ordination within the Commission

Consultation during the policy formulation process implies much more than just contact with policy actors and institutions outside the Commission. Using conventional checks and balances, co-ordination and consultation practices written into the Commission's internal rules of procedure aim to ensure consistency and at least a measure of agreement among the Commission's services on a given draft proposal. Although consensus-building is normally thought of as a function that the Commission must perform in its relations with other EU institutions and national actors, it is imperative that consensus is first of all constructed within the confines of the Commission itself.

Within the Commission, consultation mechanisms are organised both vertically and horizontally. Vertically, draft proposals follow a conventional route up through the DG's hierarchy. At each step, objections may be raised or improvements suggested. The draft will be passed back to the *rapporteur* for reworking if necessary: indeed this may happen several times before agreement is reached and the draft is passed up to the next step – where the process begins once again. This is a time-consuming procedure which can mean frustrating delays for the *rapporteur*. Additional delays may be caused as nearer the top of the DG hierarchy line managers may be unable to respond quickly to the draft, as many spend a high proportion of their time in meetings or away from the office on 'missions' (some sort of fact-finding trip, for example). Nevertheless, this vertical communication chain generally works well.

More criticism tends to be laid at the feet of the Commission's horizontal co-ordination mechanisms. The Commission's internal rules of procedure demand that all relevant departments work together and are consulted before a draft proposal is discussed in the college. Where a proposal is straightforwardly the *possession* of one DG, there is a fairly basic form of consultation, involving the circulation of the *dossier* (file) to potentially interested services and to the LS. The DGs are required by their internal rules of procedure to consult certain DGs in certain cases. The dossier includes an attached note which states that if no objection is raised within a certain number of days, it is assumed that there are no fundamental technical problems identified. Of course, this procedure does not mean that *political* stumbling-blocks are necessarily avoided, but it can highlight differences in interest and thinking on a subject early on in the formulation process. If there are objections or reservations, comments will be attached to the dossier which will then be transmitted to the commissioners' cabinets informing them of potential opposition. This may of course mean that the *rapporteur* has to rethink certain aspects of the draft.

Not surprisingly perhaps, the inter-service consultation process does not always run smoothly. 'Tight working deadlines ... mean that some parts of the Commission may be unaware, until a relatively late stage, of the detail of forthcoming policy initiatives relevant to their own work.'[20] This can cause friction between DGs, especially if it becomes a frequent occurrence. As the formal co-ordinator within the Commission, the SG is responsible for ensuring that relevant services have been consulted before a proposal is submitted to the college of commissioners, and that rules and timetables have been complied with. This is not always an easy task for it to perform. It is clear therefore that the existence of a formal process of consultation does not itself mean that relations between DGs on a particular policy matter will necessarily be amicable. Policies proposed in one DG may well serve to counter or undermine legislation in another. Such sources of tension, exacerbated by the fragmentation of the Commission's internal structure will no doubt end up by being shunted upwards to the college. There are numerous examples of this. DG IV's insistence on a pro-competition policy has, for example, frequently run counter to sectoral policies that have tended to place more emphasis on reviving European competitiveness. This has often led to much publicised friction not just amongst the DGs, but also within the college itself.

But what happens if responsibility for a new piece of legislation seems to fall under more than one DG? As well as posing additional problems of horizontal communication, the initial problem of who is to hold the file must be resolved. This can mean a struggle for control over a dossier, especially where several DGs see the possession of the proposal as part of a larger policy strategy. The frequency of such disputes should not be overstated, however. In the majority of cases, one DG will clearly be in a position to take the lead, in which case an inter-service working group will normally be established. It is much rarer to find that no DG is eligible to take sole responsibility. But where this is the case it is for the SG to recommend the setting up of a special Task Force outside the DG framework. This would normally become the additional responsibility of one of the commissioners, and would draw its staff from existing services.

This dossier approach is a way of working within the Commission that underpins much of the day-to-day life of officials, to the extent that it is taken for granted by those that have been socialised into Commission practice. The approach is essentially a juridical one, resting on the notion of individual responsibility for specific cases and on the technocratic expertise of officials who tend to become immersed in one small area of policy, becoming indeed experts in their own right. The internal politics of the dossier is fascinating. Questions such as where the files are kept may seem dull and of administrative concern only. They are, rather, key political matters affecting the relative importance and status of particular DGs, directorates and units over others.

Although decision-*taking* is the responsibility of the college of commissioners, decision-*making* rests largely with the Commission services, at least in the first instance. In the case of the Directive on machine safety standards, for example, the first identifiable stage in the process involved the DG concerned sending a questionnaire to all member states. It then produced a working paper based on the feedback it received. The next stage involved the setting up of a working party which included representatives from the member states, relevant institutions and other sectoral interests. Subsequently, other DGs and services with a potential interest were consulted, after which the draft proposal was finalised. It was only at this stage that the proposal could be transmitted to the cabinets and then on to the college of commissioners for approval.[21] Although this sort of summary is helpful as a framework, it begs many more questions than it answers. There is a whole lengthy story to be told about the genesis of any piece of EU legislation. Only thorough empirical research can expose the detail and the reality of how any policy proposal comes to be agreed in the college.

Decision-taking in the college: the internal rules

The perceived dichotomy between the work of the college (and their personal staffs, the cabinets),[22] and the work undertaken by the Commission's services is rather tenuous. Nevertheless, it is still true to say that the sponsoring DG does focus much more on technical aspects, leaving the cabinets and commissioners to their more political or nationally-oriented perspectives. One commentator has gone as far as to claim that 'Intergovernmentalism starts in the cabinet. They're mini-Councils within the Commission'.[23] It would be wrong, however, to assume that once a proposal is agreed at director-general level, it disappears or is swallowed up into the cabinet/college machinery. There is nothing to stop a proposal which is *with* the cabinet being sent back to the services; nor is there anything preventing Commission *rapporteurs* representing their DG and their proposal in meetings at this level.

Before cabinet members are willing to display their services' handiwork to other cabinets, they will want to make sure that the proposal is in line with their own policy strategy, whilst at the same time ensuring that it stands a chance of being acceptable to at least a majority of the college. The political acumen which is present amongst the cabinet staff is not always evident within the DG, other than perhaps at the most senior levels. As such, cabinet members are likely to see a draft proposal from a different point of view, which will mean that it is often likely to need further substantial redrafting after yet more consultation, this time often conducted informally amongst members of different cabinets. This informal process may begin even before the DG has formally launched the proposal, something that is certain to irritate DG officials. There have also been complaints that cabinets have at times cast aside proposals after *rapporteurs* have devoted months of hard work to them. Complaints and grumblings about cabinet staff interfering in the work of the services are nothing new of course, but they have tended to increase over recent years.

Once cabinet members are happy with a proposal, it is time to allow for a more formal process of consultation with other cabinets. In any normal week of Commission work, six or seven meetings of cabinet officials will be held on specific topics (and there are sometimes as many as ten meetings if the Commission agenda is particularly full). These meetings can last up to a whole day. The cabinet members present will usually have a specific responsibility for the area under consideration. Even so, they may call upon DG officials (especially the *rapporteur*) to be present, perhaps sitting more or less behind the cabinet member, ready to answer specific technical points. These so-called *special chefs* meetings allow cabinets across the Commission to have their say on up-and-coming legislation. They also allow proposals to be considered for the first time from a wider political perspective. The meetings have, since 1985, been chaired by a member of the President's cabinet, emphasising that one of the main objectives here is horizontal co-ordination at a political level.[24]

It is the job of the weekly (usually Monday) *chefs de cabinet* meeting to prepare for the meeting of the college of commissioners which usually takes place a couple of days later on a Wednesday. For this purpose, the meeting reviews the likely Commission agenda, seeking to reach an agreement on proposals that are not particularly controversial or sensitive, that is, those that need not be referred to the commissioners for discussion. This means that the agenda of the meeting of the college can be kept to a manageable size. In addition, the weekly *chefs* seeks to highlight questions that are particularly controversial, honing down and debating points that have been made in the more specialised and technically detailed *special chefs* meetings. Any cabinet member can ensure that an issue is raised at the meeting of the full college by placing a 'reserve' on the conclusions of preliminary discussions. The work done by the *chefs* is crucial for the effective functioning of the decision-making process. Without this intermediary stage between DG sponsorship and collegiate decision-taking, the college would certainly suffer from an enormous overload, with the decisional process almost grinding to a halt as a result.

The cabinet members acting together can use their discretion to decide to implement the so-called 'written procedure'. This is a process that largely mirrors inter-service consultation at the DG level. It involves the circulation of a draft proposal to all commissioners, outside the formal framework of the Commission meeting. If no commissioner objects to the proposal within a particular time limit (usually a week or so) it may be adopted without having to be discussed at the meeting of the college, though the decision will be noted in the minutes of the following meeting. This is only allowed with the agreement of the director-generals concerned and after the LS has given its approval. If there are any reservations or amendments, however, a commissioner might wish to place the matter on the agenda of the next meeting of the college. The procedure can only be used where a proposal is likely to be uncontroversial, as demonstrated by the results of inter-service consultation, and by informal soundings-out between cabinets. Where there is a need for extremely speedy action on a proposal, there is an even quicker procedure, the 'accelerated written procedure'. In addition, decisions may be taken via a delegated procedure. Here, one commissioner is permitted by the college to take responsibility for a specific measure. With the agreement of the President, it is then for that commissioner alone to authorise the definitive text, though its content has usually been agreed by the college in some detail beforehand.

It is clear that once a DG has formally drafted a proposal, the style and speed of its future progress is determined by the *chefs*. Indeed, individually, an effective cabinet can make a big difference to the success of a commissioner's term of office, just as a weak cabinet can be a real handicap. As such, there are some who claim that it is the cabinets that wield the real power within the Commission. Clearly their role in deciding where the controversial issues lie, and in highlighting those questions that need not be dealt with by the college does give them a certain amount of discretion. In a sense, their role is a hybrid one. On the one hand they act as political advisers; whilst on the other, their work parallels much more the work of senior civil servants at national level, those who routinely lay the groundwork for political meetings. Cabinet members are far from being civil servants in any conventional or formal sense, however. Their position is much more overtly political. In the 1970s, it was argued that cabinet prerogatives should not be overstated. 'By being able to communicate with all parts of the organisation, they give the impression of having power, without really being able to control decisions.'[25] This may well have been the case in the early 1970s, but it is not at all clear that it is still the case in the 1990s. In the sense of co-ordinating decision-taking it is clear that the cabinets are now much more important than the SG, for example. However, effective cabinets are no substitute for a unified political leadership amongst the ranks of the commissioners.[26] Even so, cabinet officials have in certain respects adopted a political brokerage role which results from the absence of party political activity at the Community level.[27] This role includes maintaining contacts with national governmental representatives and interest groups, although only those with political clout have this sort of privileged access. Neither cabinet staff nor the commissioners have time to deal with every little group that wishes to lobby the Commission, although, as it happens, through meetings with interest group representatives, cabinet staff may be provided with useful insights into potential trouble brewing in other parts of the Commission. Interest groups, for their part, may wish to lobby cabinets that are *not* responsible for the proposal in question, so that their interests have more chance of being represented in the *chefs* and in the college. The large majority of interest groups will none the less have to make do with contact at the official level.

Given the pivotal role of the cabinets within the Commission, it is not surprising that the importance of the college itself in the decision-taking process has been questioned. At the end of the day, one begins to imagine that there is little left for the college of commissioners to do. In fact, the cabinets, albeit with a certain amount of discretion in hand, act as filters through which the less controversial proposals pass. This means that the proposals that are eventually discussed in the weekly meetings are the most politically significant and potentially controversial. And as such, it is the 'heavy' work which is reserved for this forum. This is, after all, the only occasion on which all members of the college will be present, although invariably some will be away on 'mission' at any one time. As long as a majority are present the meeting is considered quorate, with *chefs de cabinets* requested to represent and speak on behalf of commissioners who are not able to attend. Likewise, if the President is not able to attend, one of the vice-presidents or another commissioner can deputise.

The meeting of the college is convened by the President, with the assistance of the SG. The agenda is controlled to a certain extent by the President's cabinet, though it is constrained by both the Commission's annual working programme and by a quarterly rolling programme. Nine days notice is required if commissioners wish to add an item on to the agenda, other than in exceptional circumstance. This allows enough time for relevant papers to be circulated. Other than where legal deadlines are involved, commissioners may also be able to get an item removed from the agenda, deferring discussion to a future meeting, though where a deadline is affected or a late item is suggested, it is for the college itself to decide whether to discuss the matter.

By this stage, the technical details and policy issues contained within a proposal will already have been chewed over by numerous bodies. Indeed, 'the Commission ... receives issues for decisions on which the DGs concerned will have at least exchanged views, Commissioners, cabinets, experts will have discussed at length, and Commissions' Chefs de Cabinet will have explained the scope for broader political agreement'.[28] But attention at this level does allow commissioners to focus specifically on what is likely to happen to a proposal once it leaves the Commission. Commissioners must be conscious that the image of the institution will be tarnished if controversial draft legislation is produced that will not make it through the Union's increasingly rigorous decision-making process. They must also be concerned to ensure that the consultation that takes place within the Commission has pre-empted many of the criticisms likely to be thrown at the legislation. In this way, the internal decision-taking function of the college of commissioners is closely allied to the external and more public role that has to be performed by the

Commission. This involves the presentation of a unified Commission policy line to the widest possible audience. There is a good reason why commissioners spend a great deal of their time travelling within the EU and beyond its borders, making speeches on Commission policy, and representing the European institutions more generally.

The Commission is a collegiate body and as such decisions taken at the Wednesday meeting are made on the basis of an absolute majority. However, it is always preferable to aim for consensus around the table. This is especially important as commissioners must defend all decisions taken – even if they voted against them. Because of this desire to maintain collegiality throughout the decision-taking stage, it is almost impossible for outsiders to find out how individual members voted. Indeed this would seem to go against the spirit of the Commission's treaty-given powers. Minutes of the meeting are kept of course, noting who voted for and against a proposal (and who abstained). But these minutes are confidential and not at all available for public scrutiny. It is only on odd occasions that the details slip out, and even then it is not easy to verify a claim that a particular commissioner voted in a particular way.

The college has a number of choices when it comes to voting on a draft proposal. It can accept it, reject it, refer it back to the DG or even defer taking a decision at all. There is, in addition, no limit to what the college can or cannot discuss at the meeting. In other words, it is important to bear in mind that commissioners may wish to go back to basics and unpack the logic and approach of a particular proposal, or simply focus on one or two controversial aspects. Commissioners may feel that this is necessary, especially if the proposal has been launched with some haste. However, if there are too many detailed points still at issue, commissioners are likely to push the proposal back to the *chefs*, who in turn may return it to the *rapporteur* for further redrafting. Only after an agreement has been reached can the proposal be authorised. Agreements are authenticated by the signatures of the President and the Secretary-General, or by the commissioner and a member of the Secretariat in the case of a delegated procedure. It is for the SG to ensure that decisions are notified officially, and that they are published in the Union's Official Journal (OJ).

Checks and balances are crucial to the internal functioning of the Commission as it performs its decisional functions.

The upward funnelling of all matters, and collective decision-making, are devices to assure that few, if any, decisions can escape the attention of any commissioner or his political advisors, and that consequently any action that may be interpreted as being rashly unfair or biased can be attacked by other nationalities.[29]

Thus, treatment of draft legislation within the college to a large extent pre-empts its treatment by both Parliament and Council. But before looking at what happens to draft proposals after the Commission's decision has been taken, we turn first of all to the adoption of a different type of decision by the college.

Executive decision-making: implementation and comitology

Decision-making within the Commission takes a number of forms. These include the regulatory or executive tasks of issuing binding rules, that is, filling in the details of broader laws already agreed. So, while Council legislation provides the framework, the Commission lays down the ground rules. It does this by issuing decisions, directives and regulations, based on powers delegated from the Council. Although this sort of administrative law may well be considered as less important than the policy law agreed by Council and Parliament, it still allows the Commission staff and the commissioners a certain measure of discretion, even if the large majority of the decisions taken are undoubtedly routine. Not surprisingly, governments are concerned that they should retain a fair amount of oversight over the procedures involved.

There is nothing unusual in 'civil services' being endowed with responsibilities in executive matters of this sort. Although there is no question of officials being allowed a truly legislative role, it is often difficult, in individual cases, to see where the line between policy and executive decision-making is drawn. There is surely a grey area between the two. The assumption that policy law is more 'political' than administrative law can mean that at the end of the day the administrators have a fair amount of freedom of manoeuvre. As such, this discretionary power is often considered as one of the most controversial areas of Commission influence over domestic politics.

It is in this sense alone that the Commission deserves to be called an 'implementer' of policy. For when it comes to street-level implementation, the Commission's role is in fact a small one. Even before the subsidiarity principle took root, 'actual' implementation was very consciously left to national and subnational actors and their agents. The Commission's role is thereby one limited to the supervision of implementation. Inevitably, perhaps, there are one or two notable exceptions to this generalisation, the most important being in the competition policy field.[30]

The policy formulation process charted above is to some extent replicated at this stage, as the Commission services again draft proposals, see their handiwork transmitted up and down the Commission hierarchy and worked through the consultation process. On first sight, the main difference seems to be that here the process stops with the college's decision and that the Commission is thus an autonomous actor in this process. As such, even though national governments are often keen to see the Commission's executive powers restricted, there are limits to what the Council can do in this respect. If the Council is to avoid being overloaded with legislative decisions, it is clear that some of the more *technical* rules must be delegated. But this is not as objective an argument as might at first appear. It has been suggested for example that the Council could begin to spell out its own legislation so thoroughly that the Commission would be left with little room for manoeuvre. Effectively, then, 'the Commission would gradually come to lose its ability to take the initiative'.[31] The question of Council control needs to be considered in more detail, however.

Largely to counter fears that the Commission might become unnecessarily politicised in performing its executive function, and in order to minimise the impact of administrative discretion in such cases, the Council has instituted a complex and far-reaching system of checks on Commission activity. It has done this through the extension of a network of committees. 'A feature common to all the implementing powers conferred upon the Commission by the Council is that they come with "strings attached".'[32] These strings demonstrate that the issue of this expansive committee network and the question of Council delegation to the Commission are inextricably linked.

The importance of what has come to be called 'comitology', the spread of a network of advisory, management and regulatory committees that oversee and in some cases seem to control the rule-making function of the Commission has only relatively recently been subject to outside scrutiny. This has emerged as a big issue over the last decade or so since both the Commission and the Council themselves began to acknowledge that the situation was getting out of hand. By the mid 1980s there was no clear idea of how many committees there were and no clear explanation of the procedures they followed. This messy state of affairs meant that there could be no real assessment of the implications of this committee network. It was unclear who the winners were and who might have lost out as a result of this growth in comitology. It should come as no surprise therefore that the drafters of the Single European Act should seek to address some of these issues.[33] The result was generally considered disappointing, however. The SEA merely required the Council to establish rules and principles that would in future govern the operation of implementing committee procedures through an amendment of the relevant treaty article (Article 145).

The Council decision of 13 July 1987, the so-called *comitology* decision, was the outcome of that new treaty provision. It set out rules for three types of committees (advisory, management and regulatory), but failed to say anything about the principles behind their operation.[34] The decision caused an inter-institutional crisis, with the EP attempting (and failing) to get the decision annulled in the European Court.[35] On the surface, it looked as though the Parliament should have had a good case, as in allowing implementing committees to demand the referral of legislation back to the Council, but not to the Parliament, the Council could effectively find a way round the EP's involvement in an important area of decision-making.

This issue is certainly crucial for the EP. For the Commission, the implications are quite different, touching as they do upon its independence from the Council and its function as Community executive. In this sense, the SEA appears to have pushed the Commission further away from any aspirations it may have had to become a fully-fledged European-level executive. Nevertheless, the SEA did for the first time make it clear that the delegation of executive powers by the Council is obligatory, something which 'constitutes an important step towards redefining the separation of powers between the Community institutions, concentrating the bulk of executive powers in the Commission'.[36] Whether this actually strengthens the Commission's position *vis-à-vis* the Council is dubious. There have none the less been doubts raised over the extent to which these committees really do act as a constraint upon the Commission. In 1991, the Commission got a favourable opinion from regulatory committees in 98 per cent of cases, with similar results emerging from the management committee network. It may in fact be the case that it is the Parliament and not the Commission that is the real loser from 'comitology'.[37]

However, the jury is still out on the real implications of comitology. It is clear that its importance is now generally acknowledged, and that this has thrown a rather different light on the Commission's executive functions. Rather than stressing the autonomy and discretion of the Commission in performing its executive tasks, attention has increasingly turned to inter-institutional relationships and the meshing of institutional contexts. It is no longer adequate to see the European institutions as distinct entities with fixed borders. If comitology tells us anything, it tells us to be cautious of ignoring what might at first be seen as 'institutional messiness'. Behind what might appear as 'messy', are lessons to be learnt about the European institutions and their relationships with one another.

The Commission and the Parliament in the policy process

Agreement on a piece of draft legislation in the Commission heralds the beginning of a new phase in the policy process. But although it is true to say the Commission's policy formulation work is now complete, it would be far from accurate to see the Commission stepping back from the legislative process at this stage. Indeed, the Commission's role continues to be a very visible one as its policy proposals come to be considered by the EP. Here, the Commission is often seen to act much more as a lobbyist for its own position than as a consensus-builder between diverse interests. As the Commission seeks, almost simultaneously, to deal with both parliamentary and Council processes, it often finds itself in a rather ambivalent position. Although its 'heart' might lie much more with the Parliament, its 'head' is often more attentive to the concerns of Council, to the extent that 'parliamentary idealism must on frequent occasions be tempered by what might be termed legislative/executive pragmatism, with the Commission often finding itself in an uneasy intermediate position'.[38] This has been particularly difficult for the Commission during the IGCs, where the Parliament has in the past had no representation. In such cases, the Commission has been in a rather peculiar position of having to represent both its own views and those of the Parliament. It is hardly surprising that the EP and the Commission have found this a most unsatisfactory state of affairs.

It is impossible to separate the question of Commission participation in the parliamentary process, from the decision-making procedures that define that participation. The specific role that the Commission plays is largely dependent upon the policy area under consideration, and upon the decision-making procedure used. Hence the issue of legal base (the relevant treaty provision) becomes all-important, as it determines the role of the Parliament *vis-à-vis* the other European institutions, including the Commission. As such, the Parliament scrutinises with great care the legal base upon which every Commission proposal is made. There have on several occasions been intense and often bitter disagreements between the two institutions over the treaty base proposed. Not surprisingly perhaps, the Commission has argued that while *it* takes an objective 'legal' approach, the Parliament refuses to see the choice other than as a reflection of its own political role in a particular policy area. Undoubtedly, however, for both institutions, this is a political as much as it is a legal question.

Essentially, there are four broad legislative procedures,[39] although three of these have two distinct variants, and there is also a quite different budgetary procedure. The classic consultation procedure which formed the basis of most Community decision-making up until the mid 1980s foresaw the EP as little more than a 'sounding board' for Commission proposals. In this procedure, the Parliament has only one opportunity to provide an Opinion on a Commission proposal, after which the Council takes its decision. Although this appears to place the Commission-Council relationship centre-stage, there is still a possibility that the EP will be able to wield some influence. When the MEPs vote on amendments to the proposal before them, the Commission receives a clear message about parliamentary priorities. The EP may well delay a vote on the resolution (the Opinion) until after the Commission has agreed (or not) to their amendments. As such, the Commission can find itself under a great deal of pressure to take on board some, at least, of the Parliament's concerns. For if the EP is not happy with the Commission's response, it may make use of its power of delay, sending the proposal back to the relevant parliamentary committee indefinitely.

Clearly, this power is all the more potent when the Commission hopes to push a proposal through fairly urgently.

Much depends upon the extent to which the EP can use its influence subtly, to achieve the objectives it seeks. The indefinite delay of a proposal, for example, is rarely what MEPs want to see. Nevertheless, the use of extreme tactics may be necessary in cases where, otherwise, the EP's voice is unlikely to be heard. Even so, the Parliament cannot veto a proposal. There have in the past been times when the EP view has in effect been ignored. However, the European Court's *Isoglucose* ruling in 1980[40] made it clear that the Council had to wait for an EP Opinion before taking a decision (although this does not mean it has any obligation to take on board its advice). Rather, the effect of the *Isoglucose* ruling was to encourage the Commission to take much more notice of the Parliament. This is important as the EP, even now, is dependent on the Commission's goodwill when the consultation procedure is used. As the Commission can withdraw a proposal at any stage in the decision-making process, the Parliament has to make sure that it does not push its 'partner' institution too far. The record of the EP within the consultation procedure is mixed. Around three-quarters of amendments are agreed to by the Commission, but its ability to influence the legislator, the Council, is extremely constrained.[41] Under the consultation procedure, decisions in the Council are taken either by a qualified majority or by unanimity. This procedure was extended under the Maastricht Treaty in a number of areas, including the decision on transition to Stage Three of EMU, the nomination of individuals including the Commission president, and on matters covered by the 'pillars' of the Union, namely, foreign policy and justice and home affairs.

The co-operation procedure was introduced in the SEA. This procedure sought to increase the involvement of the EP in decision-making by adding a second reading to the legislative process. At the same time, the procedure went hand-in-hand with the extension of qualified majority voting in all matters to do with the single market project, though the Council can still have the last word if it can reach a *unanimous* decision. While the first reading of the procedure largely mirrors the conventional consultation procedure, the second stage potentially gives the Parliament more of a say in determining final outcomes. While there is little for the Commission to do if the Parliament approves the draft legislation, or if it rejects it outright, its position is quite different if the EP proposes amendments. In such cases, the Commission has one month in which to re-examine the proposal in light of EP comments. After so doing, it then passes the draft, along with any proposed amendments, to the Council. If the Commission decides to incorporate the Parliament's amendments, the Council may accept these with a qualified majority vote, or reject them unanimously. If it does not, then the Council can only approve the amendments acting unanimously. If the Council has not acted within three months the proposal falls.

The Commission's role during the course of the co-operation procedure is often rather delicate. The first reading is most important since a lack of agreement at this stage would mean timetable restrictions, as well as inevitable bad feeling at the second reading. Not surprisingly, therefore, both institutions are keen to see agreement reached at an early stage. However, this is far from implying that the Commission always takes on board parliamentary amendments. The Commission also has to bear in mind the likely Council reaction. 'The Commission frequently finds itself in the invidious position of regretfully refusing parliamentary amendments because they upset the delicate balance of a Common Position qualified majority in the Council.'[42] Once again, the Commission finds itself having to balance, in such cases, parliamentary concerns against those of the Council. Nevertheless, the debate over whether the procedure has actually diminished or enhanced the role of the Commission now seems to highlight its overriding advantages. Since the co-operation procedure requires unanimity in the Council for a Commission proposal to be rejected, but only a qualified majority to accept it, this clearly works in favour of the Commission's draft.

One of the most important consequences of the introduction of the co-operation procedure has been the mentality shift that has taken place within the Commission (and to a lesser extent, within the Council). Increasing awareness of the importance of the Parliament has led to a variety of organisational and procedural responses on the part of the Commission.[43] Changes made since 1986 have certainly helped to inculcate a closer, more co-operative relationship between the two institutions. As the Maastricht Treaty increased the number of policy areas in which the co-operation procedure is used, the scope of constructive parliamentary input into the European policy process has expanded. Most areas previously covered by the procedure now fall under the co-decision procedure.

This new procedure, introduced in the Maastricht Treaty, extends the Commission's procedural 'gate-keeping roles'. The co-decision procedure is thus an extension of the co-operation procedure, even though at present it involves only a small number of policy areas. It gives the EP the right to veto proposals as a last resort, introducing at the same time a complex system of inter-institutional conflict resolution so as to avoid, if at all possible, that very eventuality. Again, Commission involvement in the procedure is much more important in the early stages, as by the time the (new) third reading is to start there is little the Commission can do to shape outcomes. The same is true of the final conciliation stage, though the Commission is present, acting formally as a consensus-builder between the two legislative actors, the Parliament and the Council.

Where no EP-Council agreement is possible, the Commission has been asked, as a rule, to withdraw its proposal, although this does not happen automatically. At the first reading, to heighten tension, and to attempt to draw the Commission towards *its* way of thinking, the Parliament has asked the Commission to make its position clear on EP amendments *before* a vote is taken in committee. The Commission has balked at this, claiming that it is only at the plenary stage that the discussion reaches a political level and that, as such, the Commission could not justifiably pass comment until the final stages of the parliamentary process. In spite of this, both Commission and Parliament do agree that it is crucial to try to get a decision at the earliest possible stage in the process, so as to allow the draft legislation to pass smoothly through the EU decision-making machinery. Clearly 'How effective the Article 189b (co-decision) procedure proves to be will depend partly on the nature of the collaboration between the Parliament and the Commission'.[44]

Furthermore, the Maastricht Treaty extended the assent procedure, first introduced in the SEA. Although most of the changes did not directly impact upon the Commission, there has been an attempt by the Parliament to make its powers of delay and rejection in this area less blunt. This is a common way of proceeding for the Parliament. It introduces new procedures for itself within its internal rules, carrying no obligation (other than a moral one) on the other EU institutions. In this case, the Parliament unilaterally introduced a form of conciliation which was not written into any Treaty. Before rejecting a Commission proposal outright the EP would issue a report suggesting potential amendments, thus putting pressure on the Commission to alter its proposal, even without recourse to a Council-EP conciliation approach.

The moral pressure often brought to bear on the Commission puts it in a difficult position in such cases. It does not want its own independence compromised by the EP, simply because it wishes to show its 'partner' institution a certain amount of goodwill. Although the Commission often appears to feel obliged to take the parliamentary line, it has at the same time continued to stress that there must be nothing 'automatic' about this. It is for the Commission to decide (with the Community interest in view) what its own course of action should be, though it is constrained further by the introduction of the subsidiarity principle into the equation.

Regardless of the procedure used, the Commission is represented at all stages of the parliamentary process. At the EP's committee stage, there will always be one or more Commission representative present. Top officials from relevant DGs or, in many cases, the commissioners themselves will be called upon to explain and defend a draft proposal. The discussion or question-and-answer sessions are fairly informal (as compared to the plenary sessions), although it is clear that the purpose of Commission representation at this stage is to iron out technical difficulties, rather than to engage in any political debate, which is normally reserved for the plenary, that is, the full meeting of the Parliament. It is also clear that the committees expect DG staff to keep them informed of progress within the Council working groups where they themselves have no representation.

The relationship between sponsoring Commission services and the responsible EP committee is often a close and symbiotic one, with the Commission staff responsible for providing information to the committee as and when it is needed. The archetypal example of this is found in the relationship between the EP's Budgets and Budgetary Control committee and the Commission's DG XIX (budgets). But although the relationship between these two bodies is particularly close, it is not out of the ordinary. Not surprisingly, personalities are also important, especially that of the person chairing the committee. Informally, meetings are likely to be held between the Commission *rapporteur*, and the *rapporteur* responsible for the proposals within the EP committee. These so-called 'bi-laterals' mean that misunderstandings over intentions or, more specifically, over text should be avoided. These informal meetings can even 'help in the drafting of mutually-acceptable technical amendments',[45] though this is not as collusive as it might sound. In any case, most Commission DGs now have some sort of co-ordinator whose responsibility it is to oversee relations with the Parliament. These officials provide a link between the Commission's SG and the EP committees.

In plenary, commissioners will often be quizzed on specific proposals and called upon to defend the line previously argued by the Commission. This process is important, as one of the main responsibilities of the Commission towards the EP involves keeping that body well informed of its line of thinking. Commission representatives are always present when parliamentary votes are taken in plenary, as the Parliament may wish to ask the Commission to accept certain amendments on the spot. Commissioners are given a delegated right to answer EP concerns. But if the Parliament is not satisfied with the response it receives, it may of course refer the proposal back to the committee.

The Commission and the Council in the policy process

Once the proposal has been agreed in the college of commissioners, it is forwarded by the SG to the Council Secretariat, to the Committee of Permanent Representatives (COREPER),[46] and then on to the Council working groups. Thus, at the same time as the parliamentary committees are drafting their report on the draft proposals, the Council's working groups are also beginning their assessment. These working groups undertake a thorough examination of all the technical aspects of the proposal from a variety of national perspectives. The process of negotiation that takes place here is by definition detailed, and assumes that those involved have a certain amount of expertise in the policy area concerned. This is important, as if national representatives in the working groups are to hold their own with the Commission officials (usually the drafter of the proposal and a representative from the SG – both of an equivalent grade to the national officials), they must have a profound knowledge not only of the technical detail, but also of the political and national context in which the legislation will have to be implemented. In many cases the national representatives in the working groups have been involved with the proposal from the very start, often having attended the earlier expert group meetings in the Commission. But this does not necessarily mean that a political perspective dominates here, although not surprisingly it has been noted that 'these government experts generally tend to take a stricter attitude towards Commission proposals at this stage than at the preparatory stage under the auspices of the Commission'.[47]

The importance of working groups should be neither exaggerated nor understated. After all, around 90 per cent of the final text of the legislation will be decided at this stage.[48] Even so, the 10 per cent that remains to be bargained over will include the most controversial and politically sensitive elements of the draft proposal. As such, since the Commission is in a better position to influence at this point in the Council process, there is a clear impetus for officials to ensure that a decision is reached. The Commission representatives have an incentive, therefore, to couch their proposals in a technical rather than political language, as in many instances opposition to technical standards (for example) can be dealt with in the working groups, rather than at a later stage in the Council process.

The function performed here by the Commission officials differs greatly from the formulation stage. Even so, it is still worthwhile for interests to keep in contact with Commission representatives. Indeed, on occasion, the Commission may even join forces with interest groups in order to push forward a specific lobby point.[49] The Commission now has to make use of a mix of its formal functions. On one hand, it remains the proposer or initiator of the policy, hoping to convince the member state representatives of the worth of the original draft. On the other hand, however, it is in the interests of the Commission officials to try to get as much agreement as possible amongst the national government representatives. Hence promotive and brokerage functions work simultaneously to the extent that 'The roles of proposer and mediator merge almost imperceptibly once the Council commences work. Cleavages within working groups do not occur simply on a Commission *versus* member state basis, but, inevitably perhaps, cross-national cleavages are also prevalent'.[50]

Where agreement is not forthcoming, and in areas that are essentially political rather than technical, proposals are transferred up to COREPER. The groundwork for meetings at this level is undertaken by the so-called *Antici* groups. In these forums the Commission is represented by an official from the SG. New Commission proposals are discussed here for the first time, so that they do not come to COREPER without some prior warning. Meetings usually take place a couple of days before the COREPER meeting, and as such, allow the Permanent Representatives to judge the state of play as the working groups process comes to an end. A different *Antici* meeting takes place within the Commission, allowing the Permanent Representatives an opportunity to question officials on the position of the college. This also allows national officials an insight into the potential timing of future proposals and initatives. All in all, there is plenty of contact between the Commission and the national representatives. Indeed, for the Commission staff, contacts are not only made with officials in the Permanent Representations, but will also involve direct links with officials from the lead departments in the member states themselves. Good contacts are certainly helpful. Indeed, constant Commission-COREPER interactions are essential if the Commission is to continue to influence decision-making throughout the Council process.

However, when it comes to the COREPER meetings themselves the Commission is in a fairly weak position. The balance has shifted somewhat by this stage, and the debate takes place on much more of an intergovernmental basis, with the officials from the Permanent Representatives and from national ministries playing more of a political-national game than they did in the working groups. Nevertheless, Commission officials from the relevant DGs, and representatives from the SG are present both in COREPER I and II,[51] and are expected to defend their proposal over again in this different forum. There is a real possibility that a final decision could be reached at this stage, which makes it all the more important for Commission officials to be present and defend their position effectively. Even so, the cards are largely stacked against them in terms of brute influence on the proceedings.

It is needless to say that the Council of Ministers meetings are also intergovernmental in their approach. The role of the Commission here varies, though. On some occasions, especially where informal discussions take place, the commissioners or President of the Commission, who at this level represent the Commission as a whole, may be useful sources of information or assistance for the Council Presidency chairing the meetings. But this can only really happen when some form of personal relationship is allowed to develop between Commission members and national ministers. In general, it has to be said that commissioners have little external input at this stage.

The role of the Commissioners in this political bargaining process often seems limited. With the exception of particularly strong personalities, such as Jacques Delors or Sir Leon Brittan – or in the past, Vicomte Davignon – members of the Commission do not play a major role in shaping the final decision. The threat to withdraw a Commission proposal happens rarely.[52]

So at this point, the Commission's work is largely done. This may seem odd, as the original purpose of COREPER having the authority to deal with the less controversial 'A' points, was to allow for greater Commission-Council dialogue over the 'B' points remaining on the agenda. However, it is clear that this logic is rarely apparent in COREPER meetings now. In any case, what comes before the Council usually differs substantially from the original proposal agreed in the Commission (after the working parties and COREPER officials have worked through all their technical and political objections). As such, the draft legislation that the commissioner may end up having to defend usually bears little resemblance to the proposal issued by the college. This places the Commission in an even more vulnerable position when it does participate in Council sessions. It is not surprising therefore that most of the Commission's influence must come well before this stage in the process.

Enforcement and the Commission-Court relationship

Although it is questionable whether the enforcement of legislation constitutes an element in the European decision-*making* process *per se*, it is worth commenting briefly on the Commission's role at this stage in the policy process, drawing as we go some general conclusions as to the Commission-Court relationship. The constraints upon the Commission's role as implementor of legislation have been remarked upon at various junctures above. Other than in exceptional circumstances, the Commission is restricted to the filling out or execution of legislation that has already been agreed in the Council. This reliance on what is effectively only a legal form of implementation has meant that the Commission has had to rely upon its enforcement function to achieve ends normally achieved through the control of implementation. Indeed, 'the legal watchdog role acts, to some extent, as a substitute for ... detailed application of policies'.[53] Here too, however, the Commission is in a vulnerable position.

From a political perspective at least, the Commission's position in the enforcement process rests heavily on its relationship with the European Court of Justice. This relationship is naturally governed by legal rules and norms. But there is much more to it than that. In spite of the fact that a legal literature on the European Court has been around for a long time, it is only relatively recently, in the last decade or so, that political scientists have 'discovered' this important Community institution. In terms of inter-institutional relationships, there is still very little written about the relationship between Court and Commission, for example. This is certainly an area of institutional research that needs to be further explored.

It is clear that the legal capacity of the Commission to enforce European policy is one of the features that distinguishes it, and the system as a whole, from conventional international organisations. The Commission is not the only actor here (national governments, national courts and individuals are also heavily involved), but it is pivotal in some areas. In the broad Community framework for enforcing legislation, much of the work of the Court is now taken up with preliminary rulings. These occur when national courts ask the European Court to rule on and thereby clarify a particular question of European law under Article 177. In these cases the Commission is involved only indirectly. Of more direct relevance, for our purposes, are so-called 'direct actions', cases brought to the Court by the Commission and other bodies, as well as those brought against the Commission and its partner institutions.

In the case of the former, the Commission can bring an action when a member state fails to abide by a particular piece of European legislation. There are about a hundred of these cases every year. When it comes to the Commission's attention that a member state is breaching Community law in some way, there is a clear procedure to follow. The first thing it does is send a letter to the government concerned. Usually in these circumstances, contact is made through the Brussels-based Permanent Representation, who will henceforth act as a sort of go-between between Commission and government. The letter is known as the 'reasoned opinion'. This is important, as it formally begins the Commission's enforcement procedure. However, it would be wrong to assume that this will be the first contact the Commission has had with a member state on the subject. Indeed, informal contacts may well have started long before the reasoned opinion, with warning letters and perhaps telephone calls to ministers and responsible officials. This generally means that the member state has had ample time to correct an error, or to account for their failure to implement. In spite of this, there are still currently around 700 reasoned opinions sent out each year.[54]

In the reasoned opinion, the member state government is once again given an opportunity to respond to the criticisms that have been put to it by the Commission. But if it refuses to comply with the opinion within a stated period, the Commission can take the matter to the European Court. With the case inside the Court system, the Commission continues to act as a sort of prosecuting council. Only in the case of competition policy does it act more like judge and jury. Of course, such a time-consuming and costly step as involving the Court may not be necessary. In the large majority of cases that warrant a reasoned opinion, the member state gives the Commission adequate guarantees that they will comply (usually explaining at the same time the how and the when of it). As such, the Commission, beyond making sure that the member state does what it says it will do, will not need to take the matter any further.

Commission staff have a fair amount of discretion in this area. For example, it is for the Commission alone to decide whether a case should be brought before the Court. The Commission's rationale in taking such action may be more complex than at first appears, and may go beyond simple crime-and-punishment or, rather, breach-and-sanction motives. The Commission may wish to de-politicise potentially damaging disputes between member states by taking on an action itself.[55] Not surprisingly, this may mean that the accused member state then turns on the Commission as a target for its hostility. There may be even more far-reaching ambitions within the Commission when the decision is taken to pursue a particular case. These may involve a desire on the part of Commission staff to publicise the law in a particular area, to establish norms of behaviour in a certain field, or simply to make an example of a particular party. For reasons of diplomacy, this latter is likely to happen much more in cases not directed at national governments, however. Whatever the motive, it is clear that the Commission has more potential cases to bring than it has resources to bring them. Some element of prioritisation (using its discretion, that is) is essential as a result.

The matter of a Court judgement against a member state always begs the same question: what if the member state fails to comply with the judgement? What, then, is the next step? To respond to this problem more effectively, the Maastricht Treaty added a supplementary procedure to the powers of the Commission. What this means in practice is that if there is evidence that a state is not complying with a Court judgement, the Commission can begin a new procedure. This will involve a second warning, a second reasoned opinion and a second referral to the Court. On this second occasion the Commission has to specify a lump sum or penalty payment (i.e. a fine) that the member state must pay if the Court finds against it.

In certain circumstances the Commission will find itself on the other side of the legal fence, accused by a member state, another EU institution or indeed any interested party of any number of illegalities. Often this will involve an action against a piece of legislation which, it is claimed, should not have been issued. Such 'proceedings for annulment' are usually argued along the lines of the Commission having acted in an area where it has no competence, or of the Commission having misused its power in some manner. Cases may also be brought against the Commission for failure to act under Article 175. On top of all of this the Commission also has to contend with cases in which damages are being claimed, as well as cases that involve members of its own staff.

Although we have been talking about the Commission's enforcement powers here, when we look more specifically at the Commission-Court relationship what we are usually talking about is the involvement of one part of the Commission, the Legal Service. DGs and other services will rarely have a direct contact with the Court. It is not surprising therefore that the LS wishes to keep the DGs on a close rein as they draft and administer their policies. For at the end of the day, it is often the LS staff that have to pick up the pieces.

Generally speaking, the relationship between the Commission and the Court is a mutually reinforcing one. Both institutions look to the other to consolidate their position within the European political arena. In the case of the Court, it 'follows the lead of the *commission*, using it as a political bellwether to ascertain how far member states can be *pushed* toward the Court and the commission's vision of maximum integration'.[56] The Court looks to the Commission to provide its maximalist position. It also suggests to the Court the limits of what is likely to be politically acceptable within the Council. In this way, the Court feeds into (and off) the Commission's relationship with other Community institutions, using the Commission's consensus-building experience to judge the outer boundaries of its own judicial activism. The Commission's interest in the Court seems more straightforward. The Commission looks to the Court to legitimise legally and politically the decisions it takes. More broadly, the Commission also sees the Court as an institutional symbol of the European rule of law and as such an actor that legitimises the broader European integration process. It is certain that this must have repercussions on the Commission's own activity.

In spite of the good relations that often exist between the two institutions, there also exists an implicit tension. After all, it is the Court that is often seen to defend the rights of the individual (the 'little person') as against the powers of the 'monolithic' European (and national) institutions. In this respect, there is a certain irony in the fact that cases brought against the Commission may well serve to legitimise the Union, though at the expense of the reputation and the prestige of the Commission itself. As such, the Court strengthens its own role in the Community system by 'building a constituency beyond the Brussels bureaucracy'.[57]

Conclusion

Making policy in the EU is a complicated business. Not only are the processes and procedures difficult to follow, but there are numerous actors to consider, actors whose roles are different at different stages in the game. Agenda-setting, policy-formulation, consultation and consensus-building, implementation and enforcement, all involve the Commission in one way or another. Different Commission functions are salient at different times, and combinations of roles are made use of simultaneously so as to ensure that Commission participation is maximised. To some extent at least, the characteristics of the EU policy process mirror those specifically at work within the confines of the Commission. The bargains struck, compromises reached and consensus built are not only outcomes of intergovernmental deliberations in the Council, they also feature heavily within the internal Commission process. Likewise, disagreements and disputes over institutional (or departmental) boundaries and responsibilities are as much a feature of internal Commission decision-making as they are of the broader EU policy process. It is only in examining the role of the Commission within the European policy process, as we have done, that we can see at one and the same time the internal dynamics at play within the institution, and the impact and influence that can be brought to bear by the Commission on its external environment. Indeed, the boundaries between the Commission and the outside world are never as clear-cut as we might at first imagine.

Notes

1   Peters (1994).

2   *Ibid.* (p. 13).

3   Mazey and Richardson (1993, p. 22).

4   Donelly (1993, p. 81).

5   There are many case studies of the policy process that involve coverage of the Commission's role. See Rosenthal (1975); Wallace, Wallace and Webb (1983), Cram (1994), and Skjaerseth (1994) for a few recent and not so recent examples.

6   See Cram (1994) on this.

7   *Ibid.* (p. 211).

8   This point was made by Coombes in 1970 (p. 234).

9   Hull (1993, p. 83).

10   *Ibid.* (p. 87).

11   Spence (1993).

12   On the Commission's advisory network, see *The European Citizen* (1991), and Nugent (1994).

13   Also see Buitendijk and Van Schendelen (1995) on the Commission's advisory committees.

14   Hay (1989, p. 28).

15   According to Cawson, Holmes and Stevens (1987, p. 31), agency capture exists 'where private interests succeed in turning public power to private ends'.

16   Mazey and Richardson (1993, p. 22).

17   Greenwood and Ronit (1994, p. 43).

18   Commission (1993), 'An open and structured dialogue between the Commission and special interest groups', OJ 93/C63/02.

19   This was suggested as reasonable by Coombes, even in 1970 (p. 88).

20   Donelly (1993, p. 77).

21   This example was given by Hay (1989, p. 28).

22   See chapter four on the organisational aspects of the college and the cabinets.

23   Peterson (1995, p. 74).

24   The *chef de cabinet* meetings were previously chaired by Emile

Noël, the former Secretary-General.

25   Peterson (1972, p. 125).

26   This is a point that was made by Coombes in (1970, p. 257).

27   See Michelmann (1978b, p. 485).

28   Donelly (1993, p. 79).

29   Michelmann (1978a, p. 16).

30   For more on the specific case of competition policy see Cini (1994), Goyder (1988) and Swann (1983).

31   Coombes (1970, pp. 291 and 326–7).

32   Docksey and Williams (1994, p. 120).

33   Delors himself was very interested in the issue, and as noted in chapter two, argued vehemently for it to be considered seriously in the Treaty.

34   For a detailed breakdown of the procedures in each of the committee types, see Bradley (1992).

35   Case 302/87, the so-called 'comitology' case. *European Parliament v. Council* [1985] ECR 5616, 5627.

36   Bradley (1992, p. 720).

37   Bradley (1992).

38   Westlake (1994a, p. 1.1).

39   There is no space here to provide a comprehensive assessment of the main decision-making procedures. See Nugent (1994), for example, for further details.

40   Cases 138 and 139/79 of October 1980.

41   Nugent (1994, p. 309).

42   Westlake (1994a, p. 3.5).

43   See chapter four on the relationship between the Commission and the European Parliament.

44   Duff (1994a, p. 151–2).

45   Westlake (1994a, p. 2.1).

46   COREPER pass on the draft to national government departments. It is often at this stage that the press will get hold of a proposal, sometimes causing a storm over unforeseen implications.

47   Sasse (1977, p. 217).

48   Rometsch and Wessels (1994, p. 213).

49   Donelly (1993, p. 81).

50   Rometsch and Wessels (1994, p. 213).

51   COREPER I comprises the Deputy Permanent Representatives and deals with the more routine policy matters. COREPER II is more political and is comprised of the Permanent Representatives themselves. See Nugent (1994, p. 130).

52   Rometsch and Wessels (1994, p. 216).

53   Nugent (1994, p. 42).

54 This is according to Usher (1994).
55 Burley and Mattli (1993, p. 71).
56 *Ibid.* (p. 51).
57 *Ibid.* (p. 64).

THE NORTHERN COLLEGE
LIBRARY

BARNSLEY

6

Jacques Delors and the internal management of the Commission

When Jacques Delors arrived in Brussels in 1985, he inherited the leadership of an institution that was not only failing to perform its original function as motor of the European integration process, it was also suffering from an organisational malaise that was proving an insuperable barrier to the emergence of the institution's leadership capacity. Problems such as the inflexibility of formal procedures, the stultification of hierarchies and the inadequacy of horizontal communication flows were nothing new, of course. Commentators, such as David Coombes, writing as far back as the end of the 1960s, had highlighted the self-same characteristics.[1] There had, since then, been little real attempt to reform the Commission, however, with the changes that had been made only serving to tinker with specific and usually intra-DG structural deficiencies. In addition, the departmentalisation of the Commission appeared to be intensifying. Again, this was not a new phenomenon. But it did seem to be more worrying now, as individual Commission services increasingly followed different policy directions, many of which were potentially or even blatantly contradictory. It is hardly surprising, then, that the reputation of the Commission as an overly bureaucratic, byzantine and inefficient organisation was one increasingly difficult to contradict.

One might imagine, then, that in 1985 the reform of the Commission would be high on the new President's agenda. This was far from the case. Administrative difficulties were to be 'skirted around' rather than resolved; and inefficiencies sidelined rather than removed. Institutional reform, for most of Delors's presidency, was not on the agenda at all. Instead, a variety of less arduous, less costly and more informal changes (in terms of time and other resources) were initiated, which, it was hoped, would serve the same ends. What these amounted to was an informal process of centralisation instituted by Delors and his personal staff, which served temporarily to offer a short cut to organisational effectiveness, whilst at the same time providing a solid foundation on which to construct a revitalised European Community and a new European Union. In examining the changes that took place after 1985 this chapter draws together some of the key themes of previous chapters to consider the internal Commission questions of leadership, organisation and process during the years of the Delors presidency.

Presidentialisation and personality politics

One of the most important prerequisites for establishing a more dynamic policy role for the Commission was the tackling of internal organisational constraints which had prevented the institution from projecting itself as a unified and coherent political actor. The starting-point was the presidency itself. Focusing on Delors, on his political style and personal characteristics, the introduction of personality politics into the supranational political arena was relatively new.[2] Many of Delors's predecessors had deliberately kept a low profile, staying out of the limelight so as to avoid antagonising national political elites. Delors changed the perception of the Commission presidency and the perception of the Commission itself, a shift that would later have a knock-on effect on member governments' own appointments to the college of commissioners. At the time, however, there was little to suggest that the apparently not-so-charismatic figure of Jacques Delors would come to symbolise and represent the federalisation of the EU in the way that he eventually did.

Delors's character certainly coloured the way in which he organised his work, and, by implication, this affected the position that the presidency of the Commission was soon to adopt. He was very much an 'ideas man', keen to grapple with complex political, economic and social concepts. Yet at the same time he was well able to grasp the finer details of technical policy issues, seeing the connections to be made between his conceptual thinking and technical problem-solving. It was his ability to retain at one and the same time a broad vision and strategic plan of action, whilst also dealing with

the nitty-gritty of day-to-day political life in a practical and pragmatic way that made him well suited to the job of Commission President. So although Delors seemed to possess a clear picture of the
Europe he wanted, his approach was essentially a reformist one,
dealing with specific projects in a step-by-step manner.[3]

It is said that Delors spent a certain period every day reading and
thinking (although he often bemoaned the fact that there was never
enough time for this). This may be considered a rather unusual
occupation for a political actor. But what Delors was not good at,
or did not enjoy, he delegated. He did not presume to act as a manager of Commission affairs, leaving this to his *chef de cabinet*, Pascal
Lamy. It became Lamy's job to 'protect' the President from too
heavy a schedule which would have meant that he would have been
unable to fulfil his key function – innovation.[4] As a result, Lamy
often ended up standing in for Delors in internal Commission business. The President, in the meantime, was more concerned with the
Commission's external face, hoping to project a unified institutional
image to the outside world. This became all the more important in
view of the Community's developing international role.

There is a certain irony in that Delors never really considered
himself a politician, in spite of being generally recognised as such
(and as a very skilful one at that) by many national leaders. On the
contrary, much of Delors's rhetoric revolved around the term 'management', as describing the role he was to perform.[5] Strangely perhaps, Delors did not seem very concerned about his media image,
although he did take personal offence when verbally attacked in
public, whether by politicians or by journalists. In such cases, he had
a long memory and was not particularly forgiving.[6] Yet as President
of the Commission, Delors was severely constrained in what he
could do. These formal constraints did not mean that the Commission presidency could not change *informally*, however.[7] Indeed,
'For effective leadership to occur, a president must find ways to
acquire power which he or she is not formally entitled to have'.[8]
The fact that the President had few formal powers over and above
those of any member of the college did not pose serious problems
for Delors. It did not hamper his plan of turning the rather weak
position of President into one that symbolised Commission authority and influence both within the institution and outside it.

In spite of formal constraints, then, Delors instituted a process of
'presidentialisation', as a means of mobilising Commission

resources in favour of his own vision of an integrated Europe. He tended to stay out of the maelstrom of internal Commission politics, however, so as not to be tainted by it. As such, he often remained above the administrative wrangles that Lamy coped with so forcefully, even though everyone involved was well aware that Lamy always acted with Delors's blessing. The increasing presidentialisation of Delors's role had much more to do with the image he presented to the outside world than with how he was perceived inside the Commission. Indeed although there was a great deal of respect for Delors amongst Commission staff, at least during the first half of his presidency, he was not particularly well liked. The enhancement of his role and standing externally was in part the result of the length of his presidency. It was, as such, not until his second term that his international political stature increased. Indeed, it has been said that Mrs Thatcher's biggest mistake when dealing with the Commission was to have allowed Delors to speak for Europe. This was exactly the position he wanted to be in. Delors's skills in managing, or at least influencing the essentially intergovernmental forum of the European Council are well documented. His ability to make himself heard during summit meetings arose from his skill at explaining complex issues in clear terms, whilst at the same time arguing vehemently for his own case. Indeed, on many occasions it was left to Delors to introduce European Council discussions, and as such to set the terms of the debate.

The role of the Delors cabinet

The presidentialisation process that occurred during the late 1980s cannot be understood in isolation, as it is clear that Delors's personal staff, too, were crucial to the changes taking place within the Commission at this time.[9] Indeed, the role performed by the Delors cabinet in the Commission's revitalisation was 'the best-kept secret in the story'.[10] Individuals are important here, none more so than Pascal Lamy, Delors's second-in-command and *chef de cabinet*.[11] But others too were instrumental in serving and servicing the broad objectives of the Commission President, slotting neatly into the administrative framework envisaged by Lamy for that purpose.

Lamy's role was generally understated. While Delors hogged the limelight, Lamy seemingly understudied the reorganisation of the Commission along lines with which he was familiar. But Lamy's input should not be negated just because it occurred behind the scenes. The relationship between the two men was complementary, and became fundamental to the running of the Commission after 1985, such that, 'Delors was the commander-in-chief: visionary, intellectual and a statesman. Without his contributions, little or nothing would have occurred. Lamy was the general who drilled the divisions into line'.[12]

Lamy was *chef de cabinet* to Delors from his appointment in 1985 to May 1994 when he left the Commission to take up a senior banking post back in France. To many, and even to some commissioners, he was a rather frightening figure. It was clear that he held more power that anyone else in the Commission, second only to Delors himself. His quick brain and his efficiency were awesome and almost legendary.[13] The fact that he expected everyone else to work as hard as he did, forgoing time with their families and social engagements, made for a cabinet that was consistently one step ahead of all other cabinets and services. Indeed, the general understanding was that the President's cabinet *had* to be better informed than any other group, if the dynamism of the Commission and the leadership of the President were to be maintained. This had its disadvantages, though. The problem of 'burn-out' amongst cabinet members was common, with many staff failing to see out more than one term of office before moving to a less stressful and less time-consuming job of work.

Although Lamy agreed with Delors about most of his strategy towards European integration, he was much more of a free marketeer than was the President, though this did not prevent the relationship between the two men from being extremely close. With Lamy given responsibility for administration, he sought to shape the Commission to complement Delors's way of working, whilst also taking into consideration the inherent structural and procedural weaknesses therein. This side of Commission life was of little interest to the President. It was important to him that the Commission functioned smoothly, but this was not an end in itself. So, while Delors concentrated on 'ideas', Lamy was much more concerned with management, control and 'power'.[14] Whereas Lamy's strength lay in his ability to delegate, one could justifiably argue that Delors's influence stemmed from his ability to keep a check on an extremely wide range of issues, focusing on the big European picture, as much as on the detail.

The starting-point for a more effective managerial system within the Commission was the more effective operation of the cabinet itself. Functions divided amongst Delors's personal staff were fairly rigid as was the informal yet soon-to-be deeply ingrained hierarchical structure of the cabinet. It was put together very much with Delors as its focus. The Commission President was not much of a team player, however, and this indirectly imposed his own solitary working practices on his staff. Although some senior members of the cabinet had high-level overview roles, the majority were responsible for very specific policy areas, and hardly ever had anything to do with matters beyond their specialism. However, the cabinet members flourished, as they soon came to possess a virtual monopoly of control over their own particular field of expertise. They could also be assured that when disputes arose between them and the services responsible for their policy fields, they could rely on the backing of Delors and Lamy in all matters.[15]

The main objective of this approach to the organisational life of the cabinet was to provide Delors with a continual flow of intellectual fodder. Cabinet staff were expected to produce reams of notes and detailed briefing papers to help Delors place his general ideas about society and economy into a practical context. They were aware that Delors's starting-point for dealing with any specific policy issue was conceptual or theoretical, so that rather than taking a deductive approach to problem-solving, the parameters in which the debate was begun were clearly defined from the outset.[16] This made life easier for the cabinet members as they sought to develop their own practical solutions to problems in line with Delors's earlier thoughts on the subject. Hence a prerequisite for the effective working of this system was that the cabinet members should be of like mind to Delors, or that they should at least be amenable to the basic underlying values he espoused. Without a doubt, they were worked extremely hard. A lot was expected of the cabinet in terms of both the quality and quantity of their work. To some extent this same work ethic applied to all senior staff throughout the Commission. Very early on, Delors had tried to encourage a commitment to hard work as a way of countering accusations that Commission staff were overpaid and underworked. For example, Delors tried to ensure that no one went on holiday unless their desks had been cleared before their departure.[17]

But although the internal dynamics and organisation of the cabinet was important, it also had a wider role to play in the internal life of the Commission. The Commission services had to be convinced, if possible, of the validity of the Delors line on the policies they administered, for example. This was not always an easy task, as DGs usually had their own extremely fixed notions of how their policy area should be run. Not only was it important to convince, where possible, key operators within the services, it was also crucial that the lines taken by commissioners and their cabinets should be consistent with the stance likely to be taken by Delors and his staff. Given the wide variety of political backgrounds from which the commissioners were drawn, this too was not an easy task. Although their relations with the services and with the other cabinets were not always harmonious, the members of the President's cabinet were nevertheless respected both for their grasp of policy detail and for their efficiency. Indeed their reputations reached almost mythical levels. 'The Delors team was everywhere co-ordinating, arguing, and insisting upon ideas, generating proposals, monitoring the work of others, obliging institutional "flexibility" and simply presuming to get its way.'[18]

However, the tactics used by the Delors cabinet to get its own way at times verged on bullying and coercion, giving the cabinet led by Lamy the reputation of an 'elite squad of commandos, dedicated to enforcing the President's will'.[19] This, not surprisingly, became a rather delicate matter. So as not to implicate Delors in the rather underhand manoeuvres that would not infrequently serve to undermine the position of an obstreperous commissioner, individual cabinet members (and Lamy in particular) were often entrusted with the job of dealing with what were simply considered to be awkward administrative problems. Although Delors was rarely present on such occasions, it would have been naive to imagine that his personal staff were acting without his or at least Lamy's tacit approval. The figure of Delors was assumed to be behind most of the shadier activities of the cabinet.

The enhancement of the role of Delors's cabinet, especially in the first term of the Delors presidency, was important in that it allowed Delors himself time to think about the bigger European picture. It was also just one element in a broader process of centralisation. Across the board, there was criticism, especially from director-general level, that the status of the commissioners' personal staffs was growing, largely at the expense of the Commission services. Many cabinet members were employed at a lower grade than the director-generals and their senior staff, though the Commission officials were often forced to deal with them as equals or superiors. To many director-generals, cabinet members were little more than political 'cowboys', with little 'real' knowledge of how the Commission worked, or of the policy area for which they were ultimately responsible.[20]

As a result of this growth in the status of the President's cabinet, the *chef de cabinet* meetings, which did much of the groundwork for the meeting of the college,[21] also became more pivotal. Later in his presidency Delors and Lamy tried to play down this development so as to respond to some of the director-generals' concerns. Indeed, after 1992, even the grip of the Delors cabinet loosened in line with the generally more cautious approach taken by Delors. As the Delors decade neared its end, long-standing high-profile cabinet members began to leave. François Lamoureux, Delors's forceful and federalist deputy *chef de cabinet*[22] left in July 1991; others, Joly Dixon and Jean-Charles Leygues, for example, also moved on after seeing through the Maastricht process, though it was not until the middle of 1994 that Pascal Lamy himself was to leave.

The command-control approach applied

If the fundamental weakness of the Commission was seen to lie in its inability to project a unified view of its objectives, then the most important administrative task of Delors and his cabinet was to provide the Commission with strong leadership. In addition, some sort of centripetal organisational process was required to consolidate this new era. Co-ordination was to be of a top-down or vertical nature, with Delors seeking above all to run a 'tight ship', side-tracking inefficiency and ignoring dissent. His success would depend upon his control over individual DGs, as well as over the college. In many cases, the absence of countervailing leadership within the Commission meant that this was not difficult to achieve. However, DG IV, which dealt with competition policy and which was headed effectively first by Peter Sutherland (from 1985 to 1989) and then by Sir Leon Brittan (from 1989 to the end of 1992) was an exception. Its deserved reputation for being one of the few services that continued to possess a measure of autonomy meant that it was a continual source of irritation to the Commission President.

Naturally, the main instrument for implementing this process of centralisation was the Delors cabinet. But this was not the only means of command and control at Delors's disposal. An opportunity for tightening up the relationship between the Commission's Secretariat-General and the presidency came in 1987 with the retirement of Emile Noël, the long-standing head of the SG, a larger than life character who had run the service in a quasi-independent fashion since the setting up of the Community. Noël's replacement, David Williamson, a former British civil servant did not seek to continue the high-profile role adopted by his predecessor, preferring to concentrate on more neutral administrative functions of co-ordination and information-sharing. As such, the SG became the administrative base of Delors's presidential regime.

Delors also attempted to monopolise expertise within the Commission. He did this in a number of ways. He set up (in 1989) an internal Commission think-tank, the *Cellule de Prospective* (Forward Studies Unit) which was headed by Jérome Vignon, a personal friend. This unit's job was to provide working papers on long-term priority policy areas for Delors's own perusal.[23] In the past, this was work which would only have been done by the Commission's services. But in forming an alternative organisational source of ideas, alongside his cabinet, Delors created a new channel for information and was thus able to circumvent many of the ingrained policy stances that emerged time after time from certain DGs. At the same time, Delors was also able to avoid dealing with services he considered inefficient, or whose policy lines did not coincide with his own. Informal networks were established as a means of bypassing the more ineffective or reluctant formal hierarchies. This proved a real source of contention for officials who felt, justifiably, that their authority was being undermined. But Delors had no control over the choice of commissioners with whom he had to work, and it is clear that their effectiveness (and the compatibility of their ideas with those of the President) did vary considerably. Delors developed some skill in marginalising ineffective commissioners, whilst profiting from the intellectual weight of others.[24] The standards within individual cabinets were also variable, making it difficult to achieve consistency across the spectrum of Commission policies. Delors sought to get round this by developing contacts throughout the Commission with staff who could be trusted to follow the Delors line. At the same time, he chose to work closely with individuals who would be dynamic and innovative in their particular areas of expertise. The Delors cabinet became increasingly involved in the replacement of senior officials at director-general level and even below. The newly appointed head of the Legal Service, M. Dewost, was for example a friend of Delors. It was claimed that after his appointment the LS was less inclined to oppose Delors-backed proposals.[25] Examples such as this are not uncommon. It is hardly surprising that these Delors-sponsored appointees should support the Delors policy approach – after all these newcomers were not only hand-picked; they also owed their positions to Delors personally.

This network was crucial when it came to the drafting of key policy documents. The Delors package of budgetary plans of 1987, the proposals of the Commission on EMU and the plans put forward for aid to Eastern Europe[26] were all the work of a close-knit group of trusted officials, working outside the framework of the Commission hierarchy, and in some cases outside the control or oversight of the college of commissioners, although this was more difficult to sustain. However, the college could be 'tamed' by various means: the mobilisation of agreement in advance of college meetings and the pre-packaging of proposals before a vote, for example.[27] In spite of the existence of an effective network of supporters, there were times when Delors, Lamy and other members of the President's cabinet would act as surrogates for ineffective commissioners, initiating a *de facto* take-over of a portfolio. Reluctance to allow commissioners any freedom of manoeuvre went further, however, with the agendas of the weekly Commission meetings tightly controlled by Lamy. Commissioners hoping to propose an item were often encouraged to withdraw it at the last minute. It is hardly surprising then that many commissioners resented the command and control approach that Delors applied. Moreover, the fact that he kept himself to himself, rarely consulting his colleagues, did not help matters. Indeed, fellow commissioners often found it very difficult simply to get to talk to Delors. And it was clear that in many cases, Delors felt a certain disdain for those with whom he was forced to work. This attitude was particularly marked in the period after the Maastricht summit when the President was keen to ensure that the Commission and the commissioners kept a low profile. The outspoken manner of the environment commissioner, Carlo Ripa de Meana, at the time, was therefore a source of great annoyance to Delors.[28]

But in spite of evidence that commissioners' portfolios were being usurped by Delors, cabinets across the board continued to play an increasingly important role within the Commission. As a consequence, the director-generals, whose roles *vis-à-vis* the commissioners had often been ill defined, felt their powers further slipping away. The average size of the cabinets increased in 1989 from five to six senior staff, allowing them greater scope to act as shadows of their services.[29] This approach to Commission management is very much in a French administrative tradition that would have been familiar to Delors and to Lamy, both of whom had had direct experience of it.[30] By importing this French approach towards the informal organisation of administrative life to Brussels, the trend begun by Monnet and by Emile Noël, that is, the mimicry of the French model at the European level, was to continue.

As time went on there came to be a blurring of the boundaries between the President's cabinet, the SG, the *Cellule de Prospective* and, more generally, the informal Delors network. Key players, such as David Williamson, were closely tied into what came to be known rather disparagingly as the 'Delors Mafia'. Yet, the existence of such a network is perhaps part and parcel of the transformation of the Commission's role over the early years of Delors's presidency. Where there *was* criticism in the early years, it was not that Delors leapfrogged over formal Commission structures that had been labelled as inefficient well before Delors's arrival in Brussels, but that his network was largely a French-speaking one.[31] Whether, during his ten years in office, Delors acted as an advocate for French interests was an issue often raised at the time. There are clearly differences of opinion on this. There were certainly occasions on which Delors backed the French government against his Commission colleagues and against the usual Commission conventions, especially where matters of French state aid were concerned. But it is debatable whether this demonstrated a blatant adherence to the French line, or whether Delors was in fact displaying his pro-interventionist pro-competitiveness, which just happened to fit a French case. There is less-publicised evidence of Delors backing similar schemes benefiting Italian industry, for example. Indeed, it was not unusual for commissioners to adopt a more nationalistic line in these sorts of cases. Perhaps Delors was just acting as 'commissioner' rather than 'President' on such occasions.

Morale within the Commission was to be crucial if Delors was to maintain the support of his officials during this period of change and hard work. The task of filling in the details of the White Paper on the internal market was a momentous task, for example. And there was subsequently a huge amount of work required in advance of the IGCs and as a result of other new policy initiatives. All this fell on top of the routine administrative work that continued to mount up as before. The increased workload imposed upon the Commission's services had to be compensated for in some way. It was expected, however, that the benefits for staff would lie in their association with a revitalised Commission. As such, individual morale would emerge from an ever-growing sense of institutional status. But this was a rather vain and optimistic hope. Although Delors was respected in the early years of his presidency, a more activist Commission role was not enough to sustain the unquestioning commitment of all senior officials. The idealism and Europeanism of the Hallstein Commission could not be revived in the 1980s and 1990s.

The failure of Delors to sustain morale within the Commission administration meant that his staff were quick to blame their President when the Commission's involvement in the integration process began to wane. As the Delors decade progressed, there was an all-pervading sense of disillusionment both internally, and with the way the Commission was perceived externally. The continual onslaught from certain national presses did not help matters. Generally, there was a feeling that Delors's failure to invoke any team spirit had in the end come to exacerbate the weaknesses of the Commission, so that although 'Mr Delors's achievement has been to impose some top-down cohesion on the bureaucracy',[32] it later became clear that this came at a heavy cost.

Reform of the Commission?

The need to make permanent changes to the formal structure of the Commission was on the Community agenda long before Delors's arrival in Brussels. It was clear from the very start, however, that this was not considered a priority by the new Commission President. As restructuring could be little more than a means to an end, it was soon very clear that that end, the revitalisation of the European integration process as a means of reviving European society, economy and polity, could be achieved without the upheavals of a major project of institutional reform. This gap in the Delors programme has since made the legacy of his presidency uncertain. For although he and his team were able to find alternatives to formal Commission reform, it was clear that informal networks could not necessarily survive his departure.[33]

Nevertheless, it would be unfair to claim that no reform took place under Delors. In addition to those highlighted above, changes were also made to the structure of certain DGs during this period. For example, the organisation of DG I, the external relations department, altered dramatically over the course of the Delors presidency.[34] Efforts were also made to improve obvious areas of weakness, such as horizontal communication between the services. Instead of cabinets continuing to deal with co-ordination, the job became the preserve of the SG. Likewise, later in his presidency, Delors tried to respond to the specific concerns of his director-generals, by allowing them to meet as a group and have greater control over the organisation of their own departments. But in all these cases, and in the numerous other examples of minor reform, there was nothing to suggest a strategic vision.

The closest the Commission came to major reform was after 1991. The growing fears that improvements in Commission activism were unlikely to continue after Delors's departure, provoked what came to be known as the 'screening exercise', a service-by-service evaluation of the internal operation of Commission structures and procedures, orchestrated by Pascal Lamy. This was led by an internal Commission Task Force which included David Williamson, Carlo Trojan, who was the Deputy Secretary-General, and other members of the Delors team. The logic of such an investigative process at this particular time was clear. As the burden of Commission work shifted from policy formulation to policy implementation, formal internal procedures and their effectiveness became more and more of an issue. Whereas the Commission had had a relatively good record in applying itself to solving strategic and policy questions, it had had less success when it came actually to putting those policies into practice and ensuring that member states implemented them in line with the commitments they had made. This had to be addressed.

The process of assessing each DG was undertaken by a small team which included officials at the grade of director. Over the course of the investigation, over 700 interviews took place.[35] Matters arising covered aspects of Commission life such as the duplication of tasks between services; budgeting and evaluation for common policies; and internal communication. There were clearly important conclusions to be drawn from this research, although many of them seemed to involve 'stating of the obvious' for those already in the know about how the Commission operated.

The main priority was the anomaly in staffing levels within individual DGs. As services guarded their complements jealously, it was almost impossible for the gap between overstaffing in some DGs and understaffing in others to be resolved. The screening process concluded that there were too many DGs and services in the first place, and that the division of labour between them was often rather opaque. This had led to embarrassing and pointless demarcation disputes. Standards and reputations varied enormously amongst services, leading to associated problems of inconsistency and ineffectiveness. As a result, co-ordination had to be the key to resolving many of the problems identified.

The recommendations that were made at the end of the screening process, had they been implemented, would have led to a major reorganisation of the Commission. Within this, there would also have been more attention paid to specific intra-DG problems. Lack of resources was, not surprisingly, one major bone of contention. But most important of all was the realisation that the process of centralisation that had been put into effect informally over the course of the late 1980s had not, under the surface, countered the process of fragmentation earlier identified within the Commission. As one of Delors's senior cabinet members stated at this time: 'There isn't satisfactory co-ordination in any area of Commission activity, and the "culture of the DG or of dossiers" takes precedence over Commission culture'.[36] Clearly, co-ordination is not just about structures and procedures, but it is also about the particular mind-set of officials. Delors's team had tackled many aspects of institutional life, but cultural questions were rarely considered.

'Screening' was little more than a means to an end, however, in that it allowed the public airing of organisational problems which inside the Commission were common knowledge. The ultimate objective had to be the creation of a momentum towards reform, a momentum that in fact never materialised under Delors. Maastricht was the first excuse for inaction, perhaps justifiably. And after Maastricht, the question of reorganisation once again seemed to take second place to other administrative and policy tasks. There is a certain irony in this, as the strategic role previously played out by the Commission began to diminish post-1991. The argument that the ineffectiveness of the Commission in the later years of the Delors presidency was in part due to the constraints placed upon it by the institutional system,[37] should certainly be taken seriously.

Conclusion

The centralisation of the Commission that took place after 1985 has to be understood as a process that was largely 'a fiendishly complicated set of informal practices with new links continually added to remedy weaknesses as they emerged'.[38] This does not detract from the fact that it was also largely effective, at least during the first and more activist half of the Delors decade. The changes that occurred involved much more than the politicisation or presidentialisation of the upper echelons of the Commission; they also rested upon the orderly and controlled administration of the Commission machinery as a prerequisite of the substantive metamorphosis of the Commission's role in the European integration and policy process. So while the shift that took place over this period was said to transform the top of the Commission hierarchy from an *administration de gestion* to an *administration de mission*,[39] it is clear that in fact both elements were present simultaneously.

But while this process was effective for a short period, it also served to provoke a sense of alienation and disillusionment amongst officials and commissioners whose formal roles within the hierarchy were persistently undermined. Indeed, there is a certain irony in the fact that while the French newspaper, *Libération*, claimed that Delors's political ideas were based on the building of compromises through negotiation, there is little evidence of this approach being applied to his relations internally within the Commission.[40]

Nevertheless, the changes that did take place allowed Delors and his trusted network of officials to keep a tight hold, not only of general Commission strategy, but also of the minutiae of policy content. Instead of devoting energy to the institutional reform of the Commission, a matter that would have certainly been time-consuming and costly, ways were found to sideline and leapfrog over the inefficiencies and rigidities that had previously acted as barriers to the evolution of a coherent Commission strategy. Even though it was recognised that these *ad hoc* measures should serve only as temporary solutions to recurrent problems, there was little political will and no firm commitment within the upper echelons of the Commission for overarching institutional reform. The consequences are potentially immense. It is now for Jacques Santer to tackle these institutional issues, either by reinventing informal networks in his own image to shadow the less effective formal ones, as Delors himself did, or to follow through a fully-fledged commitment to the structural reform of the Commission. The concluding chapters below review the question of institutional reform in light of changes in emphasis that occurred over the first months of the Santer presidency.

Notes

1 Coombes (1970).

2 Both Hallstein and Jenkins also relied on personality politics, though perhaps to a lesser extent than Delors. See chapter two above.

3 Ross (1995, p. 29).

4 *Ibid.* (p. 64).

5 Middlemas (1995, p. 219). Delors talked specifically about the 'management of democracy'.

6 There are many accounts of Delors barring journalists from press conferences or personal interviews after they had written rather critical reports.

7 Middlemas (1995, p. 214).

8 Ross (1995, p. 27).

9 Middlemas (1995, ch. 6, fn. 10) notes that the cabinet was largely made up of French staff, but that there was also one German, one British and one Dutch official.

10 Ross (1995, p. 34).

11 *The Economist*, 3 March 1990.

12 Ross (1995, p. 34).

13 *The Economist* on 3 March 1990 wrote of Lamy: 'He has a piercing mind and a forceful, occasionally explosive style'. It also noted that commissioner Sutherland labelled him 'Delors's exocet'.

14 Grant (1994, p. 100).

15 *Ibid.* (p. 97).

16 Middlemas (1995, p. 217) talks of the 'delphic hints' given by Delors which were to be fleshed out by the cabinet through a process of argumentation.

17 *The Economist*, 27 July 1985.

18   Ross (1995, p. 158).

19   Grant (1994, p. 86).

20   *The Economist*, 25 March 1989.

21   See also chapter four on the meetings of the college.

22   Lamoureux was the author of much of the text of the SEA. He also drafted many of the Commission's submissions to the political union IGC in the run up to the Maastricht summit.

23   Papers produced by the *Cellule* included those on the effects of the internal market; and on the links between technology, industrial and trade policies. See Middlemas (1995, p. 225).

24   *Ibid.* (pp. 218 and 220) mentions Vasso Papandreou, Manuel Marin and Bruce Millan as those who were often sidelined.

25   Grant (1994, p. 101).

26   See chapter three on Delors's policies during these years.

27   Middlemas (1995, p. 223).

28   On the Ripa-Delors rift, see Grant (1994, p. 108).

29   Ross (1995, p. 161); Grant (1994, p. 112) and Edwards and Spence (1994, p. 46).

30   Delors had less experience of the French administrative state, at least from an elitist (*énarque*) perspective. He had not pursued a formal career in administration, taking a less conventional career path. See Grant (1994), amongst others, on Delors's early (pre-Commission) life and career.

31   Middlemas (1995, pp. 221–2).

32   *The Economist*, 3 March 1990.

33   See chapter seven below on the question of institutional reform.

34   DG I was divided into DG I and DG IA in 1992, for example.

35   Much of this section is taken from Ross (1995, p. 163).

36   *Ibid.* (p. 164).

37   Edwards and Spence (1994, p. 15).

38   Middlemas (1995, p. 223).

39   Edwards and Spence (1994, p. 14) make this distinction.

40   *Libération*, 8 November 1994.

III
Reform and adaptation

7

Institutional reform and the Santer Commission

The reform of the Commission has long been talked of as a matter of some urgency. From the 1960s on, there emerged a consensus based on a realisation that serious changes to the internal functioning of the institution were imperative, even though this consensus broke down quickly once substantive elements of reform were proposed. A spate of reports issued over the 1970s and 1980s confirmed this received wisdom, and proposed what often amounted to far-reaching recommendations which would, it was expected, improve the Commission's performance.[1] Yet, in spite of the reams of paper used up setting out these criticisms and laying down detailed proposals for action, few recommendations were acted upon. Commissioners and officials alike managed to live with the organisational weaknesses, and either seemed resigned to them (with a grumble), or, as in Delors's case, were able to sideline and ignore them, creating new informal structures and networks that were more manageable and more flexible. The first few months of the new 1995 European Commission were dominated by thoughts of the coming IGC, to begin a year or so later. As such, sloganeering about the importance of institutional reform preoccupied much of the new Commission President's time. All the same, it remains to be seen whether the Santer Commission will have either the political will or clout to introduce fundamental change. This chapter reviews the prospects for institutional reform and introduces the 1995 Commission and its President.

Jacques Santer: a successor for Delors

The appointment of a new Commission President to replace Jacques Delors, who had earlier announced his departure, posed a number of problems both for the Commission and for the national governments. On one hand, governments could try to use this transition to weaken the Commission's position in the run-up to the IGC. Not surprisingly, the activism of the Delors Commission over the previous decade had made some governments, especially the British, wary of acceding too readily to a reputedly *federalist* candidate. On the other hand, however, there was a well-worn procedural route to be followed. And although in principle all governments had a veto over any presidential candidate, in practice the application of the *common accord* principle meant that there would be subtle intergovernmental (as well as supranational) pressures at work in the process of appointing a new Commission President. These pressures came to dominate the early summer months of 1994. The outcome of what many considered at the time to be a grave Community crisis was the appointment of Jacques Santer, formerly the Prime Minister of Luxembourg.

It has often been said that after the experience of a strong high-profile Commission President, governments will invariably appoint a weaker, more consensual figure. This piece of accepted wisdom has had a lot to answer for. For whether it accurately sums up the motivation of the EU's national leaders, the fact that it was perceived to be the case by most of the European media meant that whoever was to be appointed as Commission President after Delors would be assessed from this starting-point. However, judgements as to the likely effectiveness of Commission Presidents early in their term of office (or indeed before they take up their posts) often bear little relation to the assessments made at the end of their presidency. We need only remember that Delors himself was originally a compromise candidate back in 1984.

The events leading up to Jacques Santer's appointment were certainly controversial. The candidate originally proposed, Jean-Luc Dehaene, the Belgian Prime Minister, had had his nomination informally endorsed by both Mitterrand and Kohl. And, at the start of 1994, it was clear that most of the other member states were prepared to go along with this. The British government, largely to appease the Euro-sceptic lobby within the Conservative Party, opposed Dehaene's nomination, and supported their own candidate, Sir Leon Brittan. Dehaene was formally vetoed by the British government at the European Council meeting in Corfu in June 1994, causing a panic within German governmental circles, as it was the Germans who held the EU presidency at the time. There was a frantic flurry of activity[2] before Jacques Santer was proposed as an alternative compromise candidate.

As for Santer, he claims that when he heard that Dehaene was likely to be vetoed, he thought he might indeed be in with a chance of taking his place. This seemed ever more likely as the German Chancellor continued to argue that the next President should come from one of the small member states and should be a christian democrat. Santer, it was said, was attending a wedding when he heard that Kohl wanted to see him immediately at the G7 (Group of Seven) summit in Naples. He says he knew straight away what was about to happen.[3] When the news broke of agreement over Santer's appointment, the press reports were predictable. Why was Santer acceptable to the British government when Dehaene was not? And what were the substantive political differences between the two men? There was much speculation. Santer, throughout, stressed the similarities, claiming, for example, that: 'Mr Dehaene and I come from the same political family and we have the same commitment to European union.'[4] The British Prime Minister, by contrast, stressed what he considered to be a key difference. Whilst he acknowledged that both men might label themselves as federalists, Santer 'is a federalist in the sense that he is a decentraliser and a great believer in subsidiarity',[5] whereas Dehaene (implicitly) was not. Few seriously believed that this distinction really held up. Dehaene had clearly been sacrificed on a British Euro-sceptic altar.

Even so, that Santer had been acceptable to the British government as a *compromise* candidate led to a lot of speculation about whether he would be able to provide effective leadership not just within the Commission but for the wider Union. The implications of weak leadership would be clear. Without a forceful and assertive President, the Commission would revert to cautious pre-1985 mode, leaving national governments to battle it out amongst themselves during the 1996 IGC, something some member states at least would not be too unhappy about. This rather simplistic assessment ignores a great deal, however. Firstly, it ignores the fact that Delors and his commissioners had themselves been playing a rather cautious political game since at least 1992. Delors's political style and approach had altered to fit the prevailing mood, what he called 'l'air du temps'.[6] It also ignores Santer himself. Was he really the helpless figure much of the media made him out to be?

Jacques Santer was born in Wasserbillig in Luxembourg in 1937. Like many Luxembourg nationals he chose to pursue his higher education in France, first in Strasbourg and later in Paris where he received his doctorate in law and a certificate from the Institut d'Etudes Politiques (the 'Sciences Po'). Initially as a practising lawyer, he worked with the social christian party and was soon heavily involved in Luxembourg politics, first as party secretary to the social christians and then in a variety of posts, including Secretary of State for Culture, General Secretary and finally, Prime Minister between 1989 and 1994. His political experience is extensive, stretching beyond the small world of Luxembourg politics. Many of his posts have involved international financial and banking matters. These have included responsibility for the Luxembourg Finance Ministry (between 1979–84 and 1989–94), Governor of the World Bank (1984–89), Governor of the International Monetary Fund (IMF) (1989–95) and Governor of the European Bank for Reconstruction and Development (EBRD) from 1991 to 1995.

More specifically, his experience of European politics is also worthy of note. Not only has Santer been involved twice with the presidency of the European Council, first in 1985, and then in 1991 as Prime Minister, but he was also, for a period of four years in the late 1970s, a member of the EP, spending two of those years as a vice-president. And in addition, he held the post of president of the European People's Party between 1987 and 1990. Although Luxembourg is a very small country, a micro-state indeed, this does not belie the fact that Santer has had a wealth of political experience. This did not necessarily make him a heavyweight candidate, but he certainly did not come to the post as a political novice. In domestic politics he seemed well liked. He was, for example, known in one local satirical newspaper as 'Jacques Champagne' or 'Jacques digestif' as he was often seen 'glass-in-hand' at public meetings.[7]

In terms of his political and personal style, Santer has been described on many occasions (and often by himself) as a convivial and affable, but tenacious, operator. He has argued that although he recognises that he can be rather opinionated at times, his methods are essentially pragmatic ones. As such, he stresses that his political style is not at all authoritarian.[8] When it comes to problem-solving his approach seems to be one of cool, calculating reflection. One political opponent has noted, for example, that Santer never acts emotionally when it comes to taking decisions. Rather, he approaches problems in a relaxed fashion, listening to advice, and 'sitting' on issues, in much the same way as Helmut Kohl does. Indeed Kohl and Santer are long-time friends.

Long experience of working in coalition governments has given Santer a feel for compromise-building, according to his former foreign minister, Jacques Poos. His 'reputation as a pragmatist and a negotiator rather than an ideologue or a man of ideas'[9] is likely to stand him in good stead when it comes to performing the consensus-building role central to much of the Commission's work. This will no doubt be important given the Commission's mediatory position in the 1996 IGC. There is some irony, however, in the fact that this consensual approach tends to be associated with weak rather than effective leadership.

If Santer's capacity for hard work was never in doubt, neither was his commitment to his new post. Indeed, in the run-up to the handover, the President-designate was travelling to Brussels twice a week, as well as continuing his prime ministerial duties at home. Intellectually, however, there have been doubts about his capacity for grand schemas and far-sighted projects. This is not a man with a vision such as possessed Delors. In this respect, Delors was perhaps exceptional. As such, it is not easy to glean any deep philosophical influences in the political thinking of Jacques Santer. Indeed, he has not been particularly forthcoming in laying out any philosophical framework for his presidency. In fact, he has even stated categorically that he has no avowed political model as such. While Santer claims nevertheless to have a very clear vision of society and a christian-democrat philosophy of life, what this means in practice is not clear. Instead, what comes across from his speeches and writings is a desire not to present a personal vision as did Delors, but to act as the voice of the collegiate Commission. In one interview, for example, when Santer was asked a direct question, he repeatedly argued that he, personally, was unable to answer, as it was for the collegiate Commission to take a decision on the matter. The contrast with Delors in this alone is notable.

A new President and a new college

The first real political test faced by Santer seemed to confirm the early press reports. Before the EP in July 1994, the President-designate gave a lacklustre performance, and was attacked on all sides by extremely critical MEPs.[10] John Palmer of *The Guardian* captured some of this feeling when he wrote that: 'A number of MEPs ... expressed alarm at the prospect of Mr Santer's appointment. They fear he does not have the intellectual capacity or political authority to lead the commission, especially in the run-up to the 1996 constitutional conference'. And to quote an MEP at the time: 'Santer's appointment would be little short of a disaster for the future of the European Union. He is a very weak leader from a very small country and is certain to be walked over by the British Conservatives'.[11] The general impression given to the EP seemed to justify the initial prejudice towards Santer. His nomination was accepted, but only within an extremely small margin: 260 in favour; 238 against; and 23 abstentions.[12] It is perhaps ironic that Santer was almost a victim of his own earlier commitment to EU democratisation. As Luxembourg Prime Minister during the pre-Maastricht negotiations, he had been adamant that the EP should be given more powers, especially in terms of its oversight of Commission appointments. As a result, though, Santer argued that he would have more legitimacy than any Commission president before him.[13] It was clear nevertheless that the treatment he received from MEPs and from the press made him more aware of parliamentary expectations. This would stand him in good stead during the investiture procedure early in 1995.

After his nomination, Santer had been asked to play down his federalist credentials for the British audience. Although he refused, he none the less gave a well-publicised speech condemning everything that was 'napoleonic' about Europe. He stressed that: 'for me, federalism is the opposite of centralism ... the European unity process should not usher in a Napoleonic Europe ... the more decentralised Europe is, the stronger it is'. This was vague enough both to be in line with his own thinking *and* to provide evidence of his anti-centralising bent to the British Euro-sceptics, though many, it has to be said, remained sceptical.

Santer's first real job as President-designate was the sharing out of portfolios amongst the commissioners nominated to the 1995 Commission. This was never an easy task for any incumbent president, and was made yet more difficult because there were now likely to be twenty-one instead of seventeen commissioners, the consequence of the imminent accession of Sweden, Austria, Finland and Norway. Santer chose to deal with this task as early as possible. The process was not without controversy, however, with squabbles occurring amongst returning commissioners on finding that their responsibilities had actually been reduced. The most acrimonious (and well-publicised) argument was between two of the 'heavyweight' commissioners, Sir Leon Brittan and Hans van den Broek over control of the foreign affairs portfolio.

Santer gathered the commissioners together for what was dubbed the 'weekend of the long knives', at the Chateau of Senningen in Luxembourg on 29 October 1994. He stressed to the new commissioners that it was essential that the collegiality of the Commission be maintained, and that no commissioner could 'own' a portfolio. And more specifically, Sir Leon Brittan, the senior British commissioner, was told that he could not have the precise portfolio he wanted – one which would include responsibility for Eastern Europe. This came close to provoking Brittan's resignation, which only the intervention of the British Prime Minister prevented, it seems. In spite of the publicity given to this affair, particularly in Britain, Santer dealt with the share-out of portfolios assertively, something which surprised many commentators (Figure 3). As such, he managed to impose some sort of authority on the commissioners from the very start. There was no guarantee, however, that this would have more far-reaching implications for his presidential style. Of course, the portfolio decisions had to be altered somewhat after the Norwegian referendum. The proposed Norwegian commissioner, already offered the fisheries job, was speedily removed from the list, his portfolio handed on to Italy's Emma Bonnino.

It is notable that Santer, like Delors, was sure to retain ultimate responsibility for a number of portfolios, namely monetary affairs, foreign policy and institutional/IGC matters. These would suggest the policy areas that would become Commission priorities. In addition to the formal allocation of portfolios, *groupes des commissaires* (commissioners groups) were also established. These mini-colleges were created in an effort to ensure that the actions of the college as a whole would be coherent and consistent. This was particularly important in policy areas that cut across the responsibilities of

Jacques Santer – President (Luxembourg): horizontal services; CFSP, monetary and institutional affairs
Sir Leon Brittan – vice-president (UK): external relations (North America and other developed countries)
Manuel Marin – vice-president (Spain): external relations (near and mid East/Med./Latin America)
Martin Bangemann (Germany): industry, IT and telecoms
Emma Bonnino (Italy): consumer policy: ECHO; fisheries
Ritt Bjerregaard (Denmark): environment; nuclear security
Edith Cresson (France): science, R&D, human resources, education, training youth
Joao de Deus Pinheiro (Portugal): external relations (ACP, S. Africa, Lomé)
Franz Fischler (Austria): agriculture/rural development
Padraig Flynn (Ireland): employment/social affairs
Anita Gradin (Sweden): immigration; JHA; anti-fraud; ombudsman
Neil Kinnock (Britain): transport/trans-European networks
Erkki Liikanen (Finland): budget; admin; translation & IT
Mario Monti (Italy): SEM; fin. services; customs and tax
Marcelino Orejo (Spain): culture/audio-visual policy, openness and information (EP & member states); institutional questions/IGC
Christos Papoutsis (Greece): energy; SMEs; tourism
Yves-Thibault de Silguy (France): econ. & financial, & monetary matters; credit & investment; statistical office
Hans van den Broek (Netherlands): external relations (CCEE and other European countries)
Karel Van Miert (Belgium): competition
Monika Wulf-Mathies (Germany): regions/COR, Cohesion Fund

Figure 3 The 1995 Commission
Source: Adapted from Bainbridge (1995)

several commissioners. It also helped co-ordinate policies that were of a horizontal rather than a vertical or sectoral nature. Six of these groups were set up: *External relations*: co-ordinating external Commission activity, especially when defining priorities for strategic action. This was to ensure that the Commission had a coherent across-the-board line when it came to dealing with actions in different geographical regions.[14] *Growth, competitiveness, employ-*

ment: co-ordinating the implementation of the White Paper on Growth, Competitiveness and Employment, as well as the White Paper on Social Policy.[15] *Trans-European networks*: this group's mandate was to make progress in getting rid of obstacles to trans-European networks, whilst ensuring that there was coherence between work in progress in different policy sectors – in particular in the fields of transport, energy and the environment.[16] The other three groups – on cohesion, the information society and equal opportunities – are self explanatory.[17]

The new Commission was relatively evenly balanced in party political terms. Although the social democrats and socialists could be considered the largest group (with nine commissioners), the conservatives, christian democrats, liberals and the one Italian radical together held a majority. However, this tells us little about potential policy outcomes, as commissioners do not always vote according to their supposed political colour. Yet the first impression seems confirmed when one considers that those on the political right tend to hold the most important jobs in the Santer Commission. The five women commissioners, now holding 25 per cent of the portfolios, gave the college the largest number and proportion of women ever. It is worth noting that the female commissioners hold the portfolios in environmental matters, regional policy, consumer policy, fisheries, science and R&D policy, immigration and home affairs and anti-fraud policy. It is perhaps not so surprising that none of the women commissioners holds the high-profile and much sought-after portfolios of foreign affairs, agriculture, competition, or industrial affairs, given that they are all new to the job.

Generally speaking, then, the commissioners appear to be a fairly good team, with several political heavyweights and experienced members. If the professional and political background of commissioners tells us anything about the status of the Commission in the eyes of national governments, it is interesting to note that the majority of commissioners have extensive political experience, as national deputies, as MEPs, or as ministers. In the latter category, seven commissioners have held posts either at prime ministerial, foreign or finance minister levels. This seems to reflect a recognition that commissioners must often play a high-profile political role, and (albeit implicitly) that national governments see it in their own interests to nominate high-profile members.

The EP was not so easily convinced of the calibre of the new

Commission, however. Although an investiture procedure was laid down in the Maastricht Treaty, there was, legally, no provision for the hearings that the Parliament had argued should precede it. However, after Santer's poor performance before the Parliament six months earlier, the new President saw acquiescence on this point a way of making amends with the MEPs. Because the three newcomers to the Commission could not be voted in before their countries officially joined the EU on 1 January, it was decided that the vote as a whole should be delayed, meaning of course that Delors would have to stay on for an extra few weeks.[18]

So as not to delay the work of the new Commission too much, the hearings were all held within a concentrated time-frame in January 1995. Prospective commissioners came before relevant committees of the Parliament and answered questions put to them largely on their European credentials; their attitude towards the Parliament; and their mastery of their new portfolios. Practice varied from committee to committee, which meant that it was difficult to draw general conclusions about what it was that the MEPs were looking for. Nevertheless, the results were decidedly patchy. While the majority of commissioners-to-be performed well before the committees, several were heavily criticised.[19] This is in spite of the fact that Santer had specifically tried to encourage his new team to be careful and to make good impressions.

Other than in one specific case, the heaviest criticisms befell the new commissioners. This, it has been suggested, reflects a bias within the system: firstly against those with no prior experience of the Commission or the EU; and secondly, potentially, against a Scandinavian political culture in which politicians are loath to make promises they are not sure that they can keep. The proposed environment commissioner, Ritt Bjerregaard, left a particularly bad taste in the mouths of the Environment Committee because of what some saw as an arrogant disregard for her portfolio, and a disdain for the EP. She had earlier been criticised for making a statement in a Danish newspaper to the effect that the EP was not a real parliament, though she said later that this comment had been misinterpreted. As a returning commissioner (and not a Scandinavian) Padraig Flynn, responsible for social affairs, had no such excuse for what many MEPs considered to be a very poor performance on his part. He was especially slated by some parliamentarians for what appeared to be a rather half-hearted commitment to equal opportunities issues. As a result, there were unsuccessful calls made for Flynn's portfolio to be altered.

All in all five prospective commissioners were considered to be unsatisfactory although, as some committee members later said, the opinions of the committees were more shaded and subtle than the comments of Klaus Hänsch, the EP President, gave them credit for in his well-publicised summary. Indeed, committees do not vote yes or no, but issue a short report for the benefit of MEPs and the Commission President. When it came to a vote on 18 January, 416 MEPs voted for the investiture of the Commission, with 103 against and 59 abstentions. Generally speaking, the main political groups (the christian democrats, socialists, conservatives, liberals and Forza Italia) voted in favour of the Commission, with the greens, extreme right and communists voting against. Compared to the previous July's vote on Santer's nomination, this was a great improvement. The vote was not just for Santer, of course. The EP cannot vote for or against individual commissioners, but must take or leave the whole – a process resting of the avowed collegiality of the Commission. In spite of this victory, the impression left was of a college of commissioners clearly on probation.

Commission priorities and strategies

The new Commission took their formal oath in the European Court of Justice in Luxembourg on 24 January 1995 and held their first meeting the following day. On 1 February, Sir Leon Brittan and Manuel Marin were named as the two vice-presidents.[20] The first few months of a new Commission are an important time. This is when priorities for the rest of the term of office (or at least for the year to come) are established. Some of these will of course be determined by the agendas of previous years. Continuity is crucial: but so is innovation.

After having faced the EP several times already, Santer had to return before the MEPs once again for confirmation of the Commission's 1995 Work Programme. The Annual Work Programme sets out the Commission's general policy intentions and provides lists of proposals and papers (with timetables for action) that are to be prepared by Commission staff over the year. As the demands of openness and transparency have increased, so too has the importance of the Work Programme. The strategies and priorities of the

Santer Commission can be divided into those substantive policy proposals that involve some legislative or agenda-setting activity, and the more procedural or institutional strategies that touch on issues of reform, effectiveness and overall Commission performance. As mentioned, substantive policy matters are initially determined by the agenda of the previous Commission. In other words, the new Santer Commission had to deal with the adoption of proposals pending at the end of 1994. There is therefore something of a limit placed on the number of new initiatives that can be made by even the most activist Commission, at least in the first few months of its existence. Several projects of this sort were indeed highlighted in the 1995 Work Programme. These included the long-awaited completion of the internal energy market in gas and electricity, a policy matter that has been on the Commission's agenda since 1988; in addition, proposals concerning environment policy; the nuclear industry; trans-European networks; the single currency; and on relations with developing countries also remained to be dealt with. Many of these proposals were confirmed by the college over the first half of 1995.

In spite of the time taken up with such proposals, there was still some potential for the elaboration of new legislative drafts and new initiatives. The Work Programme spelt out specific areas of interest, such as IT and technology policy more generally. Santer was keen to stress that in policy fields such as these, there would be no playing down of the Commission's initiative role, though he did stress the importance of focusing upon what he called '*l'essentiel*' (essential matters). In other words, he seemed adamant that the Commission should concentrate its policy formulation activity in a limited range of areas.[21] This, Santer argued, would demonstrate the Commission's commitment to the principle of subsidiarity, which (according to the Commission President), dictated that the Commission ought only to do what it could do better than the member states.

Taking the initiative does not necessarily imply the drafting and adoption of concrete legislative proposals, and the abdication of that role in certain policy fields does not mean that the Commission is likely to be weaker, less effective, or that it must by rights play less of a leadership role. In the President's inauguration speech to the EP, Santer had confirmed that his number one policy priority would be an economic one. As far as the Commission was concerned, such a priority would be tied to ongoing discussions on the implementation of Delors's 1993 White Paper on 'Growth, Competitiveness and Employment',[22] to be based on a plan of action outlined at the 1994 Essen summit. The rationale was two-pronged, with the creation of a European employment policy only part of the story. Emphasis was to be placed, in addition, on the promotion of economic conditions that would bode well for the successful implementation of EMU by the end of the decade.[23] In line with these rather broad objectives, specific policy attention was also turned to IT, the liberalisation of telecommunications and more broadly on technology and research matters, as the means of achieving higher growth levels and increased industrial competitiveness. In this case there would be new legislative proposals. A high profile was to be given to the creation of an effective European IT policy which was intended to prevent the Europeans becoming merely 'hitchhikers on the information superhighway'.[24] A G7 Conference organised by the Commission in February 1995 helped to highlight some of the more serious problems facing European industries in this field and began to establish some of the parameters within which the policy might further be developed. Second only to economic concerns, external relations were also given a high priority, with a specific focus on relations with the Central and East European states, and more broadly on the Commission's hoped-for involvement in the new Common Foreign and Security Policy (CFSP). The first evidence of this in 1995 was the publication of a Commission White Paper on the legislative and agricultural changes to be made by prospective member states before joining the EU.

But specific policy priorities and agendas are only half the story. While the 'what' was crucial, the 'how' was also to earn a high profile under Santer. Santer seemed to be suggesting that low-key changes made to the internal functioning of the Commission could be accomplished, as a means of correcting some of the institution's weaknesses. The first emphasis was to be on transparency and openness within the European policy process. Here the Commission committed itself to undertaking far-reaching pre-legislative debates, with emphasis placed on the publication of White and Green Papers which would give individuals and interests a greater opportunity to influence decision-making. It also reflected an increasing focus on the notion of the Commission as a provider of information. Here, however, the merging of an initiative with an informational role meant that it was too early to draw simplistic conclusions as to trends in Commission activism.

Clarification and simplification would also necessitate a more aggressive policy on fraud. This was tied more generally to the issue of managerial effectiveness. Very early on, the slogan 'Less action, more efficiency' came to represent the principal organisational strategy of the Santer presidency. *The Economist* witnessed this when it noted that 'Mr Santer believes in the maxim "less but better"'.[25] This approach was confirmed in the Work Programme. Here, emphasis was placed on fulfilling the most important Commission tasks *more effectively* as well as in a more simplified and open manner. Effectiveness was indeed to become a crucial theme. It was also closely linked to the belief that the Commission had to do all it could to be seen to be 'closer to the people' and to operate on a day-to-day basis in a more democratic fashion. It also recognised the pressures brought to bear on the Commission as a result of increasing responsibilities and static resources.

But, in spite of this low-key approach, high-profile institutional questions also hogged the limelight. Within the IGC context, Santer was keen to see the Commission pursue a strong line from the start. It was clear, then, that institutional reform must be debated seriously during the IGC, and that the problems caused by the proliferation of procedural mechanisms in the EU, and, potentially (if not actually), by the enlargements of the Union had to be dealt with without delay. Time and again, the need for clarity and simplification was emphasised, not just within the Commission, but throughout the EU. Santer was even arguing early in his term that a clear delineation between the responsibilities of the European institutions should be sought. The Commission's commitment to institutional reform on a grand inter-institutional, EU scale needs to be distinguished, however, from the internal fine-tuning of the Commission. As the first involves the very framework of the EU, that is, the parameters within which the institutions act and interact, it must by rights be dealt with by national governments (within the IGC). The second is largely an internal Commission matter, however, and is as such under the control of the President and the college. There are, then, two reform processes at work here, one externally determined, and the other internally motivated.

Identifying the reform agenda

A starting-point for uncovering the details of the reform agenda involves identifying the problems. The grouping together of these problems (along with, tentatively, some potential solutions) under six broad headings can help to structure an understanding of where reform might begin, and might also suggest how change could be made. The general themes dealt with below then are: the functions of the Commission; leadership and homogeneity; accountability; organisational rationality; management; and the question of the 'nationalisation' of the Commission.

It would be misleading to give the impression that dealing with these issues is merely a matter of political will. The practical difficulties in addressing reform in such a piecemeal fashion are clear. Changes which in the first instance seem to improve the situation under one heading may well lead to unintended consequences under another.[26] In addition, what the Commission does, that is, the functions it performs, remain up for grabs whenever the institutional reform of the Commission is proposed. Euro-sceptics and those who would prefer to see the Commission either as an international secretariat or as a European civil service often seek to challenge the Commission's policy-making (or initiative role), arguing that this function should be the responsibility of a different European institution, possibly the European Council, or even the EP. Yet even so, there is, now, much more of a general acceptance that it is the executive functions of the Commission that are in need of real reform. Proposed changes may include the elaboration of a clearer definition of the Commission's role in the implementation of legislation, or of its relationship with the Council of Ministers; or, more broadly, whether there ought to be a separation of functions (legislative, executive and judicial) at the European level, with the Commission's decision-making role decided constitutionally once and for all.

Secondly, questions of cohesion, homogeneity and leadership can merge to challenge the institution's capacity for coherence. The reform intention here, it seems, would be to counter tendencies towards fragmentation, which have often been identified as the main source of confusion and uncertainty for those having to deal with the Commission.[27] In this regard, the role of the presidency is frequently stressed as a potential reform issue. For although strong

presidents can forge their own agendas upon the Commission, officially at least, they remain only the first amongst equals, with little
more power than any other member of the Commission. Collegiality is important here too: whether the collegiate, collective character of the Commission should be done away with so as to instil a
sense of individual responsibility amongst commissioners; or
whether collegiality should be enhanced, in order to contribute to
the creation of a more coherent and unified body. If the latter is the
case, then this may be a good argument for slimming down the
number of commissioners, reducing the college as a whole to a more
manageable size.

Thirdly, attempts to make the Commission more accountable,
and in the process more legitimate, beg the question – 'accountable
to whom?' On occasion, emphasis has been placed on the benefits
that would accrue to the Commission from some direct accountability to the European electorate, perhaps suggesting the direct
election of the President of the Commission; the transformation of
the President of the Commission into the President of the EU; or
even, the election of the Commission as a whole (as one would elect
a government). There would at this stage be difficulties in opera-
tionalising the latter, given the only part-formed European party
system. In any case, with the direct election of the members of the
EP, such direct links between the Commission and the electorate
may be deemed unnecessary. The tightening of the oversight function, or the scrutiny of the Commission by the EP and its committees, could very well be extended, giving the parliamentarians a role
in the choice of President, for example. Ultimately, however, the
Commission needs here to consider how it can best explain itself to
the public. A more informal accountability may in fact be much
more effective.

Fourthly, looking for a more rational way of organising the Commission will appeal to organisational theorists keen to envisage
some 'near-perfect' institutional form. Given that it is not perfec-
tion that is being sought here, a more rational approach to structural and functional issues may nevertheless reap dividends, both in
terms of organisational effectiveness and in terms of cost savings.
Here, issues such as the reduction in the number of commissioners
(and hence portfolios); the reduction in the number of DGs; avoid-
ance of the splitting of portfolios for merely political reasons; a
reduction in tasks duplicated by DGs; and an improved form of hor-

izontal communication amongst services, as well as at the political level, all lead to recommendations for organisational change. Other issues, such as whether the structure of the Commission (its DGs and portfolios) should mirror that of other institutions, and most notably the EP's committee network; and whether there should be a single seat for the EU and for the Commission (namely Brussels), are fraught with political difficulty, but must all the same be addressed.

Fifthly, managerial inadequacies and an inflexible personnel policy have long been perhaps the most pressing internal institutional concern – at least as far as the staff of the Commission are concerned. There is a whole host of issues that could be raised here: the over-specialisation of staff and their remoteness from broad issues of policy (and the real policy-makers); the weakness of career structures and profiles and the difficulties involved in moving post and gaining promotion; and the absence of a real managerial ethos within the Commission. Resource problems may be at the heart of difficulties (such as in the case of the rather paltry use of up-to-the-minute IT within the Commission services), but many of these problems could be resolved with some thought as to the reallocation of resources within the institution, and some political will to do just that.

Finally, it is clear that 'nationalisation' and 'intergovernmentalisation' have long been identified as a potential threat to the Commission's effectiveness and its capacity to act independently.[28] The high number of so-called temporary staff recruited from outside the Commission (often as national experts, and often in posts more long-term than temporary); the increased role of the commissioners' cabinets, often at the expense of the director-generals; the application of national quotas, whether formally or informally; the impact of Council control through its network of committees (comitology); and the incorporation of national priorities and concerns at the policy formulation stage of decision-making. All these serve to tighten the link between the Commission and the national governments. Although complaints have long been heard that the Commission is far from being the European body the founding fathers intended to create, it is clear that the involvement of national actors and perspectives is not necessarily detrimental to its effectiveness. But whether one argues that this is acceptable, irrelevant, or negative, will largely depend, more generally, on the role one sees the Commission playing in the EU system.

So far, where evidence of internal Commission reform is found, it has been characterised by a piecemeal, incremental process, occurring undramatically and behind the scenes. Even so, the former director-general of the personnel DG has argued that since 1986 the Commission has undergone a process of 'modernisation' which has involved the improvement of staff management techniques, the simplification of procedures and the introduction of new IT facilities.[29] Indeed, it has also been noted that the Commission:

> has in a quiet manner acted to increase its efficiency through greater staff flexibility, more use of outside expertise on a temporary basis, small and less rigid internal structures, some decentralisation of management, improved lateral inter-service co-ordination and, above all, adaptation to a resource environment in which new tasks cannot automatically be met by new staff, as was often the case in an earlier period. Much remains to be done, but there is definite progress.[30]

The IGC of 1996 was foreseen in the Treaty on European Union (Article N) as an opportunity to assess the effectiveness and operability of the 'Maastricht Treaty', whilst at the same time looking to the future – most notably to the prospect of EMU and enlargement to the East. The resolution of institutional questions is a corollary of these future developments, and even though, over the course of 1995, many commentators were unsure as to the prominence that would be given to the reform of the EU's institutional framework, it is clear that this issue must remain one of the highest priorities for the EU at the end of the 1990s. There are dangers, however. Although the functions performed by the institutions have changed over the years, the institutional framework of the Community has often given the EC a sort of permanency or stability, especially in times of crisis. Although we may well have criticised in the past the absence of any strategic reform, institutional continuity has provided a solid foundation when external fluctuations, whether economic or political, have rocked the Community boat. At a period in the history of the Union when so many dramatic changes are taking place, it would not be surprising if we once again saw only the minimum necessary change, under the banner of institutional reform. However, the credibility of the Union is at stake here. The reform criteria: accountability; openness; transparency; efficiency; and responsiveness,[31] are at the heart of concerns about the institutional deficits on counts of both democracy and effectiveness. Existing structures and practices can only be fine-tuned, however, once the capacity of the inter-institutional triangle to act effectively has been enhanced. The Commission will be affected by all the issues raised during the IGC process and after: whether the voting mechanisms or the weighting of votes in the Council; the extension or simplification of the decision-making procedures; or changes made to the pillarisation of the Union.[32] Some, more than others, will have an impact upon the internal operation of the institution though, and will address (possibly) some of the issues raised in the section above. However, it is really only likely that questions relating to the number of commissioners, or the division of portfolios will be dealt with in this forum.

Conclusion

The quasi-constitutional agenda debated within the framework of the IGC and during the regular meetings of the European Council involves grand questions of inter-institutional relations that touch on the very *raison d'être* and future development of the EU. How the institutions are organised, what they do, and how they do it, are important for the very fact they dictate their relative positions within the system *as a whole* and indeed shape that system. But many of these grand questions also have an impact upon the internal dynamics of the institutions, though it is equally clear that many of the internal problems and criticisms facing the Commission cannot be dealt with in a forum such as this, but are for the Commission staff and, most notably, for the President to deal with. The implications for the current Commission President are clear. If, as Santer claims, institutional reform is a Commission priority, then a two-track approach to reform is imperative. On one hand, the President must use the mediatory capacity of the Commission to encourage the serious discussion of institutional reform by the member states, both during the IGC process and beyond it. On the other hand, he must remember that institutional reform begins at home; that is, that it is also an internal Commission matter, and that questions such as those affecting personnel policy and managerial weakness are *as* if not *more* important than how many commissioners there are, the dividing up of portfolios, and other 'big' issues of the day.

Notes

1   See for example the Tindemans Report (Bull-EC (S) 1/76); the Spierenberg Report (Bull-EC 9–1979); the report of the 'Three Wise Men' (Bull-EC 11–1979), and the Dooge Committee report (Bull-EC 3–1985).

2   Germany vetoed the first potential compromise candidate, Ruud Lubbers, who had originally been supported by the Dutch, the Italians and the Spanish.

3   *Le Monde*, 18 January 1995.

4   This was quoted in *The Guardian*, 16 July 1994.

5   This was quoted in *ibid.*.

6   This point was made by Helen Drake in her paper to the Fourth Biennial International Conference of the European Community Studies Association in Charleston, South Carolina, in May 1995.

7   *Le Monde*, 18 January 1995.

8   Santer (1995a).

9   *The Independent*, 15 July 1994.

10   Santer (1995a).

11   Quoted in *The Guardian*, 14 July 1994.

12   *The Economist*, 23 July 1994, noted that Santer won by only twenty-two votes, and that 521 MEPs were present.

13   This was Santer's argument. One could quite easily argue that legitimacy rests on more than a vote of approval from the Parliament, however.

14   Six commissioners are involved, with Santer himself presiding over the meetings.

15   The group has eight members and Santer chairs the meetings. It deals with matters relating to White Papers on Growth, and on social policy.

16   This group has eight commissioners and is chaired by Neil Kinnock, the transport commissioner.

17   They aim to promote consistency in a number of policy areas. The *Cohesion* group is presided over by Monika Wulf-Mathies, commissioner for regional policy; the *Information society* group, is presided over by Bangemann; and the group on *Equality of opportunity for men and women and women's rights* looks at equal opportunities matters both within the Commission, and more broadly. This group is chaired by Padraig Flynn, the social policy commissioner.

18   This caused some legal problems as there was officially a leadership vacuum between the end of Delors's presidency and the beginning of Santer's.

19   See Agence Europe, Europe Documents, No. 1919, 18 January 1995 for the comments of each committee on the commissioners' performances.

20   Reduced from five to two in the Treaty on European Union.

21   See *Eur-op News*, 1/1995.

22   The full title of the White Paper is 'Growth, Competitiveness, Employment: the challenge and ways forward into the 21st century', Commission (1993).

23   Note that a Green Paper on Economic and Monetary Affairs was approved on 31 May 1995.

24   B. Barnard, 'Europe gets up to speed on the information super-highway', *Europe*, April 1995.

25   *The Economist*, 13 May 1995.

26   There is no presumption that these categories are anything other that useful ways of clarifying and pigeonholing the morass of reform proposals.

27   This is not necessarily the case. There have in recent years been many suggestions that parts of the Commission should be 'hived off' to create agencies. To some extent this has already begun. The European Environmental Agency and others have been created to deal largely with technical and informational matters. As yet, the 'powers' of the Commission have not been 'hived off' into such bodies, however.

28   Ironically, the argument is also put that without national input the Commission would be a less effective body. This is dealt with below.

29   Hay (1989, pp. 41–5).

30   Fitzmaurice (1994, p. 185).

31   See Lodge (1994).

32   The three pillars are those of 'the European Community', 'Common Foreign and Security Policy' and 'Justice and Home Affairs'.

8

Conclusions

In echoing some of the themes introduced at the beginning of the book, this last chapter seeks to draw some brief conclusions about the internal dynamism of the European Commission. Institutions, it was noted in the introduction, are social constructs designed to create order where none exists, that is, in our political and social environment. As such, institutions are able to influence social, economic and political life; they impinge upon their environments in ways mere organisations cannot. Labelling the European Commission as an institution, then, recognises the constraints placed upon it, but also signals the Commission's capacity to shape and influence the European political agenda and the outputs that emerge from it.

Re-inventing the Commission

There are numerous examples of the Commission's (or its leaders') skill at imposing its agenda and its vision on European society. The SEM/SEA was clear a case in point, as was the EMS agenda introduced initially by Roy Jenkins. Yet there are still more examples of the Commission failing to achieve its full potential, merely reacting to events outside its control. This was true of many episodes over the course of the 1970s, but it might also characterise the last years of the Delors decade. We have to be careful here, however. There is an understandable tendency in studying the European Commission to assume that a Commission failing to churn out (ultimately successful) legislative proposals, or failing to assert itself *vis-à-vis* national governments, is a Commission that is essentially weak. This may be far from the case. For example, the ability to ensure that legislative acts are actually implemented on the ground must be judged as a measure of organisational effectiveness. Yet still, implementation skills and the managerial capacity associated with Commission activities of this sort are consistently underrated, denigrated and treated disparagingly as 'mere' administration. Of course, there are still times when the Commission is indeed reactive, but this ought not to be confused with a creative use of a variety of institutional roles and functions.

Perhaps what we need, then, as a starting-point is a reassessment of the Commission's history so as to emphasise that institutional success should not be defined only in terms of outputs. Out*comes* are clearly a more appropriate way of judging just how much the Commission has been able to affect and alter its environment. Indeed, we can take this even further if we consider the capacity of the Commission, not just to 'make an impact', but also to adapt to prevailing circumstances, to reinvent itself in line with changing social, political and economic conditions, and to make use of windows of political opportunity where these appear. An example of this was Delors's tactically successful drafting of a White Paper in 1993, just as his office seemed to be running out of steam. This document did not attempt to *impose* the Commission line on member governments, yet it served to reinsert issues of industrial competitiveness at the forefront of the minds of national elites, reminding them that the Commission could still be a source of useful, informative and well-researched policy ideas. This is agenda-setting pure and simple, and should not be denigrated simply because it uses the Commission's consensus-building or mediation functions to achieve its ends.

Leadership, organisation and culture

The Commission's capacity for taking advantage of windows of political opportunity focuses our attention on the importance of leadership and, more specifically, on individual leaders. The most important prerequisite for institutional adaptation or 'reinvention' may well be the existence of a leader capable of making judgements that seek out the most effective instruments and methods at the Commission's disposal at any particular time. Leadership is indeed crucial here, as it can give both direction to the institution, and at the same time forge a coherence internally within it. Institutional identity relies a great deal on the Commission's potential as a unified coherent actor. This coherence may be the work of a strong individual at the top of the institution, that is, someone who possesses vision and has clear policy objectives in mind. (Delors is of course the obvious example.) However, it may be that the college (acting collegially and collectively) could fulfil a similar role, though in practice there has been less evidence of this up to now. There have even been times when individual commissioners have taken the lead: Vicomte Davignon was a noteworthy example. Experience suggests, even so, that visionless leaders may be a liability. In the past, where strong and dynamic central leadership has been lacking, either alternative departmental fiefdoms have been allowed to develop, or the Commission has been left merely as a reactive and directionless organisation. The issue of leadership, then, leads us perhaps to the crux of understanding what it is that makes the Commission coherent or incoherent. But even the most visionary of Commission leaders need to have organisational weight behind them. The socio-structural environment within which leaders find themselves placed is, as such, extremely important. The Commission's structural and procedural evolution has witnessed an ever-growing trend towards diversity. In practice, this has meant the emergence of a multitude of cleavages, cut along various lines, leading to the conclusion that there is really no *one* Commission, but a plethora of them. For example, we may accept the Commission as forming a sort of embryonic European public administration, but this would mean ignoring the large numbers of seconded and temporary staff who currently work within the institution; we may see the Commission as a supranational European body, but this would fail to acknowledge the intergovernmentalism all too apparent in the cabinet system and even within the college itself; we may want to see the Commission as a goal-oriented, unitary body, but the distinctive identities, working practices and structures of individual DGs suggest that they too may be considered as institutions in their own right; and we may consider the Commission as a hierarchical bureaucracy, even though this fails to acknowledge the existence of more organic or informal networks and channels throughout the institution.

In addition, there are many potential threats to the effective operation of the Commission's organisation: the lack of co-ordination; the impact of the influx of temporary staff; discontent over personnel matters; unreliable communication and information flows; and the inadequate use of available resources. Inefficiencies of this sort act as barriers to the performance of the Commission's functions, and suggest that institutional reform should be more of a priority than it is. Yet the story does not end here. Leadership and organisation alone do not give a full and complete picture of what it is that makes the Commission an institution. Although institutions may well be 'actors', they are also collections of individuals, albeit in a distinctive working environment. It is this perspective that leads us to focus on administrative culture.

Cultures that exist in organisational contexts affect the way in which staff view the work they do; they affect the way they see the world and their perception of their institution within it; moreover, albeit indirectly, culture also affects policy outcomes.[1] Cultural factors are the foundations upon which all decisions are taken; the basic beliefs, values, attitudes, experiences, accepted wisdoms and learned behaviour that are, more often than not, taken for granted by those whose action is determined or affected by them. Indeed, it is what affects their sense of who, why and what they are. To ask, then, whether there is a specific Commission culture is to raise a fundamental question about the officials who work within the institution's services. It also raises questions about the institution itself: whether there is some sort of 'adhesive' which, collectively, allows, encourages or even forces these individuals to be considered as something greater than the sum of their parts. If this is indeed the case, perhaps we are closer to defining what it is that makes an institution different from a formal organisation; and perhaps this is the 'secret' to understanding the ability of an institution to act cohesively. With a cohesive cultural identity, the foundations for a cohesive, unified institution exist, foundations possibly able to survive both leadership deficits and structural-procedural weaknesses as they arise.

Yet the evidence provided in the chapters above suggests that there is only the shadow of a cohesive Commission culture, and that organisational features of the institution seem to work against the emergence of either a European public service ethic or the re-emergence of a basic belief system, based perhaps on some notion of the European ideal – that is, an emotional (as opposed to a pragmatic) commitment to further European integration. Yet, there remains, even so, certain common underlying assumptions that pervade the

entire Commission, assumptions that are largely the product of continuous processes of socialisation (for both permanent and temporary staff). However, it is doubtful whether these assumptions are
coherent enough to counter the jumble of cultural influences, the
nationally, regionally, professionally, linguistically, departmentally
and functionally based values, beliefs and identities that persist
within the Commission.

Legitimacy and effectiveness

Although internal institutional dynamics are important, the Commission does not act in a political vacuum. When external conditions are unfavourable, severe institutional constraints can make it
extremely difficult for the Commission to perform any of its more
visible functions. In practice, a variety of factors can bring this
about: governmental reluctance to relinquish control over specific
policy matters; or a more general resistance towards allowing the
Commission a greater freedom of policy manoeuvre, perhaps.
Although such national interests and perspectives are very important, it is the issue of the legitimacy gap that has come to shape
public perceptions of the Commission. Legitimacy is what gives the
Commission the *authority* to influence or compel a course of
action.[2] Political legitimacy, in the Commission's case, is founded on
an acknowledgement of the institution's distinctive quasi-governmental role, as set out in the treaties, and rests on the loyalty and
trust placed in the institution by European citizens. It is doubtful,
however, whether we would find much evidence for a legitimate
Commission role based on these criteria at present.

A different sort of legitimacy that is based much more on bureaucratic notions of delegated powers, on the monopoly of technical
knowledge and expertise, and on perceptions of effectiveness, is
also relevant in the case of the Commission. Early in the Community's history, bureaucratic legitimacy went hand-in-hand with a
conception of the Commission as a prototype European public service, based loosely along northern European/weberian lines. Yet
recognition that the Commission was something more than just a
conventional civil service transposed to the European level, and a
growing concern about the policy effectiveness of the institution,
seemed to suggest that legitimacy must rest on something more that
just a job well done. The lack of any solid foundation for either

political or bureaucratic legitimacy has since come to dominate more general discussions of the EU's democratic deficit.

Solutions to this problem have involved on one level a sort of inter-institutional 'mingling'. The Commission has tolerated (grudgingly, it has to be said) the growing involvement of or 'infiltration' by the Council in its internal business in exchange for what might be considered a rather tenuous legitimacy. Through the spread of 'comitology' and the increased number of national 'experts' appointed to work in the Commission, the control or at least the oversight of (elected) national governments has intensified. In addition, the developing decisional powers of the EP have meant that political legitimacy has also been sought through acceptance of a greater scrutiny role for elected MEPs over both the college of commissioners, and the policies pursued by the Commission.

By contrast, bureaucratic solutions towards this legitimacy gap have been sought internally, with the aforementioned emphasis on improving internal management structures. But whether solutions are to be found internally or externally, legitimacy (and the lack of it) has much to do with public perceptions. The need to alter the reality of internal Commission dynamics or inter-institutional relationships addressed only one part of the problem.

Assessment

There is little expectation that the Commission will be able to develop in the near future a common cultural identity when all evidence seems to point to further organisational fragmentation, and an absence, even within the institution, of an across-the-board consensus on the values underlying the Commission's European vocation. It would take a conscious and concerted effort by Commission elites to forge cultural change, in much the same way that industrial elites have sought to create corporate cultures to enhance their firms' performance.[3] At present, there is no evidence at all that the Commission President is thinking along these lines. Indeed, even if this were on the agenda, it would be an extremely difficult and sensitive task to undertake; one that could easily backfire, should officials understand it as a contrived process of socialisation or indoctrination.[4] Where issues of institutional reform *are* raised, they focus, not surprisingly, on structural and procedural matters. These, it seems, are currently being addressed. Leadership, too, is already acknowledged as perhaps the most crucial element in the construction of an effective, assertive institution. But without an understanding of the cultural heterogeneity of the body and the importance of legitimising the various functions that it performs, it seems as though the Commission will continue to fluctuate between coherence and incoherence.

Notes

1   For a more detailed definition of administrative culture, see the introduction to this book.

2   Lewis (1983).

3   Another example is that of the UK's Department of Trade and Industry. Whilst Secretary of State, Lord Young made a concerted effort to alter the culture within the department, turning what had been a predisposition for intervention into a neo-liberal commitment to free up industrial markets.

4   There is some evidence that there was in fact a concerted attempt to alter the culture within the environmental DG, DG XI. The objective here was to bring the DG into line with thinking in other parts of the Commission, on the subject of growth and the importance of industrial development (though in line with environmental considerations too).

Bibliography

Abélès, M. (1994), 'A la Recherche d'un espace public communautaire', *Pouvoirs*, 69, pp. 117–28.

Allaire, Y. and Firsirotu, M. E. (1984), 'Theories of organizational culture', *Organization Studies*, 5, pp. 193–226.

Azzi, G. Ciavarini (1985), 'Les Expert nationaux: chevaux de troie ou partenaires indispensables?', in Jamar, J. and Wessels, W. eds, *Community Bureaucracy at the Crossroads*, De Tempel, Bruges.

Bainbridge, T. (with Teasdale, A.) (1995), *The Penguin Companion to European Union*, Penguin, London.

Bellier, I. (1994), 'Une Culture de la Commission européenne? De la rencontre des cultures et du multilingualisme des fonctionnaires,' in Mény, Y., Muller, P., and Quermonne, J.-C., eds, *Politiques publiques en Europe*, L'Harmattan, Paris.

Beloff, Lord (1963), *The General Says No*, Penguin, London.

Blumann, C. (1989), 'La Commission, agent d'execution du droit communautaire: la comitologie', in Louis, J. V. and Waelbroek, D. eds, *La Commission au coeur du système institutionnel des Communautés européennes*, Editions de L'Université de Bruxelles, Brussels.

Bradley, K. S. C. (1992), 'Comitology and the law: through a glass darkly', *Common Market Law Review*, 20, pp. 693–721.

Brittan, L. (1994), *Europe: The Europe We Need*, Hamish Hamilton, London.

Büchner, L. C. and Sangolt, L. (1994), 'The concept of subsidiarity and the debate on European cooperation: pitfalls and possibilities', *Governance*, 7, pp. 284–306.

Budd, S. and Jones, A. (1991), *The European Community: A Guide to the Maze*, Kogan Page, London.

Buitendijk, G. T. and Van Schendelen, M. C. P. M. (1995), 'Brussels advisory committees: a channel for influence', *European Law Review*, 21, pp. 37–57.

Bulmer, S. (1983), 'Domestic politics and European Community policy-making', *Journal of Common Market Studies*, 21, pp. 349–63.

Bulmer, S. (1994), 'Institutions and policy change in the European Communities: the case of merger control', *Public Administration*, 72, pp. 423–44.

Burley, A.-M. and Mattli, W. (1993), 'Europe before the Court: a political theory of legal integration', *International Organization*, 47, pp. 41–76.

Cameron, F. (1992), 'The EC and its institutions', in Griffiths, A. ed., *European Community Survey*, Longman, Harlow.

Cameron, F. (1995), 'The 1996 IGC – a challenge for Europe', Paper presented to the Fourth International ECSA Conference, Charleston, South Carolina, 1995.

Campanella, M. L. (1995), 'Getting to the core: a neo-institutionalist approach to EMU', *Government and Opposition*, 30, pp. 347–69.

Campbell, C. and Peters, B. G. (1988), 'The politics/administration dichotomy: death or merely change?', *Governance*, 1, pp. 79–99.

Camps, M. (1964), *Britain and the European Community 1955–1963*, Free Press, Princeton, NJ.

Cassese, S. (1987), *The European Administration*, EIPA, Maastricht.

Cassidy, B. (1995), 'Britons are winning more Euro-jobs', *The House Magazine*, 20 February, p. 6.

Cawson, A., Homes, P. and Stevens, A. (1987), 'The interaction between firms and the state in France: the telecommunications and the consumer electronics sectors', in Wilks, S. and Wright, M. eds, *Comparative Government-Industry Relations: Western Europe, the United States and Japan*, Clarendon Press, Oxford.

Cecchini, P. (1988), *The European Challenge 1992: The benefits of a Single Market*, Wildwood House, Aldershot.

Cini, M. (1994), ' Policing the internal market: the regulation of competition in the European Commission', Ph.D. thesis, University of Exeter.

Cini, M. (1995a), 'Administrative culture in the European Commission: the case of competition and environment', Paper presented to the Fourth International ECSA Conference, Charleston, South Carolina, May.

Cini, M. (1995b), 'The personality, policy approach and priorities of the new Commission President: the implications for institutional reform', Paper presented to the UACES Research Conference, University of Birmingham, September.

Clergerie, J. L. (1995), 'L'Improbable censure de la Commission européenne', *Revue du droit publique et de la science politique en France et a l'étranger*, 1, pp. 210–20.

Conolly, B. (1995), *The Rotten Heart of Europe*, Faber and Faber, London.

Coombes, D. (1970), *Politics and Bureaucracy in the European Commu-*

nity: A Portrait of the Commission of the EEC, George Allen and Unwin, London.

Corbett, R. (1994), 'Representing the people', in Duff, A. *et al.* eds, *Maastricht and Beyond: Building the European Union*, Routledge, London.

Cram, L. (1994), 'The European Commission as a multi-organization: social policy and IT policy in the EU', *Journal of European Public Policy*, 1, pp. 195–218.

De Gaulle, C. (1970), *Mémoirs d'espoir*, Plan, Paris.

Dehousse, R. (1992), 'Integration v. regulation? On the dynamics of regulation in the European Community', *Journal of Common Market Studies*, 30, pp. 383–402.

Delors, J. (1975), *Changer*, Stock, Paris.

Delors, J. (1988), *La France par L'Europe*, Clisthène-Grasset, Paris.

Delors, J. (1992), *Le Nouveau Concert Européen*, Odile Jacob, Paris.

Delors, J. (1993), 'Commentary: the programme of the Commission 1993–94', *European Access*, 2, pp. 9–13.

Deprez, G. (1974), *La Commission des Communautés européennes: essai sociologique sur une institution captive*, Centre de recherches sociologiques, Université catholique de Louvain, Louvain.

Dinan, D. (1994), *Ever Closer Union*, Macmillan, London.

Docksey, C. and Williams, K. (1994), 'The Commission and the execution of Community policy', in Edwards, G. and Spence, D. eds, *The European Commission*, Longman Current Affairs, Harlow.

Donnelly, M. (1993), 'The structure of the European Commission and the policy formulation process', in Mazey, S. and Richardson, J. eds, *Lobbying in the European Community*, Oxford University Press, Oxford.

Donnelly, M. and Richie, E. (1994), 'The College of Commissioners and their *Cabinets*', in Edwards, G. and Spence, D. eds, *The European Commission*, Longman Current Affairs, Harlow.

Drake, H. (1995a), 'Political leadership and European integration: the case of Jacques Delors', in *West European Politics*, 18, pp. 140–60.

Drake, H. (1995b), 'The Commission presidency of Jacques Delors: a study in political leadership', Paper presented to the Fourth Biennial International Conference of the European Community Studies Association, Charleston, South Carolina, May.

Drake, H. (1995c), 'Defining the Commission: the politics of legitimacy', Paper presented to the UACES Research Conference, Birmingham, September.

Duff, A. (1994a), 'Building a parliamentary Europe', *Government and Opposition*, 29, pp. 147–65.

Duff, A. (1994b), 'Ratification', in Duff, A. *et al.* eds, *Maastricht and Beyond: Building the European Union*, Routledge, London.

Edwards, G. and Spence, D. (1994), 'The Commission in perspective', in

Edwards, G. and Spence, D. eds, *The European Commission*, Longman Current Affairs, Harlow.

Egeberg, M. (1994), 'Bridging the gap between theory and practice: the case of administration and policy', *Governance*, 7, pp. 83–98.

Egeberg, M. (1995), 'Organization and nationality in the European Commission services', Paper presented to the ECPR Joint Sessions, Bordeaux, 27 April–2 May.

Ehlermann, C.-D. (1985), 'Rapport général', in Jamar, J. and Wessels, W. eds, *Community Bureaucracy at the Crossroads*, De Tempel, Bruges.

The European Citizen (1991), 'Consultation committees within the Commission', February.

European Commission (1995), *Budget*, Office of Official Publications, Luxembourg.

Fitzmaurice, J. (1994), 'The European Commission', in Duff, A. *et al.* eds, *Maastricht and Beyond: Building the European Union*, Routledge, London.

Franklin, M., with Wilke, M. (1990), *Britain's Future in Europe*, RIIA, London.

George, S. (1991), *Politics and Policy in the European Community*, Oxford University Press, Oxford.

George, S. (1995), 'The European Commission: opportunities seized; problems unresolved', Paper presented to the Fourth International ECSA Conference, Charleston, South Carolina, May.

Gower, J. (1993), 'EC relations with central and Eastern Europe', in Lodge, J. ed., *The European Community and the Challenge of the Future*, Pinter, London.

Goyder, D. G. (1988), *EEC Competition Law*, Butterworths, London.

Grant, C. (1994), *Jacques Delors. The House that Jacques Built*, Nicholas Brearley, London.

Grant, W. (1993), 'Pressure groups and the European Community: an overview', in Mazey, S. and Richardson, J. eds, *Lobbying in the European Community*, Oxford University Press, Oxford.

Greenwood, J. and Ronit, K. (1994), 'Interest groups in the European Community: newly emerging dynamics and forms', *West European Politics*, 17, pp. 31–52.

Haas, E. (1964), *Beyond the Nation State*, Stanford University Press, Stanford.

Haas, E. (1968), *The Uniting of Europe*, Stanford University Press, Stanford.

Hallstein, W. (1972), *Europe in the Making*, Allen and Unwin, London.

Hay, R. (1989), *The European Commission and the Administration of the Community*, Commission, Luxembourg.

Hellman J. (1981), *Emmanuel Mounier and the Catholic Left 1930–1950*,

University of Toronto Press, Toronto.

Henderson, W. O. (1962), *The Genesis of the Common Market*, Frank Cass, London.

Henig, S. (1980), *Power and Decision in Europe*, Europotentials press, London.

Henig, S. (1994), 'Europe's institutional morass – can the Union escape?', Paper presented to the ESRC Single Market Conference, Exeter, September.

Hix, S. (1994), 'The study of the European Community: the challenge to comparative politics', *West European Politics*, 17, pp. 1–30.

Hoffmann, S. (1966), 'Obstinate or obsolete: the fate of the nation state and the case of Western Europe', *Daedelus*, 95, pp. 862–915.

Holt, S. (1967), *The Common Market*, Hamish Hamilton, London.

Hrbek, R. (1985), 'Relations of Community bureaucracy with the socio-political environment', in Jamar, J. and Wessels, W. eds, *Community Bureaucracy at the Crossroads*, De Tempel, Bruges.

Hull, R. (1993), 'Lobbying Brussels: a view from within', in Mazey, S. and Richardson, J. eds, *Lobbying in the European Community*, Oxford University Press, Oxford.

Jacobs, F. (1995), 'The European Parliament's role in nominating the members of the Commission: first steps towards parliamentary government or US Senate-type confirmation hearings', Paper presented to the Fourth International ECSA Conference, Charleston, South Carolina, May.

Jamar, J., and Wessels, W. eds, (1985), *Community Bureaucracy at the Crossroads*, De Tempel, Bruges.

Jenkins, R. (1989), *European Diary*, Collins, London.

Joshua, J. (1983), 'The element of surprise: EEC competition investigations under Article 14 (3) of Regulation 17', *European Law Review*, 8, pp. 3–23.

Kirchner, E. (1992), *Decision Making in the European Community*, Manchester University Press, Manchester.

Koelble, T. A. (1995), 'The new institutionalism in political science and sociology', *Comparative Politics*, 27, pp. 231–43.

Kohler-Koch, B. (1993), 'Changing patterns of interest intermediation in the European Union', *Government and Opposition*, 29, pp. 166–80.

Lenchow, A. (1995), 'Policy and institutional change in the European Community: environmental integration in the CAP', Paper presented at the Fourth International ECSA Conference, Charleston, South Carolina, May.

Lewis, P. G. (1983), 'Introduction: legitimacy and the state', in Held, D. *et al.* eds, *States and Societies*, Martin Robinson, Oxford.

Lodge, J. (1994), 'Crisis or opportunity? Institutional affairs', A discussion paper of the Jean Monnet Group of Experts, Centre for European Union

Studies, University of Hull.

Lopès, A. de F. (1990), 'CEE: la spécificté de la fonction publique communautaire: l'exemple de la Commission', *Revue française d'administration publique*, 55, pp. 497–503.

Louis, J. V. (1989), 'La Désignation de la Commission et ses problèmes', in Louis, J. V. and Waelbroek, D. eds, *La Commission au coeur du système institutionnel des Communautés européennes*, Editions de L'Université de Bruxelles, Brussels.

Ludlow, P. (1991), 'The European Commission', in Keohane, R. O. and Hoffmann, S. eds, *The New European Community. Decision Making and Institutional Change*, Westview, Oxford.

Majone, G. (1991), 'Cross-national sources of regulatory policymaking in Europe and the United States', *Journal of Public Policy*, pp. 79–105.

March, J. G. and Olsen, J. P. (1989), *Rediscovering Institutions: The Organizational Basis of Politics*, Free Press, New York.

Mazey, S. and Richardson, J. (1993), 'Introduction: transference of power, decision rules, and rules of the game', in Mazey, S. and Richardson, J. eds, *Lobbying in the European Community*, Oxford University Press, Oxford.

Mazey, S. and Richardson, J. (1994), 'The Commission and the lobby', in Edwards, G. and Spence, D. eds, *The European Commission*, Longman Current Affairs, Harlow.

McLachlan, D. J. and Swann, D. (1967), *Competition Policy in the EC*, Oxford University Press/RIIA, Oxford.

Medefind, H. (1975), *Organisation Europe*, Europa Union Verlag, Bonn.

Menindrou, M. (1994), 'European Community fraud and the politics of institutional development', *European Journal of Political Research*, 26, pp. 81–101.

Metcalfe, L. (1992), 'After 1992: can the Commission manage Europe?', *Australian Journal of Public Administration*, 51, pp. 117–30.

Michalski, A. and Wallace, H. (1992), *The European Community: The Challenge of Enlargement*, RIIA, London.

Michelmann, H. J. (1978a), *Organisational Effectiveness in a Multinational Bureaucracy*, Saxon House, Hants.

Michelmann, H. J. (1978b), 'Multinational staffing and organizational functioning in the Commission of the European Communities', *International Organization*, 32, pp. 477–96.

Middlemas, K. (1995), *Orchestrating Europe: The Informal Politics of the European Union*, Fontana Press, London.

Milward, A. S. and Sørensen, V. (1993), 'Independence or integration', in Milward, A. S. and Sørensen, V. eds, *The Frontiers of National Sovereignty*, Routledge, London.

Monnet, J. (1978), *Memoirs*, Collins, London.

Moravscik, A. (1991), 'Negotiating the Single European Act: national interests and conventional statecraft in the European Community', *International Organization*, 45, pp. 19–56.

Moravscik, A. (1993), 'Preferences and power in the European Community: a liberal intergovernmentalist approach', *Journal of Common Market Studies*, 31, pp. 473–534.

Moussis, N. (1993), *Access to Europe: Guide to Community Policies*, Edit-Europe, Rixensart, Belgium.

Neunreither, K. (1972), 'Transformation of a political role: reconsidering the case of the Commission of the European Communities', *Journal of Common Market Studies*, 10, pp. 233–48.

Neville-Jones, P. (1985), 'Comment', in Jamar, J. and Wessels, W. eds, *Community Bureaucracy at the Crossroads*, De Tempel, Bruges.

Nugent, N. (1991), *The Government and Politics of the European Community*, Macmillan, Basingstoke.

Nugent, N. (1994), *The Government and Politics of the European Union*, Macmillan, London.

Nugent, N. (1995), 'The leadership capacity of the European Commission', *Journal of European Public Policy*, 2, pp. 603–23.

Nutall, S. (1992), *European Political Cooperation*, Clarendon, Oxford.

Nutall, S. (1994), 'The Commission and foreign policy-making', in Edwards, G. and Spence, D. eds, *The European Commission*, Longman Current Affairs, Harlow.

O'Toole, R. (1989), 'La Commission et l'exercise du pouvoir législatif: les rapports avec le parlement européen', in Louis, J. V. and Waelbroek, D. eds, *La Commission au coeur du système institutionnel des Communautés européennes*, Editions de l'Université de Bruxelles, Brussels.

Padoa-Schioppa, T. ed. (1987), *Efficiency, Stability and Equity: A Strategy for the Evolution of the Economic System of the EC*, OOP, Luxembourg.

Page, E. C. and Wouters, L. (1994), 'Bureaucratic politics and political leadership in Brussels', *Public Administration*, 72, pp. 445–59.

Page, E. (1995), 'The problem of nationality in the administration of the European Union', *Insight*, 6, January.

Pedersen, T. (1991), 'EC-EFTA relations: an historical outline', in Wallace, H. ed., *The Wider Western Europe: Reshaping the EC/EFTA Relationship*, Pinter/RIIA, London.

Pentland, C. (1973), *International Theory and European Integration*, Faber, London.

Peters, B. G. (1991), 'Bureaucratic politics and the institutions of the European Community', in Sbragia, A. M. ed., *Euro-politics. Institutions and Policymaking in the 'New' European Community*, Brookings Institution, Washington, DC.

Peters, B. G. (1994), 'Agenda-setting in the European Community', *Journal of European Public Policy*, 1, pp. 9–26.

Peterson, J. (1995), 'Decision-making in the European Union: towards a framework for analysis', *Journal of European Public Policy*, 2, pp. 69–94.

Peterson, R. L. (1972), 'Personnel decisions and the independence of the European Communities', *Journal of Common Market Studies*, 10, pp. 117–37.

Pinder, J. (1968), 'Positive integration and negative integration: some problems of economic union in the EEC', *The World Today*, 24, pp. 88–110.

Pinder, J. (1991), *The European Community and Eastern Europe*, Pinter/RIIA, London.

Plumb, Lord (1989), 'Building a democratic Community: the role of the European Parliament', *The World Today*, 45, pp. 112–17.

Putnam, R. D. (1988), 'Diplomacy and domestic politics: the logic of two-level games', *International Organization*, 42, pp. 427–60.

Quermonne, J.-L. (1993), *Le Système politique européenne*, Montchrétien, Paris.

Rollat, A. (1993), *Delors*, Flammarion, Paris.

Rometsch, D. and Wessels, W. (1994), 'The Commission and the Council of Ministers', in Edwards, G. and Spence, D. eds, *The European Commission*, Longman Current Affairs, Harlow.

Rosenthal, G. (1975), *The Men Behind the Decisions*, Lexington Books, Farnborough.

Ross, G. (1993), 'Sidling into industrial policy: inside the European Commission', *French Politics and Society*, 11, pp. 20–44.

Ross, G. (1994), 'Inside the Delors cabinet', *Journal of Common Market Studies*, 32, pp. 499–523.

Ross, G. (1995), *Jacques Delors and European Integration*, Polity, Cambridge.

Sampson, A. (1971), *The New Europeans*, Panther, London.

Sandholtz, W. and Zysman, J. (1989), '1992: recasting the European bargain', *World Politics*, 42, pp. 95–128.

Santer, J. (1995a), 'Petit pays contre grands états', *L'Année européenne: revue du groupe des belles feuilles* (interview with Christine Holzbauer-Madison).

Santer, J. (1995b), 'Points de vue de responsables politiques – Jacques Santer', *Revue des affaires européennes: la réforme institutionnelle de 1996*.

Santer, J. (1995c), 'Une Europe pour les citoyens', *Europe sans frontières*, Commission (DG X), Brussels.

Sasse, C. (1975), 'The Commission and the Council: functional partners or constitutional rivals?', in Dagtoglou, P. D. ed., *Basic Problems of the European Community*, Blackwell, Oxford.

Sasse, C. (1977a), 'The internal functioning of the Commission', in Sasse,

C., Poullet, E., Coombes, D. and Deprez, G. eds, *Decision Making in the European Community*, Praeger, London.

Sasse, C. (1977b), 'The Commission's ability to dictate choices within the Community system', in Sasse, C., Poullet, E., Coombes, D. and Deprez, G. eds, *Decision Making in the European Community*, Praeger, London.

Sbragia, A. M. (1991), 'Thinking about the European future: the uses of comparison', in Sbragia, A. M. ed., *Euro-politics. Institutions and Policymaking in the 'New' European Community*, Brookings Institution, Washington, DC.

Scheinman, L. (1966), 'Some preliminary notes of bureaucratic relationships in the European Economic Community', *International Organization*, 30, pp. 750–73.

Sharp, M. and Shearman, C. (1987), *European Technological Collaboration*, Routledge & Kegan Paul, London.

Sharp, M., Freeman, C. and Walker, W. (1991), *Technology and the Future of Europe: Global Competition and the Environment in the 1980s*, Pinter, New York.

Simon, H. A. (1976), *Administrative Behavior*, 3rd ed., The Free Press, New York.

Skjaerseth, J. B. (1994), 'The climate policy of the EC: too hot to handle?', *Journal of Common Market Studies*, 32, pp. 25–45.

Smith, A. (1995), 'L'Intégration communautaire face au territoire. Les fonds structurels et les zones rurales en France, Espagne et au Royaume Unie, Thèse de doctorat, IEP de Grenoble, March.

Smith, Michael (1994), 'The Commission and external relations', in Edwards, G. and Spence, D. eds, *The European Commission*, Longman Current Affairs, Harlow.

Smith, Mitchell (1995), 'The Commission made me do it: policy preferences and domestic political capacity', Paper presented to the ECSA Conference, Charleston, May.

Spence, D. (1993), 'The role of the national civil service in European lobbying: the British case', in Mazey, S. and Richardson, J. eds, *Lobbying in the European Community*, Oxford University Press, Oxford.

Spence, D. (1994a), 'Structure, functions and procedures in the Commission', in Edwards, G. and Spence, D. eds, *The European Commission*, Longman Current Affairs, Harlow.

Spence, D. (1994b), 'Staff and personnel policy in the Commission', in Edwards, G. and Spence, D. eds, *The European Commission*, Longman Current Affairs, Harlow.

Spinelli, A. (1966), *The Eurocrats*, Johns Hopkins University Press, Baltimore.

Steinberg, M. S. ed. (1990), *The Technological Challenges and Opportunities of a United Europe*, Barnes and Noble, Savage, MD.

Suleiman, E. N. (1984), 'From right to left: bureaucracy and politics in France', in Suleiman, E. N. ed., *Bureaucrats and Policy Making: A Comparative Overview*, Holmes and Meier, London.

Swann, D. (1983), *Competition and Industrial Policy in the EC*, Methuen, London.

Taylor, P. (1975), 'The politics of the European Communities: the confederal phase', *World Politics*, April, pp. 336–60.

Taylor, P. (1983), *The Limits of European Integration*, Croom Helm, Kent.

Thygesen, N. (1989), 'The Delors Report and European economic and monetary union', *International Affairs*, 4, pp. 637–52.

Trojan, C. (1989), 'La Commission et l'exercise du pouvoir législatif: les rapports avec le Conseil', in Louis, J. V. and Waelbroek, D. eds, *La Commission au coeur du système institutionnel des Communautés européennes*, Editions de l'Université de Bruxelles, Brussels.

Tugendhat, C. (1986), *Making Sense of Europe*, Viking, London.

Tutt, N. (1989), *Europe on the Fiddle*, Christopher Helm, Bromley.

Urwin, D. W. (1991), *The Community of Europe. A History of European Integration since 1945*, Longman, Harlow.

Usher, J. (1994), 'The Commission and the law', in Edwards, G. and Spence, D. eds, *The European Commission*, Longman Current Affairs, Harlow.

Vahl, R. (1992), 'The European Commission on the road to European Union: the consequences of the Treaty on European Union for the Commission's power base', *Acta Politica*, 3, pp. 297–322.

Van Kraay, F. (1989), 'The strengthening of the executive powers of the European Commission', *The Law Teacher*, 23.

Vibert, F. (1989), 'Europe's constitutional deficit', *IEA Inquiry*, 13, Institute of Economic Affairs, London.

Wallace, H., Wallace, W. and Webb. C. (1983), eds, *Policymaking in the European Community*, John Wiley and Sons, London.

Wallace, H. (1985a), *Europe: The Challenge of Diversity*, Routledge/Kegan Paul, Boston.

Wallace, H. (1985b), 'General report', in Jamar, J. and Wessels, W. eds, *Community bureaucracy at the crossroads*, De Tempel, Bruges.

Wallace, H. ed. (1991), *The Wider Western Europe: Reshaping the EC/EFTA Relationship*, RIIA/Pinter, London.

Wallace, W. (1991), 'Introduction: the dynamics of European integration', in Wallace, W. ed., *The Dynamics of European Integration*, RIIA/Pinter, London.

Weaver, R. K. and Rockman, B. A. eds, *Do Institutions Matter?*, The Brookings Institution, Washington, DC.

Weber, M. (1978), *Economy and Society*, 2 vols, University of California Press, Berkeley.

Weber, S. and Wiesmeth, H. (1991), 'Issue linkage in the European Community', *Journal of Common Market Studies*, 29, pp. 255–67.

Weigall, D., and Stirk, P. eds, (1992), *The Origins and Development of the European Community*, Leicester University Press, Leicester.

Weiler, J. (1982), 'Community, member states, and European integration: is the law relevant?', *Journal of Common Market Studies*, 21, pp. 39–56.

Wessels, W. (1985), 'Community bureaucracy in a changing environment: criticism, trends, questions', in Jamar, J. and Wessels, W. eds, *Community Bureaucracy at the Crossroads*, De Tempel, Bruges.

Westlake, M. (1994a), *The Commission and the Parliament: Partners and Rivals in European Policy-making*, Butterworths, London.

Westlake, M. (1994b), 'The Commission and the Parliament', in Edwards, G. and Spence, D. eds, *The European Commission*, Longman Current Affairs, Harlow.

Willis, V. (1983), *Britons in Brussels. The Officials of the European Commission and the Council Secretariat*, PSI, London.

Wise, M. and Gibb, R. (1993), *Single Market to Social Europe: The European Community in the 1990s*, Longman, Harlow.

Index

THE NORTHERN COLLEGE
LIBRARY
CANCELLED
7113 BARNSLEY

creating a more integrated European market. Its role was increasingly one of partnership with the member states, with Delors acting simultaneously as consensus-builder, policy initiator and policy player in his own right and on behalf of the institution he headed. But it remained to be seen whether this momentum could be sustained during the period in which the treaty was to be implemented.

Keeping up the momentum

The Delors strategy did not have as its sole focal point the creation of a Europe-wide market. As such, the Commission President wanted to make sure that the post-SEA integrative momentum was sustained. Arguments for EMU, as a next step in the integration process, possessed a logic which appeared unchallengeable. Not only would EMU complement and complete the single market programme by ridding the European market of barriers to trade not touched upon by the 1992 programme, it would also help to advance the cause of European union by placing the essentially deregulatory '1992' objective on a more 'positive' footing.[24] Delors saw EMU, therefore, both as the next crucial stage in the creation of a federal Europe and as the solution to problems of economic competitiveness that continued to plague the member states.

It was not until 1988 that interest in EMU rose to a predominant position on the European political agenda. Crucial was the growing realisation by economists working with Delors that the policy of liberalising capital movements, foreseen in the SEA, was very likely to pose a serious threat to the Exchange Rate Mechanism (ERM) and to the wider EMS.[25] As such, Delors, with the help of President Mitterrand, managed to convince Helmut Kohl that a committee of central bank governors should be established to examine the steps that could be taken towards the achievement of some sort of stable European monetary zone. But just as importantly, he also managed to convince Kohl – much to the annoyance of several of the central bank governors – that he himself should chair this committee.

Agreement was reached on the setting up of the committee at the Hanover summit of June 1988 and the twelve central bank governors set to work, many of them with little enthusiasm for the job they had been asked to undertake. Aided by several economists from the member states, the Delors Committee, as it came to be known, met eight times in Basle from mid 1988 to spring 1989.

Delors was well aware of the hostility towards him from some of the central bankers, and, as a result, did his best to chair the proceedings in as unassuming a manner as he could. This low-key approach seemed to work well, although the most blatant opposition to his role in the drafting process, from Pöhl, the governor of the German Bundesbank, meant that there were continuous frictions throughout the Committee's life.

For most of the year, Delors played a conventional chairing role, summing up and synthesising the arguments put forward by the bankers. However, his input altered somewhat as the drafting of the final report began.[26] At this stage, Delors and Joly Dixon, the cabinet member in charge of EMU, along with a small team in Brussels made up of Ehlermann, Dewost, Mingasson and Lamoureux amongst others, wrote up drafts of text to be presented at the Committee meetings. The Commission's services were excluded from this process, with EMU dealt with largely outside formal Commission channels by a very small group of individuals.[27] Delors's role in editing the final version of the Report was crucial, with a time-consuming line-by-line revision turning the final draft into an extremely 'polished' piece of work.[28] Even *The Economist* was impressed, labelling the text as a 'surprisingly meaty document'.[29]

The Report, which came to be known as the Delors Report, proposed a three-stage move towards EMU, similar to that first suggested in the Werner Report of 1970. The third stage would involve the creation of a single currency and a single monetary policy which would be administered by a European System of Central Banks (ESCB) and a European Central Bank (ECB). There would also be a need for strict discipline in national macroeconomic policy, as well as economic policies at the European level (competition policy and structural policies, for example). This gradualist approach meant that no timetable was included in the Report, however, though this was to become a big issue later on. Entry to the first stage was recommended, however, from July 1990, with this marking 'a decision to embark on the entire process'.[30] In spite of some opposition, especially from Mrs Thatcher, the European Council, which met in Madrid in June 1989, asked the Commission to make plans for Stage One of the three-stage process to begin in July 1990. It was agreed that an IGC would then be set up with a view to taking decisions on the implementation of Stages Two and Three.

Delors was content with the outcome of the Madrid summit,

though not with the wording of the final communiqué. He had played his hand extremely well with regard to EMU. Getting the agreement of the central bank governors and involving them in the drafting of the Report had been critical, as it gave the proposal much more economic and political weight than it would have had if only Commission officials had been involved. Although the bankers did force some compromises about which Delors was not happy, it all the same remained largely true to the Commission President's vision of EMU.

Agreement on EMU was only to be achieved through a process of intergovernmental bargaining which necessitated the input of political factors into the integrative equation. The political cost of EMU, therefore, was to be some form of institutional change. For the Germans, this amounted to assurances that the federal dimension of the Community would be enhanced, while for the French, the extension of foreign and security policy at the European level was a prerequisite for agreement. Indeed progress on the foreign policy front came to be placed centre-stage after the implications of the 1989 revolutions in Eastern and Central Europe had been thought through. On one hand, if the EC was incapable of rising to the challenge posed by the changing international political scene, its role as an international actor and indeed as a political entity would be undermined, and perhaps irreparably damaged. On the other hand, however, Delors was concerned that with the focus of attention on the Eastern part of the European continent after 1989, the political momentum in favour of integration, founded upon the '1992' commitment, would be lost.

On the face of it, then, the Commission did rather well out of the end of the Cold War. Not only was it able to develop its own programmes of assistance to the Eastern European states and later to the former Soviet Union (the PHARE and TACIS (Technical Assistance to the Commonwealth of Independent States) programmes), it was also given the task of co-ordinating all aid to Eastern Europe from the G24, the OECD member countries. This only served to highlight the Commission's long-standing gripe about foreign policy co-ordination within the inadequate European Political Co-operation (EPC) mechanism – that it did little to solve the false dichotomy that existed between trade and foreign affairs, with the former supposedly 'technical' or administrative (and thus the rightful preserve of the Commission), and the latter 'political' (and outside Commission influence).[31] The Commission had long been keen to get its fingers in the foreign policy pie, as much for the sake of policy consistency as a means of extending its own institutional competence.

The end of the Cold War brought with it other unforeseen developments, however. With the fall of the Iron Curtain came a flood of applications for membership and expressions of interest from countries that in the past had been constrained either by their neutrality, their reluctance to become involved in political integration, or by their political relationship with the former Soviet Union. On the question of Community enlargement, Delors's thinking evolved gradually. At first, the 'widening' issue was considered to be a distraction from the primary objective of extending integration. The construction of the European Economic Area (EEA), which brought the EFTA countries (excluding Switzerland) into the single market but not into the broader Community, was largely a means of preventing an all-out clamour for membership.[32] The talk at the time of a 'Europe of Concentric Circles' or of a European village, with the EC as the 'house' at the centre of the village, was likewise a means of tempering demands for EC membership, whilst at the same time coping with fears that post-1989 Europe would witness a slowing down of the European integration process. It was not until much later that Delors became convinced of the need to 'widen' as well as 'deepen' the Community.

However, East Germany posed a different set of problems. In retrospect, perhaps, one of Delors's greatest successes arose from his understanding of German unification and its relevance for the future of Europe. Delors was on many occasions alone in pronouncing his support for German unity while other European leaders demonstrated extreme caution. Delors seemed to understand that Germany was going to unite, with or without the support of its West European neighbours, and that excessive caution over this sensitive matter could cause Germany to turn aside from the EC. Without the commitment of German involvement at the heart of Europe, the prospects for integration looked decidedly bleak. Delors's motives also involved the perceived need to contain a large Germany by integrating it fully into an even larger Union.

As a result, Delors went out of his way to demonstrate to Chancellor Kohl that a federal and united Germany within a federal Europe was at the heart of his plans for political union, as well as